American Exceptionalism and the Legacy of Vietnam

American Exceptionalism and the Legacy of Vietnam

US Foreign Policy since 1974

Trevor B. McCrisken
University of Warwick

First published 2003 by
PALGRAVE MACMILLAN
Houndmills, Basingstoke, Hampshire RG21 6XS and
175 Fifth Avenue, New York, N.Y. 10010
Companies and representatives throughout the world

PALGRAVE MACMILLAN is the global academic imprint of the Palgrave Macmillan division of St. Martin's Press, LLC and of Palgrave Macmillan Ltd. Macmillan® is a registered trademark in the United States, United Kingdom and other countries. Palgrave is a registered trademark in the European Union and other countries.

ISBN 0–333–97014–4

This book is printed on paper suitable for recycling and made from fully managed and sustained forest sources.

A catalogue record for this book is available from the British Library.

Library of Congress Cataloging-in-Publication Data
McCrisken, Trevor B., 1968–
    American exceptionalism and the legacy of Vietnam: US foreign policy since 1974/ Trevor B. McCrisken
        p. cm.
    Includes bibliographical references (p.) and index.
    ISBN 0–333–97014–4
        1. United States – Foreign relations – 1945–1989. 2. United States – Foreign relations – 1989– 3. Vietnamese Conflict, 1961–1975 – Influence. 4. National characteristics, American. 5. Political culture – United States – History – 20th century. 6. Nationalism – United States – History – 20th century. I. Title.

E840.M385 2003
327.73'009'045—dc21   2003051433

10 9 8 7 6 5 4 3 2 1
12 11 10 09 08 07 06 05 04 03

Transferred to digital printing 2005

For Sarah

Contents

Acknowledgements

This book has been a long time in the making and I owe countless people my thanks for their support, not all of whom can be mentioned here. Hopefully you all know who you are. This book began life as a doctoral thesis at the University of Sussex. I owe my greatest debt of gratitude to Michael Dunne, my supervisor, for his tireless support, encouragement, guidance and friendship. Many thanks also to Steve Burman at Sussex and John Dumbrell of Keele University who were my examiners and whose critical judgements helped me transform the thesis into this book. David Ryan of Leicester De Montfort University deserves special thanks for his insightful comments, support and friendship during the book's revision process. I hope the late Steve Reilly knew how much he impacted on my professional development, particularly by first introducing me to the idea of American exceptionalism. I am grateful to Lois Vietri of the University of Maryland who has contributed so much to my understanding of the Vietnam War and its legacies, as well as being a great friend and mentor. Many thanks to Bill Kincade of American University, Washington, DC, who also helped nurture some of the ideas discussed here. Thanks are due to Alexander DeConde, Justus Donecke, Matthew Jones, Thomas Paterson, and Simon Thompson who provided helpful comments on early outlines of my research, and to Fredrik Logevall for his support and asking me to write on exceptionalism for the *Encyclopedia of American Foreign Policy*. I also owe massive thanks to my colleagues at Sussex, Middlesex, Lancaster and Oxford and to all the students upon whom I have inflicted my ideas over the past few years at those institutions – you kept me very busy but you also helped keep me sane.

The research for this book was conducted at the Gerald R. Ford Library in Ann Arbor, Michigan; the Jimmy Carter Library in Atlanta, Georgia; the Ronald Reagan Library in Simi Valley, California; the University of Sussex Library; Lancaster University Library; the Rothermere American Institute and Vere Harmsworth Library at Oxford; and the Resource Centre of the United States Embassy in London. I would like to thank all the librarians and archivists who assisted my research: in particular Leesa Tobin and her colleagues at the Ford Library, James Yancey at the Carter Library, and Diane Barrie, Greg Cumming and Mike Duggan at the Reagan Library. I also wish to thank the Humanities Research Board of the British Academy for granting me three years of financial support including additional funds which made possible my visit to the Presidential Libraries in the United States.

Special thanks go to my family and friends on both sides of the Atlantic for their ongoing love and support: especially my parents, Jenny and

Ray McCrisken, who always believed in me and encouraged and supported me in ways they may never fully know. Most of all, for her limitless love, friendship, patience, pep talks, suggestions, for driving me around the US and so much more, I am forever grateful and indebted to Sarah Brammeier McCrisken.

TREVOR B. MCCRISKEN
Rothermere American Institute
University of Oxford
December 2002

1
American Exceptionalism: An Introduction

On September 11, 2001, following the terrorist attacks on the World Trade Center in New York and the Pentagon in Washington, DC, United States President George W. Bush declared that: 'America was targeted for the attack because we're the brightest beacon for freedom and opportunity in the world. And no one will keep that light from shining.' Americans would never forget this day but, Bush assured them, the US was 'a great nation' that would 'go forward to defend freedom and all that is good and just in our world'.[1] In the midst of a horrific tragedy, the president was drawing upon a long tradition in American public rhetoric that is informed by a belief in American exceptionalism.[2]

The term American exceptionalism describes the belief that the United States is an extraordinary nation with a special role to play in human history; not only unique but also superior among nations. Alexis de Tocqueville was the first to use the term 'exceptional' to describe the US and the American people in his classic work *Democracy in America* (1835–40), but the idea of America as an exceptional entity can be traced back to the earliest colonial times.[3] The belief in American exceptionalism forms a core element of American national identity and American nationalism. As a central part of the American belief system it contributes to what Benedict Anderson would call America's 'imagined community'.[4]

The ways in which US foreign policy is made and conducted are influenced by the underlying assumptions Americans hold about themselves and the rest of the world. Like most nations, the United States has a distinctive pattern of policy making that is determined by unique aspects of its national culture. Each country's historical and cultural heritage, its montage of national beliefs and experience – its national identity – has an influence, whether consciously or not, upon the way it practices politics. US foreign policy is driven by a variety of causal factors including strategic, economic, political, and bureaucratic interests; international and domestic pressures; the personalities and agendas of policy makers; and the actions of other nations. However, the belief in exceptionalism, since it is a core element of

1

American national identity, has an important underlying influence on foreign policy activity. This belief is one of the main ideas that, according to Michael Hunt, has 'performed for generations of Americans that essential function of giving order to their vision of the world and defining their place in it'.[5] The belief in American exceptionalism provides an essential element of the cultural and intellectual framework for the making and conduct of US foreign policy.

Two main strands of exceptionalist thought have influenced US foreign policy. One is that of the United States as an exemplar nation, as reflected in ideas such as the 'city upon a hill', 'nonentangling alliances', 'anti-imperialism', 'isolationism', and 'Fortress America'. The other, often more dominant strand is that of the missionary nation, as represented by the ideas of 'manifest destiny', 'imperialism', 'internationalism', 'leader of the free world', 'modernization theory', and the 'new world order'. Both strands have been present throughout the history of US foreign relations and are analysed in this book.

The concept of the exceptional nature of the United States, however, has been a matter of much debate since sociologist Daniel Bell declared the end of American exceptionalism in the aftermath of the Vietnam War and Watergate. Scholars continue to dispute whether or not the US is exceptional in some measurable way and whether the concept of American exceptionalism can be used in ways which are theoretically fruitful. This debate, however, is missing a more crucial and indeed more interesting point – that regardless of whether or not the US is actually exceptional, the *belief* in American exceptionalism persists. A large number of US citizens, including public officials, believe that their country is exceptional and this informs the way American society functions; indeed, the idea continues to be a central element of American national identity. This book shows how the notion of American exceptionalism forms part of the American belief system, the nation's cultural reality, and more importantly how this belief has informed and continues to inform US foreign policy making. It is argued that the belief in American exceptionalism was severely shaken by the American defeat in Vietnam, but that the belief survived and has remained a major influence on post-Vietnam US foreign policy.

American exceptionalism: the scholarly debate

In 1975, Daniel Bell declared the demise of American exceptionalism: 'Today, the belief in American exceptionalism has vanished with the end of empire, the weakening of power, the loss of faith in the nation's future.' Quite simply, Bell concluded, the US had become 'a nation like all other nations'. The only remaining vestige of the exceptional nature of the United States was its constitutional system, but any sense of destiny or specialness had been shattered.[6] Fourteen years later, however, Bell reopened the scholarly debate by arguing that in the US 'there has always been a strong belief in American exceptionalism. From the start, Americans have believed that destiny has marked their country as different from all others – that the United States is, in Lincoln's marvelous phrase, "an almost chosen nation" '. Despite his earlier conclusions, Bell now suggested several social and political areas in which the question of American exceptionalism continued to be prevalent and thus deserved further academic exploration.[7]

According to Byron Shafer, there are three main ways to approach the question of American exceptionalism. The first concerns the 'simple distinctiveness' of the United States, but as Shafer suggests 'all societies, observed closely enough, are distinctive'. The second contends that the US does not fit a 'general model of societal progression for the developed nations of the world'. But such a normative model of societal development does not, and never has, existed. Certainly some countries have developed in similar ways but each society has its differences in outcomes, methods, timescales and other elements determined by various factors unique to national, regional and local environments. This returns us to the first point that all nations are different, so why should American exceptionalism be of any interest or importance? Where Shafer finds his answer is in 'an effort to highlight distinctively American *clusters* of characteristics, even distinctively American ways of organising the major *realms* of social life'. Thus, the essays collected by Shafer reveal 'peculiarly American approaches to major social sectors' such as politics, economics, religion, culture, education and public policy.[8] This approach has been taken up by several scholars in recent years focusing on a wide variety of topics ranging from American political exceptionalism to the exceptional nature of American sports culture.[9] Most comprehensively, Seymour Martin Lipset has considered unique American aspects of ideology, politics, economics, religion, welfare, unionism, race relations and intellectualism. Lipset sees American exceptionalism as a 'double-edged sword' since there are many negative as well as positive traits in American society that are exceptional in comparison with other countries. Exceptionally high crime rates, levels of violence, prison populations, divorce rates, teenage pregnancies, income inequality, and exceptionally low levels of electoral participation, along with a lack of social welfare programmes, mean the US can be considered 'the worst as well as the best, depending on which quality is being addressed'.[10]

Judging particular exceptions to determine whether the US is the best or worst nation in that realm reveals another of the major problems with American exceptionalism. As Bell observes, the 'idea of "exceptionalism," as it has been used to describe American history and institutions, assumes not only that the US has been unlike other nations, but that it is exceptional in the sense of being *exemplary*'.[11] As the work of Lipset and others has shown, American differences can be identified and even evaluated but any declarations of superiority over alternative ways of approaching social realms can only be based on subjective criteria. For example, it is difficult, if not impossible, to determine objectively whether the US political system is better than any alternative forms of government. The same can be said of any other identifiable American exception. To attempt to prove that the US is indeed an exceptional nation, in the sense of being not only unique but also superior, is a highly problematic exercise. Rather than debate the truth of whether the US is actually exceptional, or indeed superior, in any measurable way, it is more important and interesting to focus on the fact that Americans generally believe in the myth or rhetoric of American exceptionalism and act on those beliefs.

American exceptionalism and US foreign policy

The focus in this book, then, is on the *belief* in American exceptionalism and its influence on US foreign policy rather than directly addressing the question of whether US foreign policy itself can be measured as exceptional. Indeed, Joseph Lepgold and Timothy McKeown have found little empirical evidence for claims that American foreign policy behaviour is exceptional.[12] Faults and blemishes riddle American history as much as that of any other nation and in foreign policy the US has a far from untarnished record. The colonization and expansion of the new nation were accompanied by the displacement or destruction of the indigenous population. Times of war have been plentiful, with the US imposing its will on peoples in countries as distant as the Philippines and Vietnam, ordering the internment of large numbers of its own citizens, and committing wartime atrocities like any other nation. Yet despite the abundance of evidence to the contrary, there has remained throughout American history a strong *belief* that the United States is an exceptional nation, not only unique but also superior among nations.

Lepgold and McKeown observe that American leaders make 'unusual internal justifications' for their actions abroad, using 'idiosyncratic symbols and metaphors ... based on national self-image and values'. It is typical in all societies for governments to garner support for their policies 'by linking them to general societal norms, usually through political symbols that have reference to deeply shared values'. For Americans these symbols are 'unusually linked to domestic rather than external values'. American society is held together by shared ideas and values more than shared culture or heritage. Lepgold and McKeown argue, therefore, that:

> American mass society has had little use for the symbols of competitive nationalism in the Old World sense or the geopolitical concepts that went with it. Lacking the shared cognitive maps that other peoples develop to deal with tangible disputes over territory and resources, Americans typically do not grasp the politics, history, and social forces out of which foreign policy is typically made elsewhere. US foreign behavior abroad is thus justified through general formulas and slogans.[13]

Lepgold and McKeown do not go on to discuss what symbols and metaphors are used by Americans in this context. The argument here, though, is that the belief in American exceptionalism most commonly provides these symbols and metaphors.

The majority of the academic works on the history and practice of US foreign relations neglect or discount the influence of exceptionalist beliefs. Nevertheless, a growing body of scholarship does recognize that the belief in American exceptionalism has been a persistent and major underlying influence on US foreign policy. These works recognize that despite the inherent contradictions and frequent circularity of exceptionalist thought, the 'recurring rhetoric' of the belief in American exceptionalism reveals it to be 'a cultural reality and potent force'.[14] Michael Hunt, for example, attempts to identify an 'American foreign-policy ideology inspired by the cultural approach'. Such an ideology would consist of 'a relatively coherent, emotionally charged, and conceptually interlocking set of ideas [that] would have to reflect the self-image of those who espoused them and to define a relationship with the world consonant with that self-image'. Hunt argues that the 'capstone idea' that has underscored US foreign policy from its beginnings is that of American greatness, an idea that reveals Americans as 'a special people with a unique destiny'.[15]

This 'self-image of uniqueness', together with a 'secular fundamentalism' and a 'strident moralism', are among the core traditions that according to Roger Whitcomb constitute the 'collective set of values that energize [Americans]' and form a national style of foreign policy.[16] Americans 'came to the view early in their experience that they were an exceptional people... From the days of Manifest Destiny to the era of the American Century, the foreign policy of the nation would be evocative of this sense of uniqueness'. Whitcomb suggests that 'Morality became the reference point of uniqueness; Americans were simply "better" than the common run-of-the-mill peoples of the world'. US foreign policy would often be underpinned by 'the belief that there is a fundamental difference between right and wrong; that right must be supported, that wrong must be suppressed, and that error and evil can have no place when compared with the "truth"'. The US was, therefore, 'uniquely qualified to lead the forces of freedom' in the world.[17] H. W. Brands agrees that: 'If a single theme pervades the history of American thinking about the world, it is that the United States has a peculiar obligation to better the lot of humanity.' He argues that 'Americans have commonly spoken and acted as though the salvation of the world depended on them'. This 'persistent theme in American thought, speech and writing about the world' could be called a 'manifestation of American exceptionalism'. Brands recognizes that the major protagonists of such thinking can be divided into two groups – the 'exemplarists' and the 'vindicators'.[18] These groupings correspond to the two main strands of exceptionalist thought examined here: the exemplary and the missionary.

Other authors have recently addressed the impact of the belief in American exceptionalism on specific periods in US foreign policy. John Fousek has explored the cultural roots of the Cold War and argues that US policy and the broad consensus that supported it were enveloped within a discursive 'framework of American greatness'. He concludes that American Cold War policy was underpinned by a discourse of 'American nationalist globalism' that combined 'traditional nationalist ideologies of American chosenness, mission, and destiny with the emerging notion that the entire world was now the proper sphere of concern for US foreign policy'.[19] The influence of the belief in American exceptionalism on US public diplomacy at the end of the Cold War has also been analysed. Siobhán McEvoy-Levy has found that during this period of 'consensus- and paradigm-shattering transition', Presidents George Bush and Bill Clinton both utilized the 'common institution' of traditional exceptionalist rhetoric to overcome the 'cognitive dissonance' among American elites and the public concerning the appropriate post-Cold War role for the US.[20]

This growing body of work on the belief in American exceptionalism and its influence on US foreign policy shows that it should not be dismissed as 'mere rhetoric'. In fact, it should be acknowledged as an important and influential idea that contributes to the framework of discourse in which 'policymakers deal with specific issues and in which the attentive public understands those issues'.[21] This is not to say that the belief in exceptionalism is the root cause of all foreign policy. Although the analysis in this book reveals the prevalence of the belief in foreign policy discourse, it should be remembered that at every turn policy was shaped and driven by more tangible determinants such as the preservation of national security, the demand for overseas markets, or, indeed, the personal ambitions of policymakers. As Anders Stephanson makes clear in his study of manifest destiny, the destinarian discourse he identifies did not 'cause' policy as such. It was, however, 'of signal importance in the way the United States came to understand itself in the world and still does'. The same is true about the broader idea of American exceptionalism – it is not 'a mere rationalization' but often appears 'in the guise of common sense'.[22] The argument in this book is that throughout American history, exceptionalist beliefs have framed the discourse of foreign policy making by providing the underlying assumptions and terms of reference for foreign policy debate and conduct. While others have acknowledged the importance of exceptionalist beliefs, no previous work has focused specifically on the post-Vietnam era and the legacy of that conflict for the belief in exceptionalism and the course of US foreign policy.

National identity and the belief in American exceptionalism

Scholars disagree over whether exceptionalism amounts to an ideology as such. Hunt contends that the belief in 'national greatness' is a central element of the ideology behind US foreign policy. Alternatively, it has been suggested that exceptionalism amounts to a 'para-ideology' because its influence underwrites much of US foreign policy but it does not have the coherence of a traditional ideology. It has also been argued that American democratic liberalism is the ideology underpinning US foreign policy but that a belief in American exceptionalism is a central element of that ideology.[23]

It was Richard Hofstadter who observed, 'It has been our fate as a nation not to have ideologies but to be one.' In the US, as in other countries, 'ideology helps to form the basis of the national identity, through which individuals find motivation to translate ideas into action'.[24] American nationalism is not built on the usual elements of nationhood such as shared language, culture, common descent or historical territory, but on 'an idea which singled out the new nation among the nations of the earth'. This idea is a 'universal message' that American values and principles will benefit the whole of humankind.[25] Being an American, or rather a US citizen, is not simply a birthright but the acceptance of a general set of principles and values that Samuel Huntington has described as the American Creed. These core values, he claims, are: liberty, equality, individualism, democracy, and the rule of law under a constitution. To be an American is to make an ideological commitment to these political values.[26] It is perhaps one of the unique aspects of American society that any person from anywhere in the world can be accepted as a true American *if* they will adhere to these values. Abraham Lincoln once declared that no matter where immigrants may have come from in Europe, by accepting the 'moral sentiment' of the Declaration of Independence they were as much Americans 'as though they were blood of the blood and flesh of the flesh of the men who wrote that Declaration'.[27]

Challenging or rejecting these core values can leave a person branded 'un-American', another concept peculiar to the United States – there is no such thing, for instance, as an 'un-British' or 'un-German' belief or person.[28] In times of trial in American history even people whose families have been American for several generations have had to face loyalty tests, most famously during the Truman administration and the McCarthy 'witch-hunt' of the 1950s, or to similarly proclaim their unwavering dedication to American values and principles. Those who would not were ostracized or even imprisoned. Various rituals are built into everyday American life to reinforce each citizen's belief in those values and principles. These rituals are examples of what Eric Hobsbawm calls 'invented tradition' which provides the foundations of national identity and nationalism. Hobsbawm suggests that 'Americanism' is 'notably ill-defined' but that the practices that symbolize it are 'virtually compulsory'. These rituals were 'invented' as 'emotionally and symbolically charged signs of club membership'.[29] The Pledge of Allegiance; the Fourth of July; Thanksgiving; the 'Star Spangled Banner' as both flag and anthem; the Declaration of Independence and the

Constitution, both reverentially displayed at the temple-like National Archives building; the national monuments in Washington, DC; the Statue of Liberty in New York; the carved faces of presidents on Mount Rushmore – these are all invented traditions that symbolize American national identity and amount to what Robert Bellah has called a 'civil religion'.[30] They fulfil each of the three purposes of invented tradition: they help to establish and symbolize social cohesion; they help to legitimize the relationship between citizens and government; and they inculcate certain 'beliefs, value systems and conventions of behaviour'.[31]

The conception of the nation as invented or imagined is particularly useful in understanding the construction of American national identity. Without the same sense of shared heritage, religion, ethnicity, culture and history that are important in the formation of many other nations, 'Americans had to invent what Europeans inherited: a sense of solidarity, a repertoire of national symbols, a quickening of political passions.'[32] Nations embody shared memories, myths, symbols and values. Newly formed nation states, especially those without a common ethnic root like the US, must 'forge a cultural unity and identity of myth, symbol, value, and memory that can match that of nations built on pre-existing ethnic ties if they are to survive and flourish as nations'.[33]

For Americans, in the 'absence of a shared past, the search for identity produced narratives of difference and exception'.[34] As Roger Whitcomb argues: 'A national myth of separateness, exclusivity, and superiority was integral to America's national formation and development.'[35] The belief in the exceptionalism of the United States is, therefore, a 'core theme of American nationalism' that has been expressed most commonly in the 'long-standing tradition of thought about American chosenness, mission, and destiny'.[36] It has been central to the formation of American national identity, and thus can be seen to have provided a significant part of the cultural and intellectual framework within which foreign policy has been made.

The belief in American exceptionalism

Exceptionalism is a fluid and adaptive idea that can be interpreted in different ways. Therefore it is necessary not only to identify its major assumptions but also to consider its two main strands – the exemplary and the missionary – and the outcomes these different views have for foreign policy.[37] Three main elements of exceptionalist belief have remained relatively consistent throughout American history: that the US is a special nation with a special destiny; that it is separate and different from the rest of the world, especially Europe; and that it will avoid the laws of history that determine the rise and fall of all great nations.

First and foremost is the belief that the United States is a special nation with a special role to play in human history. Throughout American history there have been repeated claims that the US is the 'promised land' and its citizens are the 'chosen people', divinely ordained to lead the world to betterment.[38] This notion goes back to the very beginnings of colonization. Most famously, in 1630, Puritan settler John Winthrop pronounced that the Massachusetts Bay colonists 'must Consider that wee shall be as a Citty upon a Hill, the eies of all people are upon us'.[39] Winthrop's words were circulated in manuscript form and have since become one of the main formative texts of American self-identity and meaning. Inherent in this notion of the city on a hill is the belief that the American colonists, and those who have followed them, were uniquely blessed by God to pursue His work on Earth and to establish a society that would provide this beacon for the betterment of all humankind. Americans have been charged by God with the task of reforming themselves and the world – they are a redeemer nation. As George Washington declared: 'Every step by which [the United States] have advanced to the character of an independent nation seems to have been distinguished by some token of providential agency.'[40] This and other such public expressions helped forge a permanent place in the American beliefs system for the idea that the US was chosen by God to assume its special place in history. In a country where religious belief remains higher than in any other major industrialized nation, such a claim continues to have a peculiar resonance.[41] At the same time, though, the chosen people are exposed to temptation and corruption, most often from abroad or from subversives within. Americans are thus constantly being tested and must undergo continual self-inspection.[42] When they do seem to fail or commit wrongdoing, it is because the forces of evil are working against them. But even in such circumstances, the belief in exceptionalism enables Americans to maintain their purity because their intentions are good and they will strive on with their national experiment.

The second main element of exceptionalist belief is the New World's separateness and difference from the Old World of Europe. In Europe, Americans believed, self-interested monarchies exploited the majority of their own people, then sought imperial expansion abroad to increase their treasures, boost their reputations, and increase their power relative to other monarchies. The political systems were invariably corrupt, and pandered to the needs and desires of the traditional elites, leaving little or no means for commoners to improve their lot in life. Many early Americans hoped they could escape such ills by establishing new forms of society on the American continent. Most seventeenth and eighteenth century settlers, particularly in New England, brought with them novel ideas and convictions about how a society should organize itself. In contrast to Europe, the New World would be committed to freedom, morality, and the betterment of humankind. The Americans were in a unique position. As Thomas Paine suggested in his influential revolutionary pamphlet *Common Sense* (1776): 'We have it in our power to begin the world over again.'[43] The American continent was regarded as a virgin land upon which the peoples of the world could gather to create a New World based upon ideas, values and principles untried elsewhere. As Crèvecoeur observed in his influential *Letters from an American Farmer* (1782): 'The American is a new man, who acts upon new principles; he must therefore entertain new ideas and form new opinions.'[44] In 1787, the US Constitution was written as the basis for an ambitious experiment in governing a modern civilization. Although they were relatively pessimistic about its chances, the greatest hope of the Founding Fathers was that the constitutional framework would allow the US to develop over time into the most perfect republican society in the world.[45]

This leads to the third main element of exceptionalism which is the belief that the United States, unlike other great nations, is not destined to rise and fall. If their political experiment was a success, the Founding Fathers hoped to escape the 'laws of history' which eventually cause the decay and downfall of all great nations and empires. The geographic isolation of the American continent from Europe seemed to offer hope that the US could protect itself from falling prey to the degenerative nature of the Old World. As Washington declared: 'Our detached and distant situation invites and enables us to pursue a different course.'[46] The United States, Thomas Jefferson observed, was 'Kindly separated by nature and a wide ocean from the exterminating havoc of one quarter of the globe; too high-minded to endure the degradations of others.'[47] Such leaders did not suggest that Americans would be immune from temptation but they did indicate that, with eternal vigilance, the US could be prevented from succumbing to the same vices that had destroyed other great nations. Such attitudes have led Americans to believe their nation is the leader of progress in the world. Practically everything that the US does as a nation is regarded as pushing forward the boundaries of human achievement, be it in politics, industry, technology, sports, the arts, even warfare. Certainly there are some mistakes made, but they are few, they are learned from, and they are improved upon at the next attempt. No matter how many setbacks they may face along the way, Americans believe they will continue forward resolutely, striving for progress toward forming an ever more perfect union. Americans think of themselves as exceptional, then, not necessarily in what they are but in what they could be. For this reason the sense of exceptionalism can never die, no matter how unexceptional the nation may appear in reality. Exceptionalism persists because of what it promises just as much as, if not more than, what it delivers. It is tied to what it means to be an American: to have faith in the values and principles that caused the nation to be founded and to continue to exist.

Advocates of both the exemplary and the missionary strands of exceptionalist belief tend to share each of these assumptions. Where they differ is in how they believe these assumptions should translate into American actions with regard to the rest of the world. All exceptionalists believe very strongly in the basic benevolence of their actions towards other nations. National motives are not perceived as being driven solely by the desire for material gain but also by a dedication to principles of liberty and freedom for all humankind. A corollary of this belief is that it is the duty of the United States to help the rest of the world follow the example of the chosen people.

Followers of the exemplary strand of American exceptionalism have mostly advocated that the US remain aloof from the world's troubles and lead by example. Americans should strive to perfect their own society as much as possible without interfering in the affairs of others. To intervene abroad, the exemplarists argue, not only would probably harm the other nation but also would most likely undermine the American experiment at home. Far better, then, that the US should have peaceful trade relations abroad but concentrate on building a model society for others to copy rather than forcing the benefits of American life on them.

Adherents to the missionary strand of American exceptionalism, who advocate US expansion or intervention in the affairs of other nations, nevertheless believe that, unlike other nations, the United States is incapable of seeking dominion over other peoples in its self-interest. As John Quincy Adams proclaimed in 1821, the US 'goes not abroad, in search of monsters to destroy'. Adams insisted that America's 'glory is not *dominion*, but *liberty*' and that: 'She is the well-wisher to the freedom and independence of all.'[48] Washington will, therefore, project its power abroad not to subjugate other nations but to help them become like the United States, to become free and democratic. These Americans seem to believe that inside every foreigner there is the potential, even the desire, to be an American. After all, to be an American is not a birthright but the willingness to believe in a certain set of political and social principles and values. The missionary strand of American exceptionalism suggests that all the people of the world want to be like Americans, whether they realize it or not. This assumption has led Americans to find it very difficult to understand that other peoples may place different values on things and have different perceptions from Americans of how the world should be. In fact, both forms of exceptionalism hold, rather paradoxically, that the unique American political values and principles are actually universal in their nature. The US is regarded as the embodiment of universal values based on the rights of all humankind – freedom, equality, and justice for all. It is the exceptional champion of these rights but they are shared by all humans, whether they are Americans or not.[49]

Exceptionalism and the history of US foreign policy

In the early years of the republic it was initially the exemplar strand of exceptionalism that dominated US foreign policy. The United States would provide a model of freedom, liberty, and democracy from which the rest of the world could learn. Both Washington and Jefferson famously called upon Americans to actively seek to preserve their nation's unique position of aloofness from the world's ills. In his Farewell Address, Washington declared:

> The great rule of conduct for us in regard to foreign nations is, in extending our commercial relations to have with them as little *political* connection as possible. So far as we have already formed engagements let them be fulfilled with perfect good faith. Here let us stop ... It is our true policy to steer clear of permanent alliances with any portion of the foreign world.[50]

Jefferson reinforced these sentiments, recommending that the US should seek 'peace, commerce, and honest friendship with all nations, entangling alliances with none'.[51] Such pronouncements laid the foundations for a foreign policy characterized by high levels of unilateralism and so-called isolationism.

As the republic became stronger and more successful, however, the dominant notion of the US as a separate, aloof nation was challenged by a growing sense of 'sacred mission' and 'sanctified destiny'.[52] By the 1840s, with the US expanding westward, the missionary strand of exceptionalism was in the ascendancy in the form of 'Manifest Destiny'. Albert Weinberg defines manifest destiny as 'in essence the doctrine that one nation has a preeminent social worth, a distinctively lofty mission, and consequently, unique rights in the application of moral principles'. The idea soon became 'a firmly established article of the national creed'.[53] Territorial expansion was justified by Americans because they believed theirs was a special nation chosen by Providence to spread its virtues far and wide.

At the end of the nineteenth century, however, the two main strands of exceptionalism came into direct conflict with one another as Americans debated the future direction of US foreign policy. Following the highly popular Spanish–American War of 1898, a 'Great Debate' erupted between expansionists who sought the annexation of former Spanish colonies and 'anti-imperialists' who opposed such a policy. The nature of the debate is illustrative of how, even when there are disagreements over the course of foreign policy, advocates on all sides tend to frame their arguments around the notion that there is something exceptional about the United States. They may differ in their perceptions of the exact nature of American exceptionalism but its basic sentiment provides the framework for their discussions.

The commercial and strategic advantages of annexation provided the rationale for most expansionists. Yet many of them also expressed their conviction that annexation was a morally acceptable policy because it was the duty of the United States, as God's emissary, to extend freedom and democracy whenever possible.[54] Expansionists, drawing upon the tradition of manifest destiny, were strong believers in and advocates of the missionary strand of American exceptionalism. The anti-imperialists, meanwhile, had a different view of the special American role in the world that reflected the exemplar strand of exceptionalism. They were more concerned that, having ousted the Spanish, the US should leave the liberated states to determine their own destinies, in keeping with the American dedication to the idea that governments derive their power from the consent of the governed. As Charles Norton Eliot made clear, he and his fellow anti-imperialists believed the transformation of the US into an imperial power 'sounded the close of the America exceptionally blessed among the nations'.[55] Although their individual opposition varied, the essence of the anti-imperialists' protest was that they feared the US was acting in a manner inconsistent with the principles laid down by the Founding Fathers. Thus both imperialists and anti-imperialists believed they were arguing for conduct consistent with the idea that the US was an exceptional nation with a special role to play in human history. They both agreed that the US was different from – indeed, better than – other nations; where they disagreed was on the precise nature of that exceptionalism.

The question of which strand of exceptionalism would dominate US foreign policy was gradually resolved in the first half of the twentieth century, but not without further debate. Woodrow Wilson, for example, seemed to personify the belief in American exceptionalism. He believed firmly that the 'force of America is the force of moral principle', that the 'idea of America is to serve humanity', and that while other nations used force 'for the oppression of mankind and their own aggrandizement', the US would only use force 'for the elevation of the spirit of the human race'.[56] Although he frequently employed force abroad it was in what he considered efforts to help other peoples become more democratic and orderly. He best expressed his attitude in 1914: 'They say the Mexicans are not fitted for self-government and to this I reply that, when properly directed, there is no people not fitted for self-government.'[57] Wilson was a clear advocate of the missionary strand of American exceptionalism.

Wilson is best remembered for taking the US into the First World War to 'make the world safe for democracy' and for his efforts to build a peaceful post-war international order based on American values and principles. The US Senate, however, rejected Wilsonian idealism and turned back to the tradition of non-entanglement with the affairs of Europe. In the interwar years, the so-called 'isolationists' and 'internationalists' again played out the debate between the exemplary and missionary strands of exceptionalism. The isolationists believed the US should remain aloof from the petty squabbles and adversarial alliances common in Europe while maintaining its traditional interests within its own hemisphere. The internationalists, on the other hand, believed the US had a duty to intervene in world affairs. The latter finally won the argument after the Japanese attacked Pearl Harbor on December 7, 1941.

The Second World War established the US as a fully engaged world power. Although security threats, strategic imperatives and economic interests drove much of his policy, Franklin D. Roosevelt still made clear that a central US war objective was to establish and secure 'freedom of speech, freedom of religion, freedom from want, and freedom from fear everywhere in the world'.[58] The 'Four Freedoms' and their contrast to fascism rooted the war effort in one of the central ideas of American political culture and remained dominant in public discourse and official rhetoric throughout the war.[59] To win the war would not be enough. An allied victory must lead to lasting peace and security in the world based upon universal values and principles traditionally espoused by Americans. To lead such a future was an American responsibility and duty that would promote not only American interests but also those of all humankind.

As this brief summary indicates, the belief in American exceptionalism has long had an influence on US foreign policy, its presentation and conduct.[60] It has not had a set content but has varied over time, with the exemplary and missionary strands often framing debate over the direction of policy. At the end of the Second World War and during the formative years of the Cold War, as the next chapter shows, exceptionalist beliefs continued to underpin US foreign policy. The events of that period, however, would cause Americans to question whether American exceptionalism had come to an end.

Challenges to exceptionalism

Certainly not all Americans believe wholeheartedly in all aspects of American exceptionalism. Many are all too aware that major problems exist within their society, many of which they may never adequately solve. Scholars, officials and the public alike debate the apparent decline of American power in the world, the corruption and scandal rife within the political system, and the gradual breakdown of civil society under the strains of crime, violence, drugs, poverty, divorce and other social ills. Many Americans acknowledge that in an increasingly interdependent world the US cannot claim dominion in international affairs and that when they do intervene abroad, Americans very often undermine the very principles they claim to be defending. Americans understand that their nation is not without its problems. Yet equally, public opinion polls show that Americans usually retain a great faith and confidence in their system's ability to ultimately overcome any challenge. This faith does not diminish the public anxiety that is felt each time a substantial challenge arises, but Americans are assured that their existing system, based on a relatively adaptable constitution and traditional values and principles, has proved itself time and again to be extremely resilient. For example, despite the impeachment proceedings against President Clinton in 1998–99 and the attendant disruption to the political process, a significant majority of Americans maintained their confidence in the ability of the Federal Government to handle effectively both domestic and international problems.[61] The debacle over the result of the 2000 presidential election also divided the country and raised serious questions about the efficacy of the electoral system, yet once the Supreme Court had settled the issue a vast majority of Americans accepted the legitimacy of George W. Bush as their president.[62]

Questions of race, ethnicity, gender, class and even regionalism also raise problems for the kind of conclusions that Huntington, Lipset and others have drawn about American exceptionalism. Many black Americans, for example, feel less than accepted by the dominant culture regardless of whether they adhere to traditional American values and principles. Fears that mass immigrations are somehow diluting the American values system are also nothing new. Each periodic wave of new immigrants has raised similar anxiety within the dominant culture. Although varying degrees of discrimination and inequality may persist, successive immigrant groups have found that conducting their lives in ways consistent with traditional American values and principles can facilitate a relatively rapid assimilation into the dominant culture.[63] Although such questions and challenges to the mainstream are obviously important, the focus of this book is upon core beliefs to which immigrants have traditionally been expected to adapt.

It is also important to note that many of the voices from the American past that provide Americans with the root references for their assumptions about the special nature of their country are actually taken out of context and given new meanings or greater importance than was originally intended. Selective quotation over the years has meant, for instance, that much of John Winthrop's original message has become lost. In his 'city on a hill' sermon, Winthrop was warning his fellow colonists that God would only grant them his favour if they conducted themselves according to his principles. Winthrop's use of the city on a hill was not a proclamation of the superiority of the colony but a warning that the whole world would know if the settlers did not live strictly in accordance with God's laws. If they failed in this commitment they would 'shame the faces of many of gods worthy servants, and cause theire prayers to be turned into Cursses upon us'.[64] The responsibility granted to the Americans was, therefore, very great. Winthrop's warning, though, became less and less heeded as the belief in the nation's special destiny grew.

Alexis de Tocqueville is remembered for his observations of the 'exceptional' qualities of US citizens. However, he also made many less-often quoted criticisms of the Americans and their ways. He was particularly critical of American national pride which he believed 'descends to every childishness of personal vanity' whenever an observer makes a negative appraisal of some aspect of American society. The majority of Americans lived 'in a state of perpetual self-adoration' he contended. Tocqueville was quite damning of the inability of most Americans to accept criticisms. It was their very sense of exceptionalism that Tocqueville found so objectionable: 'they have an immensely high opinion of themselves and are not far from believing that they form a species apart from the rest of the human race.' Yet despite Tocqueville's extensive criticisms of Americans' 'grandiose opinion of their country and themselves', most Americans tend to focus on the positive elements of his observations of American society, politics and morals and his affirmations of their special role in the world.[65]

Cultural myths and beliefs often grow from interpretive or selective readings of reality. It should come as no surprise that elements of famous American speeches, documents and works of literature have been taken out of context and given deeper cultural meaning as elements of the belief in American exceptionalism. As David Ryan observes: 'Cultural stories stabilise and organise society around acceptable ideas.... [M]yths integrate the national experience and serve as vehicles to overcome internal contradictions.'[66] Such ideas, whether grounded in reality or not, have framed public and official discourse over US foreign policy making throughout the history of the republic.

Americans are also not unique in their belief that theirs is an exceptional nation. Many, if not all, countries have shared such national vanity at some time or another in their histories. A belief in the exceptionalism of France, for example, accompanied French colonialism in the eighteenth and nineteenth centuries.[67] Similarly, the British Empire was justified by a belief in the superiority of the English and the God-given right of the Crown to bring civilization to the rest of the world.[68] Adolf Hitler justified his expansionist policies in terms of nationalism and a belief in the exceptional nature of the German people.[69] Americans are clearly not alone in holding exceptionalist beliefs. Neither are they unique in pursuing foreign policies that are informed by those cultural beliefs. In all countries, policy making is based to a certain extent on assumptions formed from unique elements of national culture.

The fact that other nations have their own forms of exceptionalism does not diminish the effects that the belief in American exceptionalism has on policy making in the United States. As the US remains the most powerful nation in the world it is important to recognize the consequences that the belief in American exceptionalism have on US foreign policy making. Political, economic, and strategic interests are the major determinants of US foreign policy. But no matter what the root reasons for a foreign policy decision, that policy is usually couched in terms consistent with American exceptionalism. Use of this rhetoric assures substantial public support for policy and has proved very effective throughout US history. It is not, however, simply a manipulative tool employed by policy makers but provides the framework for the discussion of foreign policy, its presentation by officials, and its realization. The use of exceptionalist rhetoric is often regarded by foreign observers with either contempt or confusion, but if we are to truly understand the ways in which US foreign policy is conducted it is essential that we take seriously the intellectual and cultural framework in which it is made. If this can be done then non-Americans may find it easier to understand why the United States acts in the ways it does internationally. At the same time, such a comprehension may also allow Americans a greater appreciation of why other peoples sometimes react negatively to US actions or rhetoric.

The structure of the book

The belief in American exceptionalism has been maintained throughout US history even though it has frequently been contradicted by the realities of the American experience. On various occasions, the belief has been challenged by the course of events, yet it is very resilient and has survived and flourished. The focus of this book is on the period following the most recent major challenge to the public's faith in the idea of American exceptionalism. The Vietnam War, coupled with the Watergate scandal, shook Americans' traditional confidence in their nation's purpose and the promise of an ever better future. Hence, analysts of American society such as Bell declared the end of American exceptionalism. It will be argued that the belief in American exceptionalism in fact survived the crisis of confidence of the 1970s and continues to be believed by public and officials alike. The belief continues to provide the framework within which US domestic and foreign policy is framed, conducted and presented to the public. It also tends to provide the framework for much of the dissent against that policy.

Presidential rhetoric is a particularly useful and important source for understanding the prevalence of exceptionalist belief in the United States. The president is the only nationally elected political figure and is often regarded as an embodiment of the nation and the 'voice of the people'. Woodrow Wilson once characterized the president as 'the spokesman for the real sentiment and purpose of the country'.[70] As David Ryan suggests:

> The primary reason for according value to presidential speeches is that they capture or shape the mood of the nation through prominent annual addresses, and they certainly speak to the constructions of US identity. In foreign policy these words, coupled with the sacred documents of the nation, provide meaning and identity in an otherwise bewildering world.[71]

In order to identify the main ideas that have informed US foreign policy making, Michael Hunt agrees that 'one need only look at [the foreign policy] elite's private musings and, more important, the public rhetoric by which they have justified their actions and communicated their opinions to one another and to the nation'. Obviously such material should not always be taken at face value as public rhetoric is often cleverly constructed in order to manipulate the audience or even hide the speaker's true intentions. Hunt contends, however, that such scepticism should not prevent us from gleaning much that is useful from public expressions of policy:

> Public rhetoric is not simply a screen, tool, or ornament. It is also, perhaps even primarily, a form of communication, rich in symbols and mythology and closely constrained by certain rules. To be effective, public rhetoric must draw on values and concerns widely shared and easily understood by its audience. A rhetoric that ignores or eschews the language of common discourse on the central problems of the day closes itself off as a matter of course from any sizable audience, limiting its own influence. If a rhetoric fails to reflect the speaker's genuine views on fundamental issues, it runs the risk over time of creating false public expectations and lays the basis for politically dangerous misunderstanding. If it indulges in blatant inconsistency, it eventually pays the price of diminished force and credibility.[72]

Public rhetoric is only worthless or misleading to those seeking to understand the cultural underpinnings of policy, according to Hunt, when these rules are violated or the audience is left unconvinced. The analysis in this book, therefore, is based largely on the public expressions of US presidents and other public officials. When possible, public pronouncements have been compared with private statements in order to verify that public officials are not simply manipulating the public but that they generally share in the belief in American exceptionalism.

The main focus of this book is on the post-Vietnam era. It is important, however, to show how entrenched exceptionalist beliefs were before the US experienced defeat in Vietnam. Chapter 2, therefore, looks briefly at exceptionalist beliefs in the early years of the Cold War and then explains why the American experience of the Vietnam War appeared to shatter the belief in American exceptionalism. The remaining chapters focus respectively on the Ford, Carter, Reagan, Bush and Clinton administrations. The analysis shows how each president, in his own way, attempted to fully revive public confidence in the belief in American exceptionalism. The degree to which each president both utilized and believed the rhetoric of exceptionalism is explored. The main concern is to show the extent to which the belief in exceptionalism affected foreign policy. Particular attention is given to the use of force, as exercising the will and resolve to employ the military is a way for presidents to demonstrate that American power remains strong. The appropriate application of force is also a way for administrations to ensure their foreign policy is at least perceived as being consistent with the assumptions of exceptionalist belief. Each president's success at pursuing a foreign policy consistent with traditional beliefs and at raising public confidence in exceptionalism is assessed. The analysis focuses not only on the legacy of the Vietnam War regarding the belief in exceptionalism, but also on the conduct of foreign policy.

The concluding chapter examines how significant the belief in American exceptionalism has been in the making of US foreign policy. It is argued that American exceptionalism will continue to provide the framework for foreign policy making and debate, and that to fully understand what Americans mean by the things they say about the world and to anticipate how they might react to world events we must continue to consider the influence of the belief in American exceptionalism. It is also argued that the conduct of US foreign policy remains deeply affected by the so-called 'Vietnam syndrome'. The links between this syndrome and the belief in American exceptionalism are explored.

USE FOR BUSH
SPEECH

2
The End of American Exceptionalism? The Cold War and Vietnam

In 1941, Henry Luce published an influential essay in *Life* magazine in which he declared that the twentieth century should be considered 'the American Century'. Luce portrayed a vision of America that continued the long tradition of regarding the United States as an exceptional nation with a special destiny. He argued that the US must 'accept wholeheartedly our duty and our opportunity as the most powerful and vital nation in the world and in consequence to exert upon the world the full impact of our influence'. He insisted that 'our vision of America as a world power' must include 'a passionate devotion to great American ideals' such as freedom, equality of opportunity, self-reliance and independence, but also cooperation. The time had come for the US to cast aside isolationism and become 'the powerhouse from which these ideals spread throughout the world and do their mysterious work of lifting the life of mankind from the level of the beasts to what the Psalmist called a little lower than angels'.[1]

Luce's vision seemed confirmed by the American experience in the Second World War. Although it was the longest and bloodiest war Americans had fought overseas, it was widely regarded as a resounding success for the US. Despite questions of guilt concerning the Holocaust and the use of the atomic bomb, the war has acted as affirmation for the American belief that the US is the leader and protector of all humankind and that it represents a force of good against the evil in the world. That the US was fulfilling its special destiny seemed confirmed by the nation's position of strength at the end of the conflict. While all the other major combatants had suffered massive devastation, the US emerged from the war relatively unscathed with its industry booming, its fighting forces the largest and best equipped in the world, and with a monopoly on the ultimate new weapon, the atomic bomb.

The American experience in the Second World War had, therefore, strongly reinforced the belief in American exceptionalism. Over the next thirty years, however, events were to unfold that would seriously undermine American faith in their special destiny and special place in the world. The analysis in this chapter will first show how the belief in American exceptionalism provided the basis for much of the discourse of Cold War American foreign policy. The main focus, however, will be on how US conduct in the Vietnam War and the resultant defeat caused Americans to question whether they had witnessed the end of American exceptionalism.

The leader of the free world

With its role as an international superpower firmly established, the US seemed finally to have overcome its insular approach to the rest of the world. In October 1945, 71 per cent of Americans responding to a Gallup poll believed it was 'best for the future of this country if we take an active role in world affairs'.[2] The new internationalism that characterized the post-war period also seemed to confirm to Americans that the US was first among nations. Americans were now more than willing to accept their role in the community of nations but only as the leading light. As President Dwight D. Eisenhower declared in 1953: 'destiny has laid upon our country the responsibility of the free world's leadership.'[3] Rather than retreat to the role of exemplar, the US would participate in world affairs to an extent far greater than ever before but, in accordance with the belief in its own special destiny, do so only on its own terms.

The defining feature of the post-war world was the ideological conflict between East and West. Soviet communism and its containment soon became the focus of US foreign policy as over forty years of Cold War began. Although strategic, economic and political interests were among its central determinants, US Cold War policy and the broad public consensus that supported it were underpinned by an ideology of what John Fousek identifies as 'American nationalist globalism' that was rooted in the missionary strand of the belief in American exceptionalism.[4] Anders Stephanson agrees that the 'operative framework' of Cold War policy was 'the story of American exceptionalism, with its missionary implications'.[5] Successive presidents and other public officials and opinion leaders persistently portrayed the Cold War in stark, Manichean terms as a battle between good and evil. The US was 'the leader of the free world' that must prevail and save humanity from the 'evils' of communism.

President Harry S Truman has been described as 'a staunch exponent of American exceptionalism' who frequently referred to the US as 'the greatest nation that the sun ever shone upon'.[6] For Truman, victory in the Second World War demonstrated American greatness, but it also placed on the US the responsibility of ensuring peace and freedom in the post-war world. Truman provided the guiding principles for American Cold War policy in what became known as the Truman Doctrine. It was the duty of the

United States, he contended, to do whatever was necessary to protect the rights of free, democratic nations around the world. This task was critical, he asserted, if the values and principles that Americans held so dear were to survive the challenge of communism and truly enable the world to be led out of darkness: 'The free peoples of the world look to us for support in maintaining their freedoms. If we falter in our leadership, we may endanger the peace of the world – and we shall surely endanger the welfare of our own Nation.' Truman believed it was no longer enough for the US merely to provide an example for the rest of the world to follow. He argued that the US, as the chosen nation, must take up the gauntlet and defend the rights of free peoples everywhere against what he regarded as totalitarian aggression and subversion.[7] The Cold War ethos was, then, firmly grounded in the missionary strand of American exceptionalism. Each of Truman's successors also utilized the language and ideas of American exceptionalism to reinforce the nature of the battle with communism.

It was not only in presidential rhetoric that the Cold War was defined and discussed in terms of ideas about American destiny, duty and exceptionalism. For example, George Kennan, the original architect of the containment policy, ended his influential article in *Foreign Affairs* (July 1947) by arguing that: 'The issue of Soviet-American relations is in essence a test of the over-all worth of the United States as a nation among nations. To avoid destruction the United States need only measure up to its own best traditions and prove itself worthy of preservation as a great nation.' He claimed that the 'thoughtful observer' would not object to the Cold War but would

> rather experience a certain gratitude to a Providence which, by providing the American people with this implacable challenge, has made their entire security as a nation dependent on their pulling themselves together and accepting the responsibilities of moral and political leadership that history plainly intended them to bear.[8]

Kennan, who was often critical of moralism in foreign policy, had nonetheless used the traditional language of exceptionalism to advocate his strategy for containing Soviet communism.

During the Cold War, the private communications of policy makers and even secret national security documents were frequently 'couched in the stark and sweeping terms usually reserved for crusades'.[9] For example, the authors of the secret National Security Council Paper No. 68 (NSC 68), the document that defined the course of US Cold War policy in 1950, made clear that: 'Our position as the center of power in the free world places a heavy responsibility upon the United States for leadership.' They described the Cold War as 'a basic conflict between the idea of freedom under a government of laws, and the idea of slavery under the grim oligarchy of the Kremlin'. It was 'imperative' that the forces of 'freedom' prevail, and the US must, therefore, build up its political, economic, and military strength. NSC 68 further emphasized, however, that US strength also lay 'in the way in which we affirm our values in the conduct of our national life'. The document's authors argued: 'It is only by practical affirmation, abroad as well as at home, of our essential values, that we can preserve our own integrity, in which lies the real frustration of the Kremlin design.' The US must accept 'the responsibility of world leadership' so as to 'bring about order and justice by means consistent with the principles of freedom and democracy'.[10] NSC 68 was designed only for the eyes of other policy makers yet it drew upon exceptionalist ideas and was built around the idea of free world leadership that 'became the controlling metaphor in US foreign-policy discourse throughout the postwar period'.[11]

Not all Americans, however, accepted uncritically the tenets of the Cold War consensus. African Americans in particular focused on the apparent contradiction of the US demanding freedom and democracy throughout the world when such rights were still widely denied to large numbers of its own citizens at home. The civil rights movement used claims of America's leadership of the free world to argue that racial equality must also be achieved in the US. Such demands contributed to the many advancements made in race relations during the 1950s and 1960s.[12] On the whole, though, raising objections to the Cold War consensus was difficult, even dangerous, particularly during the earlier years of the Cold War, not least because foreign policy dissent was frequently equated with 'fundamental disloyalty to the nation and its values'.[13]

Many Cold War policies reflected exceptionalist assumptions about the American role in the world. The Marshall Plan (1947) for the economic reconstruction of post-war Western Europe was designed to revive European economies using not only American money but also practices and principles. The US, in the tradition of the redeemer nation, was fulfilling its responsibility of leadership through a programme that provided benefits not only for itself but also for the peoples of war-torn Europe. Similarly, modernization theory provided the rationale for much US Cold War policy towards the developing world, particularly during the Kennedy administration. Modernization theorists believed that all societies pass through sequential stages of progress from 'traditional' to 'modern' and that because the West, and in particular the US, was the 'common endpoint' to which all peoples must irresistibly move, Americans could help underdeveloped countries along the way from being stagnant, traditional societies to active, modern ones. American 'nation building' efforts throughout the Third World, therefore, promoted the 'continuing power of the widespread belief that America was both called to and capable of remaking the rest of the world'.[14]

The rhetoric of exceptionalism was also used to justify major uses of force during the Cold War, even when clear strategic and political justifications could be found. The Truman administration perceived the North Korean invasion of South Korea on June 24, 1950 as part of a global campaign of Soviet expansion. To demonstrate the credibility of the Truman Doctrine and to achieve the containment of communism, the administration concluded that the US had no choice but to intervene.[15] Yet Truman still couched the intervention in terms consistent with the belief in American exceptionalism. He emphasized the moral aspects of the crisis and insisted that the US was acting for the good of the South Koreans rather than out of pure self-interest: 'It should be made perfectly clear that [our] action was undertaken as a matter of basic moral principle.' According to Truman, the American objective in Korea was a benevolent one: 'For ourselves, we seek no territory or domination over others.'[16] According to Truman, the US was acting in accordance with its most deeply held principles that it had a duty to protect wherever they might be threatened in the world.

The belief in American exceptionalism was reiterated most strongly and influentially during the Cold War by President John F. Kennedy in his Inaugural Address. Kennedy drew upon all the main elements of exceptionalism in a declaration of American intent towards the rest of the world. He claimed: 'the same revolutionary beliefs for which our forebears fought are still at issue around the globe – the belief that the rights of man come not from the generosity of the state but from the hand of God.' Kennedy gave a forceful assurance that the US would fulfil its duty to defend freedom not only at home but all over the world: 'Let every nation know, whether it wishes us well or ill, that we shall pay any price, bear any burden, meet any hardship, support any friend, oppose any foe to assure the survival and success of liberty.' Echoing the sentiments of American leaders throughout US history, Kennedy asserted that American actions would be divinely blessed: 'here on earth God's work must truly be our own.' Finally, he evoked the image of America as a city on a hill: 'the energy, the faith, the devotion which we bring to this endeavor will light our country and all who serve it – and the glow from that fire can truly light the world.'[17]

Despite their expansionist history, Americans were unable to imagine that their own actions could be anything but just and moral with regard to the Cold War. In their own eyes, Americans carried out their policies towards the Soviet Union not for purely self-interested strategic reasons, but for the higher purpose of securing a better, safer future for all of mankind. In October 1962, Kennedy emphasized these exceptionalist convictions as he explained the course of action the US would follow in response to the Soviet attempts to deploy nuclear missiles in Cuba:

> The path we have chosen ... is the one most consistent with our character and courage as a nation and our commitments around the world. ... Our goal is not the victory of might, but the vindication of right – not peace at the expense of freedom, but both peace *and* freedom, here in this hemisphere, and, we hope, around the world.[18]

The US was, according to Kennedy, acting in accordance with the highest of American traditions and beliefs.

Perhaps the greatest crusade of the Cold War, and what would be its greatest failure, was the Vietnam War. The US had supported the French government's attempts to reclaim its Indochinese colonies after the Second World War and then provided major financial and military aid to South Vietnam after the French had withdrawn in 1954. The major rationale behind involvement in Vietnam was the policy of containment. Successive US presidents gradually intensified American involvement in what they saw increasingly as a test of American credibility. Lyndon Baines Johnson then embarked on a major escalation of the war by deploying ground troops in 1965. Although, as the following analysis will indicate, the Johnson administration was duplicitous in its policies towards Vietnam, the president explained escalation publicly in terms that were consistent with the traditions of American exceptionalism. Like so many presidents before him, Johnson insisted that the US had nothing but benign intentions: 'We have no territory there, nor do we seek any. … We want nothing for ourselves – only that the people of South Viet-Nam be allowed to guide their own country in their own way.' This lack of desire for dominion over others was such a strong American principle that 'no nation need fear that we desire their land, or to impose our will, or to dictate their institutions. But we will always oppose the effort of one nation to conquer another nation'. The reasons for this commitment were highly moral, Johnson declared, and very much entwined in the belief that the US was brought into existence to serve a special purpose in human history:

> [O]ur generation has a dream. It is a very old dream. But we have the power and now we have the opportunity to make that dream come true. For centuries nations have struggled among each other. But we dream of a world where disputes are settled by law and reason. And we will try to make it so.

Johnson argued that: 'Because we fight for values and we fight for principles, rather than territory or colonies, our patience and our determination are unending.'[19] Johnson was suggesting that the moral superiority of the US purpose and the purity of its conduct would ensure ultimate victory. As with all the major foreign policy actions in US history, the intervention in Vietnam was justified publicly in terms consistent with the belief in American exceptionalism.

The Vietnam War

The Vietnam War was the longest foreign conflict in which the US had been involved and the first in which it was defeated. It claimed over 58,000

American lives, left some 300,000 Americans wounded, and cost $155 billion. Vietnamese losses were even higher, with estimates in excess of two million dead. Cambodia and Laos suffered proportional losses. The region's infrastructure was left in ruins largely by an air war that saw a greater tonnage of bombs dropped on the small countries of Indochina than had been dropped by all aircraft in the Second World War.[20]

Despite the devastating effects on Vietnam, the fate of the Vietnamese since the end of the war has been largely ignored by Americans, who have tended to focus instead on what are considered to be the far-reaching effects of the conflict on the United States. The war is invariably referred to by Americans as a tragedy or a national trauma.[21] Writing in the year after the American withdrawal, Alexander Kendrick stated that the 'war created an open and suppurating wound which has not yet healed, and if it does, it may leave a permanent scar on the American body politic'.[22] The Vietnam War had divided opinion in the country like no other event since the Civil War. It contributed to the breakdown in the Cold War foreign policy consensus. It diverted resources from domestic reform programmes and caused high levels of inflation and national debt. It created an atmosphere of distrust and even hostility between the public and the government. Perhaps above all, though, the experience of Vietnam raised serious doubts among Americans about the traditional belief that the United States is a special nation with a special destiny. As Stanley Karnow observes, the names on the Vietnam Veterans Memorial in Washington, DC:

> bear witness to the end of America's absolute confidence in its moral exclusivity, its military invincibility, its manifest destiny. They are the price, paid in blood and sorrow, for America's awakening to maturity, to the recognition of its limitations. With the young men who died in Vietnam died the dream of an 'American century.'[23]

In 1975, when Daniel Bell declared 'The End of American Exceptionalism', he agreed that the 'American Century...foundered on the shoals of Vietnam'. The chastening experience of the Vietnam War had made Americans realize that they 'are a nation like all other nations'.[24] During the war itself, Paul Potter, then president of Students for a Democratic Society (SDS), argued that: 'Most of us grew up thinking that the United States was a strong but humble nation that...respected the integrity of other nations and other systems; and that engaged in war only as a last resort.' Cold War foreign policy had, though, 'done much to force many of us to rethink attitudes that were deep and basic sentiments about our country'. He concluded that the Vietnam War 'has provided the razor, the terrifying sharp cutting edge that has finally severed the last vestiges of illusions that morality and democracy are the guiding principles of American foreign policy'.[25]

What was it about the American experience in Vietnam that caused Americans to question their national values and aims? The belief in American exceptionalism had been challenged by other events in US history prior to the Vietnam War. The debate over imperialism of the late nineteenth century, the years surrounding American involvement in the First World War, the Great Depression of the 1930s, and the increasingly unpopular Korean War all gave Americans cause to question whether theirs remained the chosen nation. Through each of these periods, however, exceptionalist beliefs survived. Was there anything different between these earlier events and Vietnam? What was it about Vietnam that led Bell and other Americans to conclude that the United States was now 'a nation like all other nations'?

The main contention of those who argue that the belief in American exceptionalism ended as a result of Vietnam is that American participation in the war was immoral. The reality of defeat at the hands of Third World opponents and the nature of the conduct of the war revealed to many Americans that the US was just as fallible as any other nation. Indeed, the central arguments of those who opposed the war were based on the belief that 'in Vietnam the United States was using its immense power in ways inconsistent with the principles, the values, the ethical standards of the American people'.[26] Such arguments ranged from legal objections to accusations of immoral behaviour on the part of soldiers and public officials. The ultimate conclusion was that Americans had lost their right to claim their country was exceptional among the nations of the world.

From the outset of American military involvement in Vietnam there were questions about the legality of US actions. Unlike in the Korean War, the US did not have the backing of the UN but fought largely on its own, receiving only very limited assistance from the South East Asia Treaty Organization (SEATO). Questions were also raised over whether the US had violated the 1954 Geneva Accords on the future of Vietnam, especially when the Eisenhower administration supported Saigon's refusal to participate in national elections to reunify Vietnam in 1956.[27] As with Korea, the Vietnam War was also distinguished by the fact that it was never sanctioned by a Congressional declaration of war. The closest any administration came to such a declaration was the 1964 Gulf of Tonkin Resolution, procured from the Congress by President Johnson. The Joint Resolution allowed Johnson 'to take all necessary measures to repel any armed attack against the forces of the United States and to prevent further aggression'.[28] The Congress acted under the assumption that the resolution would deter further aggression in Vietnam and prevent the US becoming involved in an extended conflict. There was a broad understanding among the Members of Congress that they were not issuing the equivalent of a declaration of war. But the resolution had effectively given Johnson a blank cheque to wage whatever war he deemed necessary in Vietnam, and Congress was not approached for any further authorizations. Quite apart from the dubious constitutionality of such an action, the event that allowed for the resolution was itself of questionable nature. Evidence suggests that the second of two alleged attacks on the US destroyer *Maddox* in the Gulf of Tonkin never actually occurred. Johnson also misled Congress by failing to tell them that the attacks, if indeed they did take place, had most likely been provoked by secret commando raids conducted against nearby North Vietnamese islands.[29]

Americans would later look back at the Gulf of Tonkin Resolution as evidence that from the very beginning of major US involvement in Vietnam they had reason to doubt the word of their leaders and question the legality of intervention. Yet US history is riddled with examples of the US government pursuing policies based on dubious justifications, if not deceit. The mysterious sinking of the *Maine* in Havana harbour had helped to give President McKinley cause to fight the Spanish–American War. Questions have been raised concerning the relationship between President Roosevelt's desire for a pretext to join the Second World War and his prior knowledge of the Japanese attack on Pearl Harbor. Indeed, in the years following the Gulf of Tonkin Resolution, Democratic Senator William J. Fulbright would state bluntly that: 'FDR's deviousness in a good cause made it much easier for [President Johnson] to practice the same kind of deviousness in a bad cause.'[30]

In addition to challenging the American justifications for the war, opponents of the war also raised questions about the legality and morality of American conduct in Vietnam. The traditional belief that the US had nothing but benign intentions towards other peoples seemed increasingly countered by reports returning from Vietnam. American policies and conduct seemed to show a remarkable insensitivity towards the Vietnamese people whom the US was supposed to be at war to defend. Policies such as the Strategic Hamlet relocation programme of 1962–63, the hunting down of National Liberation Front (NLF)[31] cadres in 1969 under the Phoenix Program, and the establishment of 'free-fire zones' across South Vietnam, demonstrated the scant regard among American policy makers for the value of individual Vietnamese lives while they pursued what they perceived as the greater good of protecting South Vietnam from communism.

During the extensive bombing campaigns against targets in North and South Vietnam, the Pentagon was accused of repeatedly and deliberately attacking non-military targets of no strategic value in contravention of international law. Hospitals, schools, churches, 'friendly' villages, and villages containing mostly women and children were frequently targeted. That such raids were 'accidental' seemed contradicted by evidence that multiple bombing missions were run against the same targets, such as the 39 separate attacks on the Quyuh Lap leper colony and sanatorium.[32] Many Americans also found objectionable the types of weapons used in bombing runs, such as fragmentation bombs, napalm and phosphorous bombs.[33] That the

US could employ such weapons, especially against civilians, seemed an indication that the nation had lost its sense of morality. Americans were used to condemning their enemies for acts of brutality but considered themselves above such actions. Yet Americans had bombed civilians in the past, of course, most notably the firebombing of Dresden and Tokyo and the atomic destruction of Hiroshima and Nagasaki. These earlier uses of indiscriminate force had carried a heavy moral burden yet were considered justified by most Americans as they had been in the pursuit of what was considered a good cause. Political commentator Bill Moyers made clear what he considered the difference between Vietnam and those earlier American wars. In 1971, he wrote: 'Americans have fought brutally in other wars. ... We have abandoned propriety before; we have never before doubted the reason for doing so, as we doubt it now.'[34]

The general lack of consideration for the wishes and human rights of the Vietnamese was most graphically illustrated by the My Lai massacre on March 16, 1968. American soldiers massacred 347 men, women, children, and babies, and burned the hamlet to the ground despite meeting with no resistance or hostility.[35] The questionable morality of US conduct in Vietnam was also revealed by an infamous statement following the shelling of a Mekong Delta village called Ben Tre during the Tet offensive. An American officer declared: 'It became necessary to destroy the town in order to save it.'[36] The disregard for the Vietnamese as a people was further exemplified by the use of 'body counts' and 'kill ratios' as a measure for progress in a war that could not provide conventional measurements such as gains and losses of territory. As a result, it seemed that 'death and destruction had some absolute value in terms of winning the war'.[37] Such an impression raised major moral objections to the conduct of the war. To base US progress in a war on attempting to indiscriminately kill as many enemy forces as possible seemed contrary to the idea that the US was fighting a war in the highest moral spirit, to protect freedom and to further the betterment of mankind. The conduct of the war in Vietnam indicated to many Americans that the US could act in ways as unexceptional as those of any other nation.

The continued American support for unpopular, corrupt South Vietnamese governments raised many questions about the American commitment to democracy and whether the US was wrongly involved in what was essentially a civil war. However, the corrupting effects of the war in Vietnam were felt even more keenly at home. Americans became increasingly concerned about what the war was doing to freedom and democracy in the US. Johnson had lied to Congress about the true nature of events in Vietnam from the outset. As argued above, though, it was nothing new that the justifications for escalating the Vietnam War were based on dubious premises; in fact it can even be regarded as part of a long tradition. As the war dragged on, however, the sense that Americans could not trust their leaders grew as rapidly as the credibility gap between official pronouncements of progress in the war and the reports from the fighting in Vietnam. This perception was given its greatest impetus by the events surrounding the 'Tet' holiday – the time of the Vietnamese New Year – at the end of January 1968.

In late 1967, the Johnson administration launched a public relations campaign, spearheaded by General William Westmoreland, in an attempt to stem the gradual erosion of support for the war by emphasizing 'the light at the end of the tunnel'. Yet on January 30, 1968, what Westmoreland had portrayed as a 'bankrupt' enemy with 'not combat-effective' battalions launched attacks against major targets all over South Vietnam that sent shock waves throughout the United States – the so-called Tet offensive. Westmoreland claimed that Tet was actually a great victory for the US and South Vietnam since the insurgents failed to establish any firm holds on territory, did not incite a popular uprising or bring the downfall of the Saigon government, and incurred extremely heavy losses. Although the NLF was heavily depleted by Tet and became totally dependent on Hanoi for the first time in the war, the US faced even more serious consequences. As Bernard Brodie noted, the Tet offensive was 'probably unique in that the side that lost completely in the tactical sense came away with an overwhelming psychological and hence political victory'.[38] Even though US forces had been victorious, the reality of a country-wide enemy onslaught jarred embarrassingly with the confident rhetoric of the previous three months. The Tet offensive demonstrated graphically to the American people that contrary to what their government might be telling them the war was not being won and that there was certainly no end to the communist threat in sight. No matter what their generals or their president might say, the supposedly bankrupt and defeated enemy had shown its ability to strike more fiercely than ever before anywhere in South Vietnam. The war was not on the brink of victory for the US; indeed it appeared the Vietnamese communists would never stop fighting. Progress had not been made and the sacrifice of lives and resources and the war's divisive effects on the homefront had all been for naught. The official assurances of the previous year appeared now as nothing but hollow lies.

In actual fact, though, it was elite and official opinion rather than the American public that was most affected by Tet. Public support for the war shifted very little despite the surprise Tet offensive. As John E. Mueller argues: 'public support for and opposition to the war in Vietnam [had] hardened ... to the point where events were less likely to make much of an impression.'[39] Elite and official opinion, however, *did* take a significant turn against the war, with influential opinion leaders in the Congress, the media, among educators, business executives, clergymen, and other elites deciding the conflict was 'futile' and 'no longer worth the effort'.[40] This realization even penetrated the Johnson administration, with the president's advisers reassessing the situation in Vietnam and convincing him to call a halt on bombing and seek a negotiated settlement. Announcing the new policy towards Vietnam on March 31, 1968, Johnson shocked the nation by pledging: 'I shall not seek, and I will not accept, the nomination of my party for another term as your president.'[41] Johnson had perhaps been more deeply affected by the Tet offensive than any other individual in Washington. His personal standing among the American public plummeted. The 'light at the end of the tunnel' campaign of late 1967 had brought approval of the president's conduct of the war back up to 40 per cent. But after Tet this approval crashed to an all-time low of 26 per cent. Johnson's overall approval rating also fell from 48 per cent to another new low of 36 per cent. It became clear that a majority of the American public did not trust their president or believe his policies, at least in Vietnam, credible.[42] Yet if the American public could not trust President Johnson, their faith in the exceptionalism of their nation would be challenged even more severely by his successor.

The Tet offensive had revealed the reality of the inconclusive nature of the war in Vietnam. However, US involvement in Vietnam was to drag on for five more years. Republican candidate Richard Nixon won the presidential election in November 1968 pledging to end the war in Vietnam, but he was not interested in ending it immediately. He insisted that the American withdrawal must be 'honorable'. Any rapid abandonment of the commitment to South Vietnam would be callously out of character with the American tradition of defending free peoples under the threat of aggressors. Nixon and his National Security Advisor, Henry Kissinger, also argued that US credibility was at stake. According to Nixon: 'this first defeat in our Nation's history would result in a collapse of confidence in American leadership, not only in Asia but throughout the world.'[43] Nixon and Kissinger came to power determined to establish a new international order based on the primacy of the United States. They sought to improve American relations with both China and the Soviet Union. To make this possible, though, they believed the US must be perceived as acting from a position of strength. Any withdrawal from Vietnam, therefore, would have to be conducted in a manner which demonstrated to allies and adversaries that the US was still a force to be reckoned with in international affairs. As Kissinger remarked: 'However we got into Vietnam...whatever the judgment of our actions, ending the war honorably is essential for the peace of the world. Any other solution may unloose forces that would complicate the prospects for international order.'[44] Nixon shared the fears of his adviser: 'Our defeat and humiliation in South Vietnam without question would promote recklessness in the councils of those great powers who have not yet abandoned their goals of world conquest.'[45]

'Peace with honor', as defined by Nixon and Kissinger, meant that the American withdrawal from Vietnam must be carried out in such a way that it could not in any sense be considered a defeat. A withdrawal that caused the immediate downfall of the South Vietnamese government would, according to Nixon's definition, be a defeat. Although he admitted the need to extricate the US from Vietnam, there remained the hope that victory was possible or at least that total defeat could be delayed until long after a full American withdrawal.

The policy adopted by Nixon in pursuit of this honourable peace was one he had inherited from Johnson: 'Vietnamization'. American forces were gradually reduced while the strength of the South Vietnamese military was built up so that it could eventually assume the full burden of the war. While scaling down US troop levels, however, Nixon would continue to employ US firepower against North Vietnamese targets in order to force compliance at the negotiating table. Nixon portrayed Vietnamization as a policy which could secure an honourable peace while minimizing the sacrifices paid by Americans. In many ways, it had the desired effect. In the four years leading to the Paris peace accords which ended the American war, the level of US troops in Vietnam was reduced from 550,000 to 24,000, the weekly American casualty rate declined from hundreds to less than 25, and the annual expenditure on the war fell from a high of $25 billion to around $3 billion. The South Vietnamese regime had also been bolstered with military equipment and training assistance to a point where the Nixon administration believed the Saigon regime had a 'better than even chance' of holding off the communists. This was provided the US Congress continued to appropriate substantial economic and military aid to Saigon and did not rule out the possibility that US troops would return to Vietnam if the peace accords were broken.[46]

Yet Daniel Ellsberg, the former Defense Department official who helped compile the top-secret 'Pentagon Papers' and then leaked them to the *New York Times*, wrote in September 1969 that the Vietnamization policy was a 'bloody, hopeless, uncompelled, hence surely immoral prolongation of US involvement in [the Vietnam] war'.[47] His judgement seemed to be confirmed by the apparent escalations of the war under Nixon even as he withdrew American troops. Public frustrations at the inconclusiveness of the war and the sense that the nation's highest officials could not be trusted were further fuelled by actions taken during Nixon's presidency. The invasion of Cambodia in April 1970, revelations of the secret campaign of bombing that country, the killing of American students at Kent State and Jackson State universities, the extension of ground operations to Laos in February 1971, the mining of Haiphong harbour and massive increase of bombing campaigns against North Vietnam in May 1972, and the so-called Christmas bombing of Hanoi and Haiphong in December of that year, all caused various levels of public and Congressional furore.[48]

The Paris peace accords, which officially brought an end to the American war on January 27, 1973, could barely be considered to have achieved 'peace with honor'. The peace did allow for the complete withdrawal of US forces, but it was a cease-fire in place, enabling North Vietnamese troops to remain inside South Vietnam. Although the treaty presumed that the fate of Vietnam would be settled by political means, all the parties involved were certain that it would actually be resolved by force. 'Peace with honor' provided little more than a pause in the ongoing struggle for control of Vietnam. It extricated the US but it did little to ensure enduring peace and security for South Vietnam.[49]

The costs of Nixon's strategy were also extremely high. Over a third of the total American casualties in the war occurred while Nixon sought peace with honour. Between 1969 and 1973, 20,553 American, 107,504 South Vietnamese, and more than half a million North Vietnamese and NLF combat deaths were recorded. There is no adequate accounting of civilian casualties for the period but these were also very substantial.[50] The greater part of the mass of bombs dropped on Vietnam, Laos and Cambodia were unleashed during the Nixon years, killing, maiming, or destituting millions of civilians, destroying vast tracts of countryside, and wrecking much of the infrastructure throughout Indo-China.[51]

Yet four years of further expenditure of lives, money, and materiel had done little to alleviate the crisis in Vietnam. It had certainly not provided a victory for the United States. The shoring up of South Vietnam's armed forces allowed a so-called 'decent interval' between the withdrawal of the last American troops on March 29, 1973 and the fall of South Vietnam to Communist forces on April 30, 1975.[52] But it could not hide the fact that the US had failed to achieve its objectives in Vietnam. For the first time in the nation's history, the United States had lost a war. Americans could not help but feel that all the lives and resources expended in Vietnam had been wasted. The US was supposed to be an exceptional nation, above the corrupt immorality of the rest of the world. Yet in Vietnam, its leaders had conducted a war whose legitimacy was questionable and objectives often unclear and increasingly unattainable. The nation's leaders were accused of employing inhumane forms of warfare and of persistently lying to the American people about how the war was progressing and what was being done to bring about a victory. This sense that the American people could no longer trust their leaders was further compounded by the events and revelations surrounding the Watergate affair. The United States seemed to have shown itself just as fallible and unexceptional as any other nation in history.

Yet there was no consensus on any of the matters that indicated to some Americans that the US was no longer, if indeed it ever had been, an exceptional nation. The questions concerning the legality and morality of the justifications for the Vietnam War and the conduct of the fighting found just as many answers among supporters of the campaign as they did among dissenters: It was the North Vietnamese who had broken the Geneva Accords. American action was justified as it was in response to aggression perpetrated by the Soviet Union and China and was necessary to stem the spread of communism. The Saigon government may not have been immune to corruption but it was far more benign than a communist regime would be. There may have been regrettable civilian deaths but the responsibility for all the violence in Vietnam must lie with the Hanoi government for perpetrating hostilities, not with the Americans. The US military was only denied total victory by weak-minded politicians in Washington and the lack of full support from the American public. As Nixon insisted in his famous 'silent majority' speech: 'North Vietnam cannot defeat or humiliate the United States. Only Americans can do that.'[53]

In addition to there being no agreement among Americans over whether the conduct of the war signalled an end to American exceptionalism, there is further evidence to suggest that the idea of the US as a special nation with a special destiny would survive the defeat in Vietnam. As with previous times of domestic disagreement over foreign policy content and direction, advocates on both sides of the Vietnam issue utilized the rhetoric of exceptionalism in their arguments. We have already seen how Lyndon Johnson used such language and ideas. Richard Nixon also made attempts to appeal to traditional American beliefs, not least in his 'silent majority' speech:

> Two hundred years ago this Nation was weak and poor. But even then, America was the hope of millions in the world. Today we have become the strongest and richest nation in the world. And the wheel of destiny has turned so that any hope the world has for the survival of peace and freedom will be determined by whether the American people have the moral stamina and the courage to meet the challenge of free world leadership.
>
> Let historians not record that when America was the most powerful nation in the world we passed on the other side of the road and allowed the last hopes for peace and freedom of millions of people to be suffocated by the forces of totalitarianism.[54]

The war's opponents also based many of their arguments on the idea that the US is a special nation with a special destiny. Senator J. William Fulbright, who became one of the most outspoken congressional opponents of the war, believed the US had been 'generous and benevolent in intent' in Vietnam but had nevertheless fallen prey to what he termed 'the arrogance of power'. Fulbright argued that the US was not immune from the temptations that befell other nations: 'we are not God's chosen savior of mankind but only one of mankind's more successful and fortunate branches, endowed by our Creator with about the same capacity for good and evil, no more or less, than the rest of humanity.' Fulbright recognized two distinct strands of American national character, both charged with a 'kind of moralism'. He argued that: 'one is the morality of decent instincts tempered by the knowledge of human imperfection and the other is the morality of absolute self-confidence fired by the crusading spirit.' Fulbright feared the latter strand was coming to dominate and that 'much of the idealism and inspiration is disappearing from American policy'. His solution was for Americans to ensure that the 'strand of humanism, tolerance, and accommodation' remain dominant. He contended that:

> The foremost need of American foreign policy is a renewal of dedication to an 'idea that mankind can hold to' – not a missionary idea full of pretensions about being the world's policemen but a Lincolnian idea expressing that powerful strand of decency and humanity which is the true source of America's greatness.

Far from signalling the end of American exceptionalism, Fulbright continued to believe that 'America has a service to perform in the world' which is to 'do good...by the force of her own example' as a 'free society enjoying its freedom to the fullest'. Despite Vietnam, the US remained a nation '[f]avored...by history, by wealth, and by the vitality and basic decency of its diverse population'.[55] Fulbright was advocating the exemplar strand of exceptionalism over the missionary one. Although they represented opposite sides in the debate over Vietnam, Fulbright and Nixon shared the same use of language which was based in the belief in American exceptionalism. Their conceptions of the nature and consequences of America's special role in the world may have differed but their discourse was nevertheless grounded in a shared notion that there was something special about the United States.

Despite its diversity, the anti-war movement became increasingly associated in the minds of many Americans with the so-called counterculture of the late 1960s and early 1970s. Members of the counterculture were characterized as Americans who 'reject patriotism, respect for the police, puritan sexuality, the work-and-success ethic, consumerism, education as a social ladder, and, perhaps above all, the underlying presumption of Middle America that the American social order is a good and just one'.[56] The New Left anti-war activists often condemned the American system and its institutions and spoke out against what they perceived as the evils of American capitalism and imperialism. The more radical elements, such as the Weathermen, even advocated armed revolution. However, most opponents of the war did not entirely reject American values and principles. As Todd Gitlin observes, much of 'the movement's élan and language were utterly American. It did not speak in Marxese dialects. If anything...the SDS Old Guard were steeped in a most traditional American individualism'.[57]

The opposition of many of the war's protesters stemmed from a belief that the US was conducting itself in ways that were inconsistent with the values and principles upon which it was founded. But that did not mean that those opponents rejected such values. On the contrary, many believed they must oppose the war in order that those values might be reaffirmed. David Stockman, who later in life would become President Reagan's director of the Office of Management and Budget, expressed his opposition in such terms as an anti-war leader at Michigan State University in April 1967:

> A nation is not defined by the particular policy, of a particular adminis-
> tration, in power at a particular point in time. Rather, the genius of a
> nation is expressed in those lofty ideals and broad spiritual currents
> which have threaded their way through the fabric of its history. ... Many
> of us feel that American intervention in Vietnam runs contrary to the
> spirit of this historical tradition. Therefore, our commitment to the real
> core values and ideals that have made this nation great, demands that we
> oppose the war.[58]

This desire to see the US resume what was perceived as its traditional benevolent behaviour towards other nations was reflected in the arguments of
other opponents of the war. On a nationwide Moratorium Day on October 15,
1967, Democratic party activist Milton Shapp told an audience at Penn State
University: 'Ours is a peaceful protest symbolizing the determination of an
aroused people to return the nation to the true pursuit of peace.'[59] Yale
President Kingman Brewster, Jr aired similar sentiments: 'Let us say simply
and proudly that our ability to keep the peace also requires above all that
America once again become a symbol of decency and hope, fully deserving
the trust and respect of mankind.'[60]

As with the anti-imperialists of 1898, those who opposed the Vietnam War
often did so in terms that were consistent with the belief in American exceptionalism. As with the earlier 'Great Debate' over the course of American
foreign policy, advocates on both sides of the Vietnam issue utilized the
language and ideas of traditional American beliefs to further their cause.
Although the belief in American exceptionalism was certainly shaken by the
events surrounding Vietnam, the continued use of its rhetoric during the
war indicated that the belief would survive this latest 'trauma' or 'time of
trial' in American history. That the belief in American exceptionalism would
persist beyond the Vietnam experience seemed confirmed further by the
reaction to the impending impeachment and subsequent resignation of
President Nixon in August 1974. Far from concluding that their political system was just as fallible as that of any other nation, Americans generally celebrated the fact that their constitutional process of government had worked
and that a corrupt president had been rooted out and removed himself from
office before he could be ejected by the Senate.

Conclusions

Despite the lauding of the constitutional system that accompanied Nixon's
resignation, the Watergate revelations, combined with the Vietnam experience and the general divisiveness of over a decade of social and political upheaval, *did* have profound effects on American public confidence.

In 1974, opinion polls showed that Americans believed they were facing problems worse than they could remember at any other time in their lives. Of those polled by Daniel Yankelovich for *Time* magazine, 71 per cent believed that 'things are going badly in the country' while 68 per cent thought 'the country is in deep and serious trouble today'. Loss of faith in the institutions of government had almost doubled between 1968 and 1973, and 88 per cent of Americans in 1974 mistrusted 'the people in power in this country'. The public felt 'that the great national institutions command an excess of power, which they abuse for selfish ends'. The loss of confidence could, therefore, be attributed to a 'crisis of moral legitimacy'. Americans believed that the resolution of this crisis would be a restoration of American values and principles to public life but they could not see how such an end could be achieved.[61] The editors of the *New Republic* characterized the period as the 'Tarnished Age'.[62] Vietnam and Watergate had, as so many commentators, public officials and ordinary Americans declared, inflicted deep wounds in the American psyche. These psychological wounds may have been vague and largely intangible but they did manifest themselves in nagging doubts about the meaning and future direction of America. They raised the question of whether there was a need for what Democratic Senator Eugene McCarthy had termed in 1967 'a great reexamination by the American people of what our objectives as a nation are'.[63]

The American commitments in the Cold War, and specifically in Vietnam, had been framed in the language of American exceptionalism. The experience of Vietnam, compounded by the Watergate scandal, caused many Americans to doubt or even cease to believe that their nation's actions were consistent with the values and principles upon which their society was supposed to function. The Vietnam War and the Watergate revelations seemed finally to reveal that the United States was just as fallible as any other nation. As the above analysis shows, however, there were indications that the belief in American exceptionalism would survive the period intact. As with earlier periods of crisis and change in American history, advocates on both sides of the Vietnam issue continued to utilize the rhetoric of American exceptionalism in their arguments. The idea that the US was a special nation with a special destiny seemed as though it might not lose its currency in American discourse. The remaining chapters of this book will explore the extent to which the belief in American exceptionalism survived the experience of Vietnam. The administrations of each post-Vietnam presidency, beginning with Gerald Ford, will be analysed to show how each of them attempted to utilize the rhetoric of American exceptionalism to heal the 'wounds' of Vietnam and Watergate and rebuild American self-confidence.

The consequences of the Vietnam War, and indeed Watergate, in US foreign policy were also somewhat ambiguous. The US Congress attempted to reassert its role in foreign policy making in order to stem further presidential excesses and abuses of power, most visibly with the 1973 War Powers

Act. But in times of crisis, and especially when force has been deployed, the Congress has remained largely subordinate to the White House in the decision making process.[64] The Vietnam War was also credited with the breakdown of the so-called Cold War consensus in foreign policy among both the public and elites.[65] Yet this consensus would have broken down with or without Vietnam as the international situation changed through the course of the 1960s, particularly in light of the Sino-Soviet split. The questions concerning the lessons of Vietnam did, however, add to the breakdown of consensus, not least by opening much debate over the future direction of US foreign policy.

The defeat of US objectives by a technologically inferior enemy in Vietnam indicated that there were limits to American power. The nature and extent of these limits, however, continue to be a major source of debate and have come to dominate discussions over foreign policy in each post-Vietnam administration. Public officials, military strategists, journalists, scholars and the American public could find no definitive answer to the question of what the lessons of the Vietnam War were for American society. The term 'Vietnam syndrome' became widely used to describe the collective lessons and legacies of the war, particularly in the political-military realm. The syndrome has been highly criticized, especially by conservative Americans, for causing an unnecessarily stringent reluctance to employ military force as a legitimate foreign policy option.[66] Yet even those policy makers who have advocated and utilized the use of force since Vietnam have been largely restricted by a need to apply the instrumental lessons learned in that war.

The Vietnam syndrome, in its political-military sense, amounts to a set of criteria that should be met if the US is to commit troops to combat. These criteria must be satisfied if public support for military intervention is to be sustained. Presidents feel the need to maintain public support for their foreign policy largely because this grants it the moral legitimacy that became so lacking in Vietnam. To avoid 'another Vietnam', policy makers have therefore, followed the central criteria of the Vietnam syndrome, namely that the US should not employ force in an international conflict unless: just cause can be demonstrated, the objectives are compelling and attainable, and sufficient force is employed to assure a swift victory with a minimum of casualties. There has been disagreement over how these conditions should be applied, but, as the following analysis will show, they have been central to US foreign policy making in the post-Vietnam era.

In the remaining chapters, it will be shown how each post-Vietnam president attempted to revive the perceived moral legitimacy of US foreign policy, usually by rhetorically justifying actions in terms consistent with the belief in American exceptionalism. The chapters will also demonstrate that each administration's foreign policy, especially in the application of force, was conducted in accordance with the apparent lessons learned in Vietnam that would enable the US to avoid again acting in ways that were inconsistent with the ideas of exceptionalism. It will be shown how the legacy of Vietnam became further institutionalized with each administration. Finally, it will be concluded that despite the best efforts of each administration, US foreign policy action was frequently out of step with its exceptionalist rhetoric. As a result, doubts do continue to exist about American power and the American role in the world even though a general belief in American exceptionalism persists.

3
Gerald Ford and the Time for Healing

'My fellow Americans, our long national nightmare is over.'[1] With these words, Gerald R. Ford signalled to the American people that, after years tainted by civil unrest, a divisive war, the assassinations of major public figures, and widespread political scandal, his presidency would offer the United States 'a time to heal'. Ford recognized that the nation was 'caught up in a crisis of confidence' and that, like Abraham Lincoln in the Civil War, it was his job to 'bind up the wounds'.[2] As Ford's transition team concluded, the 'Restoration of confidence and trust of the American people in their political leadership, institutions and processes' would be the first priority of the new administration.[3]

Faith in the moral legitimacy of actions pursued by the US is central to the belief in American exceptionalism. It was this faith that was severely shaken by Vietnam and Watergate. Much of the United States' self-image, and much of what most Americans believed made their nation exceptional, remained intact. Few people were challenging the basic ideology of the US. The ideas of economic freedom, individualism and liberty remained central to the American beliefs system. There was also no need for an institutional revolution. The constitutional framework had proved itself capable of dealing with the various traumas Americans had suffered in the 1960s and early 1970s. The succession following the assassination of a president had been smooth and immediate; a long, bloody and unpopular war had eventually been brought to an end; and now a corrupt president had been removed from office – all within the bounds of the constitutional system without the need for the coups or revolutions that might have been expected in other countries. Americans believed the system had worked; there was no need for it to be changed. What had collapsed was the public's faith in the moral legitimacy of their nation. Those in power had fallen foul of the same abuses and excesses of power that had tarnished other great nations throughout history. The president and other officials representing the United States, both at home and abroad, had adopted means and ends inconsistent with the moral code that Americans believed had helped to make the US an exceptional nation. What was needed was not a change of the system or the values and principles that supported it, but a restoration of the moral standards by which Americans expected their leaders and representatives to conduct themselves in operating that system and furthering those ideals.

Richard Nixon had been expected to restore the strength and unity of the United States. Lyndon Johnson stepped down from the presidency having divided the nation with his Vietnam policy. Nixon was elected on the promise that he would end the Vietnam War and help restore Americans' faith in themselves. Yet he merely compounded the sense that the US was no longer a special nation. He prolonged and, in fact, expanded the war in South East Asia and betrayed the trust of the American people with Watergate. Nixon took the American public's view of the moral legitimacy of their nation to an all-time low. Following Nixon's resignation, President Ford faced a mammoth task in restoring public faith in the moral rightness of the United States and thus in the belief in American exceptionalism.

The analysis in this chapter will consider the extent to which Ford utilized the rhetoric of American exceptionalism to 'heal the wounds' of Vietnam and Watergate and rebuild American self-confidence. Did such rhetoric resonate with the American people thus indicating that the belief in exceptionalism had survived Vietnam and Watergate? In foreign policy, the focus will be upon not only the use of exceptionalist rhetoric but also the extent to which the apparent lessons of the Vietnam conflict influenced decision making and policy. Whether the reality of Ford's actions lived up to his 'heal the nation' rhetoric or whether doubts remained at the end of his presidency about the special nature of the United States will also be explored.

The American public welcomed Gerald Ford as their new president with a great wave of optimism, as though they wanted to believe that recent experiences had been aberrations rather than new norms. Three weeks into his presidency, a Gallup poll showed only 3 per cent of respondents disapproved of the way the new president was handling his job.[4] Ford appeared to have an unblemished record of public service, as a Member of Congress since 1948 and as vice president for eight months. He was widely respected as an honest and decent man with whom the public could relate. Ford seemed to them the perfect antidote to the years of suspicion and deceit preceding him.

Much of this goodwill, however, disappeared when barely a month into his presidency, Ford granted a full pardon to former President Nixon. Although it appears he truly believed the pardon was for the good of the nation, Ford had succeeded in making his task of healing the nation far more difficult. Public confidence, temporarily buoyed by the prospect of a fresh start with the honest and decent Ford, now plunged once again. The president's approval rating fell from 71 per cent to 50 per cent, the 'sharpest decline recorded for any president during his first two months in office'.[5] The pardon of Richard Nixon was one more act to add to the litany of

Vietnam, Watergate and their attendant scandals. The public concluded it could trust this administration no more than its predecessors. The American fall from grace seemed to be continuing.

The Ford foreign policy

Although his attempts at healing the wounds of Watergate may have faltered with the pardoning of Nixon, Ford assumed the presidency also believing he must do whatever necessary to restore confidence, both at home and abroad, in American foreign policy. He needed to allay the fears of allies that the US would retreat into isolation as a result of the defeat in Vietnam. He also needed to convince enemies, both real and potential, that the transition of power had not weakened American resolve and the ability of the US to defend its interests world-wide. To help achieve both these goals, Ford made clear that he would seek continuity in foreign policy and build upon the very great accomplishments he considered his predecessor had made in this area. Ford, therefore, retained most of Nixon's foreign policy making team with, most notably, Henry Kissinger remaining both national security advisor and secretary of state. In his first State of the Union address, Ford made clear that his administration would not shirk its global responsibilities: 'This is not a moment for the American people to turn inward. More than ever before, our own well-being depends on America's determination and America's leadership in the whole wide world.'[6]

Ford and his advisers also recognized that the American people demanded a return to a foreign policy that embodied the moral values that traditionally were believed to have accompanied all foreign endeavours. In his first address to Congress, Ford pledged 'continuity in our dedication to the humane goals which throughout our history have been so much of America's contribution to mankind'.[7] In a draft submitted by the National Security Council for inclusion in the speech, this point was expanded upon:

> In the long run, the measure of the power of this nation will be measured more by the texture of its moral fiber than by the strength of its military sinew. The sinew is crucial – and, as I have said, this Administration will not let that be weakened. But it is in the aspirations of our people that our foreign policy is clearly rooted.[8]

Although omitted from the final draft, no doubt partly due to its inelegant language, this passage shows clearly that Ford and his advisers recognized the need to reassert the moral legitimacy of US foreign policy, at the very least by using rhetoric that invoked the belief in American exceptionalism. Ford made clear in April 1975 that he was sure the belief in American exceptionalism would survive the experience of Vietnam:

> [N]o other country can point to two centuries dedicated to expanding and perfecting a continuing revolution in a free society. This is what

makes America unique in the history of nations. And that is why, although our experience in Indochina has been one of heroic sacrifices and great disappointments, I am convinced that we can and will emerge from this ordeal stronger and wiser as a nation, just as we have from others even greater in the past.[9]

As Ford pledged in his 1975 State of the Union address: 'Let us make America once again and for centuries to come what it has so long been – a stronghold and a beacon-light of liberty for the whole world.'[10] A central objective of the Ford administration, therefore, was to conduct its foreign policy in a manner that revitalized the traditional belief in the exceptional nature of the United States.

The fall of Vietnam

Ford's first efforts at national reconciliation through foreign policy were somewhat thwarted, however, by events in South East Asia which conspired to reinforce the views of those Americans who believed their country was no longer the strongest, greatest nation on Earth. With the economy failing and Ford's approval rating still damaged by the pardoning of Nixon, the president faced his first foreign policy crisis in April 1975. Communist forces were overrunning first Cambodia, then South Vietnam. Americans were about to be given a reminder of the trauma of Vietnam and the limits of their nation's power.

It was clear by early 1975 that the American-supported governments in Phnom Penh and Saigon would not last long without substantial aid. Ford requested additional funds from the Congress to help sustain the anticommunist regimes, arguing that the US had a moral obligation to support its long-term friends and allies, especially the Saigon government. The world was watching and, like so many presidents before him, Ford contended that American credibility, already severely damaged by the experience in South East Asia, was at stake once again.[11] Many Members of Congress, however, had come to believe that presidents had gained too much control over foreign policy making since the Second World War. Towards the end of the Vietnam War, the Congress had reasserted its Members' convictions that it was their constitutional right to be a partner in that process with legislation such as the 1973 War Powers Act. Members of Congress were also increasingly less willing to defer to presidential judgement in matters of financing foreign policy. Ford had already met with opposition to his preferred policies over continued military support for Turkey despite that nation's invasion of Cyprus.[12] The Congress was even less convinced by Ford's arguments concerning Vietnam and Cambodia and refused his requests fearing that further military aid could be the first step towards still more years of costly involvement in Indo-China. They would authorize funds for the evacuation of Americans and the provision of humanitarian aid but no further military assistance would be forthcoming.[13]

On April 17, 1975, Phnom Penh capitulated. Six days later, with the fall of Saigon imminent, Ford gave a speech in New Orleans conceding that the US would not intervene again in Vietnam. In anticipation of the final defeat of American objectives in Vietnam, Ford called upon the idea of American exceptionalism in an attempt to move the US forward and 'begin a great national reconciliation'. Making use of the recurrent healing of wounds theme, he declared that:

> Today, America can regain the sense of pride that existed before Vietnam. But it cannot be achieved by refighting a war that is finished as far as America is concerned. As I see it, the time has come to look forward to an agenda for the future, to unify, to bind up the Nation's wounds, and to restore its health and its optimistic self-confidence.

Ford admitted that: 'We, of course, are saddened indeed by the events in Indo-China. But these events, tragic as they are, portend neither the end of the world nor of America's leadership in the world.' He insisted that the 'true source of American power' was not its military strength but 'our belief in ourselves and our belief in our Nation'. The task ahead, according to Ford, was to revive the traditional belief that the US was a special nation with a special destiny, despite the defeat in Vietnam: 'Let us resolve tonight to rediscover the old virtues of confidence and self-reliance and capability that characterized our forefathers two centuries ago.' He concluded with a rousing reiteration of exceptionalist rhetoric: 'Let the beacon light of the past shine forth from historic New Orleans ... and from every other corner of this land to illuminate a boundless future for all Americans and a peace for all mankind.'[14] While most Americans would gladly have put Vietnam behind them at this point, the ignominious withdrawal from Saigon a week later would once again thrust Vietnam to the forefront of people's minds.

On April 29, 1975, Saigon fell to the Vietnamese communists. Americans witnessed yet more television pictures from Vietnam, this time of the frantic scenes in Saigon as closely loyal South Vietnamese and the last of the Americans were evacuated by helicopter from the roof of the US Embassy. Thousands of people were seen clamouring at the gates, begging to be taken away as the sound of gunfire approached ever nearer. These scenes, combined with pictures of South Vietnamese Air Force helicopters being dumped from the deck of an American aircraft carrier, signalled the end of US involvement in Vietnam and the final defeat of US objectives in the region. The episode was a reminder of the agony Americans had suffered for so long and a final indication that all the lives, material, and dollars spent, all the unrest and division the war had created at home, were for naught: they had merely delayed the inevitable. The United States had been defeated totally for the first time in its history.

The American Ambassador in Saigon, Graham Martin, had warned Kissinger that a hasty evacuation from Saigon by the Americans 'would be considered an humiliating act which may have long-term psychological effects on United States foreign policy'.[15] Commander Richard Stratton, a former American prisoner of war in Vietnam, agreed that: 'American disengagement from Viet Nam was inevitable, but the manner in which we did it was embarrassing.'[16] Roy Rowan and William Stewart observed in *Time* that the panicked drama of the evacuation was 'made doubly bitter by the fact that most Americans had made their emotional peace with Viet Nam more than two years ago'. Now Americans seemed faced with 'the only war they would have to lose twice'. The process of 'putting Viet Nam behind us' was not going to be as easy as many Americans had hoped. As Rowan and Stewart concluded: 'Ending America's mental and emotional involvement may prove as hard as ending its physical involvement. The US may have to live for some time with old – and new – nightmares.'[17] The psychological impact of this final American acceptance of total defeat of its objectives in Vietnam did not go unnoticed outside the United States. In London, *The Times* observed that events in Indo-China had resulted in 'a serious loss of confidence – not in the first instance among America's allies, but within the US itself. It is this, rather than the fall of Vietnam, that could gradually erode America's influence abroad if it is not resolved within a reasonable time'.[18]

The final abandonment of Vietnam also had other, more tangible consequences. Thousands of refugees fled the country as the communist armies advanced. Ford felt the US had a moral obligation to accept as many refugees as possible but again the Congress was unwilling to release funds to finance any resettlement. Its members appeared content to put the whole episode behind them and move on to other matters. Many of them received letters and phone calls from constituents overwhelmingly against allowing refugees into the country. Most Americans appeared concerned about the impact on an already flagging economy. Some feared, however, that communists would infiltrate the US as refugees, while others gave racist or xenophobic reasons for refusing asylum.[19] A Gallup poll found that only 36 per cent of Americans believed Vietnamese refugees should be allowed to settle in the US while 54 per cent said they should not be admitted.[20]

Ford found such attitudes 'unbelievable'.[21] He invoked the belief in American exceptionalism as he launched a campaign to secure a reversal in congressional and public opinion. He declared: 'This action does not reflect the values we cherish as a nation of immigrants. It is not worthy of a people which has lived by the philosophy symbolized in the Statue of Liberty.' Ford argued that by welcoming the Vietnamese and Cambodians, as they had Cubans, Hungarians, and other peoples displaced by communist actions, Americans would go a long way towards restoring their reputation as the 'asylum for all mankind'. He concluded that: 'To do otherwise would be a repudiation of the finest principles and traditions of America.'[22]

Ford's use of rhetoric that evoked the idea that the US was an exceptional nation with certain special duties to fulfil resonated with various groups, organizations and individuals who came out in support of aiding the refugees.[23] The president did not only use such language in public forums, but also based his argument on moral grounds when addressing congressional leaders. He told Republicans from the House and Senate in a White House meeting on May 6: 'I cannot believe that the traditional compassion of this great country is dead and that we Americans will no longer welcome those whom we encouraged to defend themselves and now seek to live in freedom.'[24] Ford's appeal to traditional ideas clearly worked. Much of the public hostility to the refugees was replaced with thousands of offers of jobs, homes and financial help that overwhelmed the volunteer agencies assisting the State Department with the relocations.[25] Following much pressure and growing public support, the Congress relented and financed the admission of almost 132,000 Indo-Chinese refugees.[26] The episode had demonstrated that the idea of American exceptionalism had not lost its rhetorical currency among Americans, whether among the public or the elite. They might have doubts that their institutions lived up to the demands of traditional American values and principles, but Americans would still be responsive to appeals based on those traditional beliefs when they were pressed to consider whether their own feelings and actions matched up with them.

The fall of Saigon had nevertheless reopened many of the old wounds just when Ford had hoped the healing process was under way. Ford had effectively used exceptionalist rhetoric in the issue of the Vietnamese refugees, but the American people needed more than words. They needed some tangible proof that their nation had not been permanently weakened by all it had gone through in recent years. They needed for their country to be seen to act decisively, powerfully, and morally before they could fully believe again in its special place among nations.

The *Mayaguez* incident

One of the major questions arising from the end of the Vietnam War was where, when and how the US would again employ force to resolve an international crisis. The conflicting lessons of Vietnam suggested different approaches to the appropriate use of force. Senator Mike Mansfield, the Democratic majority leader, represented the views of those Americans who believed force should only ever be employed again by the US as a last resort under very particular conditions: 'Military interventions, except in the interests of our own security, should become a policy of the past and should be conducted only in proper consultation between the Executive and the legislative branches.'[27] Meanwhile others, including Henry Kissinger, believed that military force remained a legitimate tool in international relations that should be used swiftly and with maximum application whenever it was considered the most effective option. President Ford would not be drawn publicly on what he considered to be the appropriate use of force in light of Vietnam. He did state that he believed the 'lessons of the past in Vietnam have already been learned – learned by presidents, learned by Congress, learned by the American people'.[28] In foreign policy, Ford admitted that:

> I think we … may have learned some lessons concerning how we would conduct a military operation. … [I]f we ever become engaged in any military operation in the future – and I hope we don't – I trust we've learned something about how we should handle such an operation.

He would not be drawn, however, on what exactly he felt Americans had learned: 'I wouldn't want to pass judgment at this time. … I simply am indicating that from that unfortunate experience in Vietnam, we ought to be in a better position to judge how we should conduct ourselves in the future.'[29] However, the response to the first foreign policy crisis after the fall of Saigon did give a clear indication of the president's attitude towards the use of force and established a precedent for the post-Vietnam application of American military power. But to what extent did this incident contribute to Ford's attempts at reviving the moral legitimacy of US foreign policy?

On May 12, 1975, the US merchant ship SS *Mayaguez* was seized by Khmer Rouge gunboats some seven or eight miles from the Cambodian-held island of Pulou Wei. Ford called an emergency NSC meeting to discuss the appropriate American response to what he considered an act of piracy in international waters. The president decided to issue a statement to the Cambodians through the Chinese government condemning the action and calling for the immediate and unconditional surrender of the *Mayaguez* and her crew. On May 14, with diplomatic efforts proving unsuccessful, US Marines were ordered to search out and rescue any Americans held on the island of Koh Tang, where the ship was anchored, and to retake the *Mayaguez*. In conjunction with the rescue operation, military targets in and around the mainland port of Kompong Som were bombed. The ship was retaken without difficulty but the crew was not found. Meanwhile the Marines were meeting heavy resistance on the island with no sign of the missing crew members. Ford ordered his Press Secretary, Ron Nessen, to issue a statement to the press revealing the rescue mission was under way and that he would call off the military if the Cambodians announced the crew had been released. Ford's hope was that, in the absence of a direct diplomatic route, the Phnom Penh government might be screening the international news wires. The move may have worked, as within an hour a small fishing vessel with the *Mayaguez* crew waving white flags on board was sighted by a navy pilot. With the crew and ship safe, Ford ordered the Marines to extricate themselves from Koh Tang, but the bombing of Kompong Som continued for another hour.[30]

The reaction to the rescue was overwhelmingly positive from almost all quarters. During the crisis, public support for a strong stand had been widespread. An NBC poll conducted on May 13–14 found 65 per cent of respondents favouring military action to get back the ship and its crew.[31] Similarly, 81 per cent of the readers of Ford's homestate newspaper, the *Detroit Free Press*, reportedly believed the president should 'use any means necessary to recover the ship'.[32] Letters, telegrams and phone calls to the White House during the crisis almost unanimously urged the president to take 'swift, decisive action'. Following the successful rescue attempt, 97 per cent of mail and 93 per cent of telephone calls to the White House supported the president's action.[33] The words of two couples from Connecticut who telegrammed the president were typical of public sentiment: 'We applaud your efforts and handling of the *Mayaguez*/Cambodia incident. Your strong, affirmative action should remove the stigma that the US is a paper tiger.'[34] Such views were shared by Members of Congress. Max Friedersdorf, Ford's Assistant for Legislative Affairs, reported an 'overwhelmingly favorable' and 'laudatory' Congressional response to the president's action. Senator Clifford Hansen reflected the views of the majority of Congress Members when he spoke in the Senate on May 15:

> This has done more to restore confidence in Washington and to repair the tarnished image of America worldwide than any event of the past year. ... America, by virtue of this action in Cambodia, serves notice on the rest of the world that we have been misjudged badly should our withdrawal from Indochina be thought indicative of a failure to stand for principle throughout the world.[35]

Republican Carroll Hubbard, chairman of the 75 House Democratic freshman members, congratulated the president on their behalf, saying: 'It's good to win one for a change.'[36] That the president's action helped restore some public confidence in their nation and its leadership seemed reflected in Ford's public approval rating which rose 11 points to 51 per cent in a Gallup survey of June 12, 1975. In a reverse of the public's reaction to the pardon of Nixon, the Gallup Organization observed that this represented 'one of the sharpest gains ever recorded in Gallup surveys going back to the middle 1930s'. Certainly the gain was also effected by an upturn in public confidence concerning the economy, but the main factor appeared to be Ford's reaction to the *Mayaguez* incident.[37]

Ford and his advisers had been well aware that no matter how they dealt with the *Mayaguez* incident, their actions would come under considerable public and congressional scrutiny. They were determined to show not only that the US still had the will to stand up to aggression but also that it would do so in a manner consistent with the values and principles that had traditionally characterized American action in the world. To this end, Ford was determined to ensure that the US appeared to conduct itself in a manner acceptable to Congress and the American public. As Ford reported to the Congress, the official line was that the seizing of the *Mayaguez* was a 'hostile act…in clear violation of international law'. The US had chosen to respond with force only after 'Appropriate demands for the return of the *Mayaguez* and its crew were made, both publicly and privately, without success'. Ford insisted that all military action was taken with the clear and limited objective of rescuing the ship and its crew. The tactical bombing of military targets in the area of Kompong Som was strictly surgical and justified 'in order to prevent reinforcement or support from the mainland' by Cambodian forces.[38]

Whether the operation was truly legitimate and whether it contributed to a revival of the United States acting within the tradition of exceptionalism is open to debate. Questions can be raised about how comprehensively the Ford administration attempted to resolve the crisis diplomatically. Such efforts were severely handicapped by the absence of official diplomatic channels, the indifferent approach of the Chinese government as intermediary, and perhaps most importantly the ambiguity of whether the seizure of the ship was officially sanctioned or the independent act of a local commander. Given these problems, 60 hours was hardly a reasonable amount of time within which to expect diplomatic efforts to bring about a resolution. Moreover, though, it seems clear from discussions within the NSC that a military resolution was always intended and that any diplomacy was seen as perfunctory.

The recently declassified minutes from the first of the four NSC meetings held during the crisis reveal that Kissinger believed from the outset that 'negotiation, even if we get the ship back,…is not to our advantage'. Kissinger and Ford agreed that the administration should 'make a strong statement and give a note to the Cambodians, via the Chinese'. However, they were both adamant from the start that 'a show of force' was the preferred option. Military action was necessary, argued Kissinger, in order to send a message, not only to the Cambodians but also the Soviet Union and others, that any such challenge to the US would not go unanswered. Although the first priority should be the swift retrieval of the ship and its crew, Kissinger stressed that the current image of the United States abroad was also a factor to be considered in how to resolve the situation. The US must be seen to act decisively for the sake of its international prestige.[39]

Vice President Nelson Rockefeller agreed, recalling the 1968 seizure of the USS *Pueblo*. In that case, failure to act swiftly and forcefully had caused the crew to suffer over a year in a North Korean prison while their release was negotiated. With barely two weeks passing since the final hurried withdrawal from Vietnam, the American people would not have the patience to endure a similar embarrassment. Rockefeller also believed the American response to the seizure of the *Mayaguez* would be regarded as a 'test case' by other foreign adversaries. He believed, as a result, that: 'we need something strong soon. ... I think a violent response is in order. The world should know that we will act and that we will act quickly.'[40] Kissinger reiterated this line of thinking in the third NSC meeting of the crisis held the following night: 'We have the opportunity to prove that others will be worse off if they tackle us, and not that they can return to the status quo.' The chosen response would affect the way not only Cambodia, but also North Korea and the Soviet Union regarded the United States. It was imperative that the administration take full advantage of this opportunity to show the world that American power and will had survived the Vietnam debacle.[41]

That seeking a diplomatic solution was a low priority is further evidenced by the lack of time dedicated during the NSC meetings to discussing non-military options. Aside from the initial suggestion of sending a demand for the ship's release via Chinese intermediaries, there was no further consideration of diplomatic efforts except to confirm that no response to the original contact had been received. Ford, Kissinger, Secretary of Defense James Schlesinger, CIA Director William Colby and others present instead focused on various options involving force. They debated the possibility of seizing Cambodian assets, establishing a blockade, mining Cambodian harbours, capturing a Cambodian ship or island, and even using B-52s to bomb Cambodia, as well as the eventual decision to take the ship back by force with supporting action against other Cambodian targets.

The Nixon administration had faced many questions concerning the legality of actions taken against Cambodia during the Vietnam War. The Ford administration was determined to avoid similar criticism and sought to ensure that its actions were justified under international laws governing the use of armed force. Ford's counsel, Philip Buchen, advised the president that under the UN Charter the United States was justified in taking military action only in self-defence against the armed attack by the Cambodians on the *Mayaguez*. This action must be 'designed to recover the ship and the crew'. Buchen warned, however, that the American response must be reasonable and 'not disproportionate in severity to the attack'. While the US could legally use force to recover the ship and crew it could not take additional punitive action against Cambodia: 'Acts of force designed to *punish* Cambodia – as opposed to *recovery* of the ship and crew – are prohibited – except as collective measures decided on by the UN Security Council.'[42] Yet it is again clear from the NSC meetings that the decision makers believed some form of punitive action was necessary in order to send as strong a message as possible to the Cambodians and others that the US would not tolerate any violations of its interests or security. Schlesinger recommended that after the ship had been rescued the US should 'attack and sink the Cambodian Navy ... in order to maximize the punishment'. Rockefeller suggested that at the conclusion of the rescue mission, the US should 'destroy the port as retaliation'.[43] Although neither option was eventually pursued,

Kissinger agreed with the sentiment, stating at the third meeting: 'It is not just enough to get the ship's release. ... I think we should seize the island, seize the ship, and hit the mainland.' When Buchen reminded the meeting of the limits of what action was justified under international law, Kissinger replied: 'I think the worst stance is to follow Phil's concern. If we only respond at the same place at which we are challenged, nobody can lose by challenging us. They can only win. ... I would hit, and then deal with the legal implications.'[44] Although the bombing of the mainland may have served tactical purposes to some degree, much of the reasoning behind it was aggressive and punitive in nature. The operation can be regarded as over-zealous and out of proportion to the original act of piracy. Such an approach can be criticized for disregarding international law and standing outside the tradition of a nation that supposedly represented the best hope for freedom and justice in the world. Strategic interests were clearly more important than any moral imperatives to Kissinger and the other decision makers in the recovery of the *Mayaguez*.

Some journalists aired concerns that the main motivation for the choice of a swift but costly military operation, rather than a longer but probably less lethal diplomatic process, was the need to bolster American credibility in international affairs. At a White House press conference on May 19, 1975, Ford's Press Secretary Ron Nessen was pressed on this issue. One reporter related how Kissinger had told a press briefing that the operation to recapture the *Mayaguez* was not an attempt to demonstrate American resolve in the wake of Vietnam but that the sole purpose was to rescue the ship and its crew. Nessen assured reporters that the latter was true, stating that 'this entire operation was designed for one purpose, and that was to get the crew and the ship back safely'. Any subsequent restoration of American credibility and confidence was a 'byproduct ... that can be considered a bonus to the operation, but it was not the original impetus behind the operation'.[45] Yet the record of Kissinger's arguments in the NSC meetings shows clearly that the perceived need to demonstrate the power and resolve of the US was a major consideration in the decision to take swift military action to end the crisis. To admit as much, though, would have diminished the effects of the mission's success in showing that the US could act with resolve in pursuit of a just cause. Had the public been aware of the decision makers' keenness to make an example of Cambodia, Americans might have further questioned whether the mission was justifiable.

As it was, some criticism did come from Members of Congress who claimed the President had not fulfilled the requirements of the 1973 War Powers Act. The Act obliges presidents to consult with the Congress whenever possible in advance of any use of military force. The files of John Marsh, Max Friedersdorf, and others in Ford's Congressional Relations Office all reveal that a large number of Senators and Representatives were telegrammed or spoken with about the *Mayaguez* on May 13 and 14.

Most of those contacted indicated their support and urged the president to proceed as he saw fit. On the afternoon before the military action began, Ford met with the bipartisan leaders of Congress, including Senator Mansfield, House Speaker Carl Albert, the Floor leaders, the Whips, and the chairs of the Foreign Affairs and Armed Services Committees, to discuss the proposed action. As noted above, most Members of Congress congratulated the president upon the success of the mission. Some, such as Senator Mansfield, were unhappy with the White House, however, suggesting they had been notified rather than consulted about the situation. House Representative from New York, Elizabeth Holtzman, the Democrat who had pursued Ford on the question of there being a deal behind the Nixon pardon, was uncompromising in her criticism: 'The President's resort to force in this case appears to have been illegal and unconstitutional. At best the situation reflects terrible intelligence. At worst it is a reflection of faulty Presidential judgment and overreaction.'[46]

Ford believed he had done all that was necessary to comply with the War Powers Act by keeping key Members of Congress informed and allowing them comment, meeting with the bipartisan leadership immediately before the rescue operation began, and giving a written report to both chambers within 48 hours of the first application of force (even though this was after the operation had been completed). The Congress, however, was far from a major participant in the decision making process. Although congressional reaction was of some concern to Ford, all the major decisions were taken within the NSC. The decision to seek a military solution was taken at the first NSC meeting on the afternoon of May 12. The subsequent consultations with Members of Congress were of little consequence in the actual planning and execution of the operation. Ford had made quite clear at the first NSC meeting that decisions taken within the Executive would have primacy no matter what the conclusion of the consultation process: 'I can assure you that, irrespective of the Congress, we will move.'[47] Kissinger confirmed this perspective when asked by Rockefeller at the final NSC meeting what the president should do if the congressional leadership opposed the decision to employ force. Kissinger replied: 'He would have to go ahead anyway.'[48] Even though most Members of Congress had aired their approval of whatever action the president chose to take, the question of how far the people's representatives in the Congress contributed to the decision making process rekindled some of the fears about too much unchecked power being exercised by the Executive and the continued influence of the old guard represented by Kissinger.

There was further disquiet following the operation that the threat posed by the ship's seizure did not warrant the relatively high human cost of the mission to retrieve it. Although in original reports casualty figures were low, it gradually became clear that the operation was very costly, with

41 Americans killed (23 of them in a helicopter crash in Thailand en route to join the rescue mission) and 50 wounded in an effort to save 39 crew members. Ford himself admitted he was greatly disturbed by the fact that more Americans died as a result of the mission than had been captured in the first place.[49] Such admissions left some Americans wondering whether such losses were morally justifiable.

The resolution of the *Mayaguez* incident indicated to the American people that, despite the reversal in Vietnam, their president was still able and willing to use decisive force in defence of American interests around the world. This belief did contribute to an upturn in public confidence in their nation and its leadership. But the operation failed to fully restore Americans confidence in their nation's ability to meet crises abroad. The *Mayaguez* operation had been swiftly executed and was relatively low risk with clear, limited objectives. On the right, some questioned whether the action clearly demonstrated that the US could stand up to any threat or aggression abroad. On the left, critics argued that the incident showed the US would continue to throw its military weight at international problems, as it had in Vietnam, without sufficient energies being directed towards the more subtle and morally acceptable diplomatic approach. Anthony Lewis observed wryly in the *New York Times* that for 'all the talk of principle, it is impossible to imagine the United States behaving that way toward anyone other than a weak, ruined country of little yellow people who have frustrated us'.[50] A Gallup poll conducted immediately before the crisis indicated the degree to which Americans were evenly split over whether the US should employ force to resolve international disputes. The poll found that 45 per cent of Americans believed that war was an outmoded method of settling international differences while 46 per cent supported the use of force when necessary.[51] The *Mayaguez* incident did not resolve this debate in the US over the moral legitimacy of the use of force. The incident did, though, set the precedent for the way in which US force could be applied abroad in the post-Vietnam era and be deemed a success. To make it acceptable to the American people, any military operation would have to be presented as having clear, morally justifiable objectives that could be achieved swiftly using the maximum force necessary at the lowest cost possible in lives and materiel.

Despite the remaining questions and anxieties about the *Mayaguez* incident and the moral legitimacy of US foreign policy, Ford felt confident in his belief that 'the American people are getting out from under the trauma of our problems in Vietnam'.[52] Ford recalls in his memoirs that 'the gloomy national mood began to fade'. He believed that: 'Many people's faith in their country was restored.'[53] Ford and others looked upon his handling of the crisis as the greatest political victory of his administration and considered that it contributed to the healing of the nation that the president deemed his most important priority.

Conclusions

The Ford presidency is often looked upon as a caretakership that for some scholars hardly seems worth a mention in their histories of late twentieth century America.[54] Yet Ford was president for two and a half years and in terms of its effects on the way Americans felt about themselves in the aftermath of a decade of social and political trauma it is an important period. Gerald Ford was relatively successful in his self-proclaimed task of healing the wounds of Vietnam and Watergate. In his candour and honesty he restored much of Americans' faith in the moral legitimacy of their political leadership. In a post-election assessment in 1976, Hugh Sidey concluded that although Ford had failed to retain office, he had during his presidency 'furnished what the nation needed – solidity, courage, common sense and honor. Ford's stewardship was a welcome change from the decade of disarray that began with the bullet that killed Kennedy'.[55] This was perhaps never clearer than in July 1976 when the nation's bicentennial celebrations gave Ford a unique opportunity to symbolically further the healing process he saw as central to his leadership.

Ford gave a series of speeches, rich in the rhetoric of American exceptionalism, on and around the Fourth of July that called upon Americans to rededicate themselves to the values and principles upon which the nation was founded.[56] *Newsweek*'s editors argued that 'the vast collective experience' of the celebrations 'seemed to rekindle a lost spirit of hope'.[57] The Bicentennial acted as 'a kind of catharsis' that offered a positive way of 'clearing the American soul'.[58] Ford himself regarded the celebrations as final evidence that the 'nation's wounds had healed. We had regained our pride and rediscovered our faith and, in doing so, we had laid the foundation for a future that had to be filled with hope'.[59]

In addition to symbolically revitalizing the faith in exceptionalism, Ford also made attempts to revive American confidence in the power, will, and moral certitude of the nation's conduct abroad through what he considered a firm approach to foreign policy. This was demonstrated in particular by the *Mayaguez* incident where Ford indicated to allies, adversaries and Americans themselves that the United States was still willing to apply military force despite the chastening experience of Vietnam. He achieved other successes too. His administration helped to ease tensions between Egypt and Israel with the signing of the Sinai Accords. His Soviet policy also went at least some way towards revitalizing detente and limiting the threat of nuclear war through agreeing the framework for a second Strategic Arms Limitation Treaty (SALT II) in November 1975.[60]

Ford did not, however, have an unblemished record in foreign affairs. Concerns remained about the extent to which foreign policy decision making was an executive prerogative and the degree to which conduct abroad was founded upon the values and principles of the nation. As we have seen, the

Mayaguez operation raised as many questions as it answered concerning the use of American military power in the post-Vietnam era. The 1975 congressional investigation of the CIA shed further light on the extent of the abuse of power during the Nixon and indeed earlier administrations, both domestically and internationally. Ford's decision to commit the CIA to the conflict in Angola even while the agency was under investigation raised further questions about his tact and moral certitude.[61] Ford's Soviet policy also met with much criticism. SALT II and the 1975 Helsinki Accords, which included a provision recognizing the permanence of post-Second World War European borders, were characterized as sell-outs to the Soviet Union by Ford's opponents. Despite his best efforts, the ignominious scramble to evacuate Saigon also cast a dark reminder of the conflict and defeat in Vietnam over Ford's presidency.

Although Ford made much use of the rhetoric of American exceptionalism, his foreign policy was largely determined by strategic, political or economic interests rather than moral imperatives. His policy towards the Vietnamese refugees following the fall of Saigon provided a rare instance, however, of how the belief in American exceptionalism can have a direct influence upon US foreign policy making. Ford did not simply couch his preferred policy of admitting the refugees to the US in exceptionalist rhetoric but, on this occasion, his belief in the special duties required of his exceptional nation actually determined the policy to be taken. Basing his policy on traditional American conceptions of the special nature of the US proved highly successful in securing congressional and public approval. At other times, though, as is clear from the decision making process during the *Mayaguez* crisis, strategic and political interests took precedence over moral considerations in the administration's foreign policy.

Ford's decision to pardon former President Nixon overshadowed all that he achieved during his term in office. Regardless of his true motivations and intent, the pardon aligned Ford with the corruption, secrecy, and arrogance of his predecessor. It left enough doubt about the sincerity of his leadership to contribute to the American public electing a Washington outsider to the White House in 1976. In James Earl Carter, the American people placed their hopes for a full restoration of the integrity of their national leadership and a return to America's place as foremost among nations.

4
Jimmy Carter – Morality and the Crisis of Confidence

Jimmy Carter was elected President of the United States largely because he was a Washington outsider, untainted by the years of torment surrounding Vietnam and Watergate. Indeed, before he sought the Democratic nomination for presidential candidate, few people outside his native Georgia had heard of this former naval officer, nuclear engineer, and peanut farmer. Carter made it clear in his election campaign that he understood and shared the people's pain, doubt and failing confidence following the defeat in Vietnam and the Watergate scandals. He believed America's moral compass had been lost, that traditional beliefs at the very heart of what it meant to be an American had been thrown into question by years of government lies, failure and corruption. Carter, though, was not about to give up on those beliefs. He was confident that by rededicating the nation to the principles upon which it was founded, Americans could once again believe in themselves and the special role their nation had to play in human history.

The healing of the nation

Carter acknowledged that his predecessor had done much to begin the healing process. In his Inaugural Address on January 20, 1977, Carter thanked President Ford 'for all he has done to heal our land'.[1] Yet Carter had made clear throughout his election campaign that he did not believe Ford's administration had done enough to restore American confidence. It had been a 'tired and worn-out administration without new ideas, without youth or vitality, without vision and without the confidence of the American people'.[2] The Ford administration was inextricably linked with the causes of what Carter called the 'unprecedented doubt and soul-searching' being experienced throughout the United States.[3] The pardoning of Nixon had demonstrated this link all too clearly. In foreign policy too, Ford's continued reliance on Henry Kissinger had made it difficult for the public to fully trust his administration's claim to have put the years of corrupt and immoral policy behind. Carter and his advisers joined the chorus of critics lambasting Kissinger's so-called 'Lone Ranger' approach to the nation's foreign policy. Such criticism has been shown to be somewhat unwarranted as Ford himself did play a considerable role in foreign policy making and was certainly unwilling to grant Kissinger a free hand in all matters. Nevertheless, the Ford administration was not seen to have broken with the secretive foreign policy trends of recent years. As Carter's National Security Advisor Zbigniew Brzezinski has written, the new administration believed they were inheriting a foreign policy 'stalemated on the level of power and excessively cynical on the level of principle'.[4] In his first significant foreign policy speech as president, given at the University of Notre Dame, Carter observed: 'The Vietnamese war produced a profound moral crisis, sapping worldwide faith in our own policy and our system of life, a crisis of confidence made even more grave by the covert pessimism of some of our leaders.'[5]

Carter was determined, therefore, that his administration's foreign policy should be as open and accountable as possible. He wanted to involve the public as much as he could and cooperate with Congress more readily than previous administrations. Above all, though, Carter found it 'urgent to restore the moral bearings of American foreign policy'.[6] He promised to return the US to a foreign policy based upon the nation's founding principles. In his Inaugural Address, Carter told the American people that historically the United States had 'an exceptional appeal' among nations, based upon its dedication to moral principles. He called upon Americans to 'Let our recent mistakes bring a resurgent commitment to the basic principles of our Nation.' He believed the US must interact with other nations only in ways consistent with the traditional beliefs of the American people. Carter committed his administration to building 'international policies which reflect our own precious values'. This would ensure a revival of American self-confidence and provide the rest of the world with 'affirmation of our Nation's continuing moral strength and our belief in an undiminished, ever-expanding American dream'.[7]

The Carter foreign policy

Much has been made of Carter's inexperience in foreign affairs upon taking office. Yet Carter had been a member of the foreign policy think-tank the Trilateral Commission since 1973. It was from the Commission that he drew his two main foreign policy appointees: National Security Advisor Zbigniew Brzezinski and Secretary of State Cyrus R. Vance. Their conflicting views on the appropriate direction and conduct of foreign affairs would become a dominant feature of the Carter administration. Brzezinski was a realist with a distaste for Wilsonian idealism, who regarded Soviet power as the main obstacle to a stable world order.[8] Vance was a patient and persistent diplomat who distrusted absolutes of any kind. He acknowledged that force was sometimes a necessary political tool but believed diplomacy was better suited to the resolution of most situations.[9] Their main point of contention was over what Brzezinski characterizes as 'the proper balance between power and principle' in US foreign policy. While Vance favoured solving international disputes and problems through compromise and diplomatic negotiation, Brzezinski regarded force, or at least the threat of force, as an 'unavoidable ingredient' which should be utilized by the administration to support its principles in its foreign relations.[10] This question of how the American dedication to traditional values and principles should be balanced with the demands and realities of international politics was central to the administration's attempts to restore the moral integrity and the international prestige of the United States in world affairs. The extent to which the administration sought and achieved this balance will be the focus of the analysis in this chapter.

On the advice of Brzezinski and other officials within the administration, Carter used his speech at the University of Notre Dame on May 22, 1977 to increase public understanding of the rationale and broader purposes of his foreign policy.[11] His main purpose was to show 'the strands that connect our actions overseas with our essential character as a nation'.[12] Carter made clear that his foreign policy was to be a marked departure from that of recent administrations. An 'inordinate fear of communism' had for too long caused policy makers to overlook the strength of traditional American values. Carter proclaimed:

> For too many years, we've been willing to adopt the flawed and erroneous principles and tactics of our adversaries, sometimes abandoning our own values for theirs. We've fought fire with fire, never thinking that fire is better quenched with water. This approach failed, with Vietnam the best example of its intellectual and moral poverty. But through failure we have now found our way back to our own principles and values, and we have regained our lost confidence.[13]

This section of Carter's speech owes much to a powerful internal memo written by speechwriter Jerry Doolittle. Doolittle was airing his frustrations over early drafts of the speech which he believed failed to adequately demonstrate the difference between the Carter foreign policy and that of his predecessors. Doolittle wrote:

> In the past, our foreign policy was based on the implicit assumption that communism is superior to democracy. ... So powerful are they [the Soviet Union] that if we give them an inch, they will take the globe. But the truth of it is that if we give them an inch, they are likely to choke on it ... And, at long last, we have come to understand this. What is new about the Carter foreign policy is that it is not based on fear. Its basis is, instead, a calm confidence in the superiority of our own system.

Doolittle then went on to outline the main reasons for that confidence in democracy, concluding with the 'fighting fire with fire' analogy. He believed this was the message the administration should be getting across to the public. The President evidently agreed with him as the substance of Doolittle's memo was incorporated almost word for word into the final draft of the speech.[14]

Carter's closest foreign policy advisers agreed that the new administration should develop a foreign policy that would fill what Brzezinski called the 'moral vacuum' in international affairs.[15] Vance affirms in his memoirs that one of the central elements of the new American approach was:

> ...the harnessing of the basic values of the Founding Fathers to our foreign policy. Historically our country had been a force for progress in human affairs. A nation that saw itself as a 'beacon on the hill' for the rest of mankind could not content itself with power politics alone.[16]

As Carter declared at Notre Dame, therefore, his foreign policy would be 'based on an historical vision of America's role... [and] ... rooted in our moral values'.[17]

Carter was adamant that the US should remain a central participant in world affairs. He was not interested in withdrawing the US from its global responsibilities; rather he would follow a policy of what Brzezinski called 'constructive global engagement'.[18] In keeping with American traditions, though, this global involvement would not be based purely on American self-interest but would also serve some higher purpose of humanity and progress – 'Our policy is designed to serve mankind,' Carter told his audience at Notre Dame.[19] The US would encourage all nations to adopt democracy and peaceful interaction with other states, but the US would not impose its will on others, let alone attempt to subjugate sovereign peoples as it had in Vietnam. Carter insisted that Americans had learned from recent experience and would recognize and respect differences in culture and beliefs while advocating universal principles. Upon taking office, Carter issued an address to the people of other nations in which he assured them:

> The United States will meet its obligation to help create a stable, just, and peaceful world order. We will not seek to dominate nor dictate to others. As we Americans have concluded one chapter in our Nation's history and are beginning to work on another, we have, I believe, acquired a more mature perspective on the problems of the world. It is a perspective which recognizes the fact that we do not have the answers to all the world's problems.[20]

Carter acknowledged that the experience in Vietnam had shown there were limits to what the US could achieve in world affairs. It was important to

Carter that Americans remember that 'even our great Nation has its recognized limits, and that we can neither answer all questions nor solve all problems'.[21] Carter believed that no single nation, including the United States and the Soviet Union, was 'all-powerful': 'We've learned that this world, no matter how technology has shrunk distances, is nevertheless too large and too varied to come under the sway of either one or two superpowers.' This fact would not, however, be faced by the Carter administration with resignation, but in a spirit of 'increasing maturity'.[22]

This new maturity would allow the administration to attempt to shift the emphasis of US foreign policy making away from the politics of superpower relations. Carter was clear that competition with the Soviet Union would continue in all forms necessary and would remain the central component of US foreign policy, but it would no longer be allowed to dominate the agenda at the expense of other priorities.[23] Carter was determined to raise awareness of the increasingly interdependent nature of global affairs and reorient US policy accordingly. Administration officials recognized that the world had undergone a great deal of change during the 1960s and 1970s. Nation states in the developing world were acquiring increasingly more important roles in world affairs. The energy crisis and the OPEC oil embargo had demonstrated that US security interests extended beyond the Cold War rivalry with the USSR. Decolonization had unleashed nationalist movements throughout the world that did not fit neatly into a global view predicated on the centrality of the geopolitical competition between East and West. India's testing of a nuclear device in 1974 raised questions about nuclear proliferation among non-aligned states. The rise of transnational organizations, global communication networks, and an increasingly interdependent global economy all added to the need to develop a more complex foreign policy that could accommodate these changes yet allow for continued American leadership.[24] As Carter observed: 'It is a new world that calls for a new American foreign policy. ... We can no longer expect that the other 150 nations will follow the dictates of the powerful, but we must continue – confidently – our efforts to inspire, to persuade, and to lead.'[25] The global interdependence approach of the Carter administration would be in clear contrast to the Nixon–Kissinger–Ford years when US foreign policy had, according to Carter and his advisers, been too greatly dominated by a *realpolitik* approach to international relations. Carter believed that returning to the basic American principles that gave the US its special role in human history would help facilitate such a policy. Complex global interrelationships required the US to cooperate with rather than dominate other nations. Carter was insistent that the US should once again lead by example with a strength 'based not merely on the size of an arsenal but on the nobility of ideas'.[26] By joining with others to protect and promote American principles throughout the world, Carter would revive the moral rightness of US foreign policy. In doing so, the administration drew upon both the exemplar and missionary strands of American exceptionalism.

President Carter's foreign policy was organized around what he called 'five cardinal principles'.[27] These were: first and foremost, a commitment to human rights as the fundamental root of all policy; second, the promotion of increased links and cooperation with other democracies; third, engaging with the Soviet Union in a joint effort to limit and then reduce their arsenals of strategic arms; fourth, to seek a lasting peace in the Middle East; and fifth, to address the threat of nuclear proliferation. The following analysis will concentrate first on the human rights element of Carter's foreign policy, as it was here that his attempts to restore America's moral compass were most pronounced.

Human rights

Carter was determined that human rights would provide the linchpin of his foreign policy. In Presidential Directive NSC-30, Carter declared:

> It shall be a major objective of US foreign policy to promote the observance of human rights throughout the world. The policy shall be applied globally, but with due consideration to the cultural, political and historical characteristics of each individual nation, and to the significance of US relations with the nation in question.[28]

Human rights were placed at the centre of Carter's foreign policy because he believed them to be the very essence of the American beliefs system. Carter accepted that from its conception the US had been dedicated to the principle that all people on earth had a natural right to lead lives based on freedom and equality of opportunity. To deny human rights a central place in US foreign policy making should be unthinkable, he believed, yet much of the floundering in recent years stemmed from the lack of concern exhibited for such rights. Carter believed 'the human rights effort … is a position that is compatible with the character of the American people'.[29] The policy was at the centre of his attempts to revive the moral core of US foreign policy by rededicating it to traditional American principles:

> We've been filled with the words of Thomas Paine and Thomas Jefferson, Benjamin Franklin and George Washington, and others – that all men are created equal, that we are endowed with certain inalienable rights, and that we have a government designed not to control us but to guarantee our rights.
>
> So, human rights is a part of the American consciousness. These kinds of commitments that I share with all other Americans make it almost inevitable that our country will be a leader in the world standing up for the same principles on which our Nation was founded.[30]

Carter was not only invoking the canon of American exceptionalism but attempting to revive and add to that tradition in order to leave behind the memories of Vietnam and Watergate. He used familiar exceptionalist rhetoric, on various occasions referring to his human rights policy as a 'beacon light' that would again 'make our people proud and say we stand for something'.[31] This 'beacon light' would shine across the globe, Carter claimed, not only making Americans feel better about themselves, but also providing 'a rallying point for us in all the democracies of the world'.[32]

It was not only at the level of public rhetoric but also privately that traditional American principles were recognized as being the primary reason for pursuing a human rights policy. Presidential Review Memorandum NSC-28 on Human Rights (PRM 28), drafted in July 1977, concludes that pursuing the overall objective of the human rights policy: 'helps fulfill a moral obligation that we have incurred by virtue of our heritage and values.' This was listed first among several 'sound reasons, based in national interest as well as our moral tradition and legal obligation, for encouraging an increase in the respect that governments accord to human rights'. The promotion of human rights would encourage widespread domestic approval for Carter's foreign policy from both the Congress, where human rights had already become a central issue, and the public 'by permitting the moral and ethical values of our people to be reflected in that policy'. PRM 28 stated that adopting a firm human rights policy would also strengthen the rule of law and respect for international agreements such as the Universal Declaration of Human Rights; promote the 'fundamental long-term American interest' of seeing governments throughout the world base their political and social systems on 'individual freedom and dignity' rather than totalitarianism; and play a central role in the 'philosophical debate' with the Soviet Union over the best way of organizing human society.[33] For Brzezinski, the human rights policy was the most effective method of balancing power with principle in foreign policy. It would meet the requirements of the nation's principles while also advancing American national interests. Emphasizing human rights would illustrate to emerging Third World nations that American-style democracy was a more attractive and beneficial system than those offered by America's adversaries. 'The best way to answer the Soviets' ideological challenge', Brzezinski writes in his memoirs, 'would be to commit the United States to a concept which reflected America's very essence.' This essence, according to Brzezinski, is 'personal freedom and individual liberty'.[34]

Precisely how this essence would be transformed into an actual policy was laid out in the subsequent Presidential Directive NSC-30. This document stipulated that the policy's objectives were to 'reduce worldwide governmental violations of the integrity of the person; ... to enhance civil and political liberties; ... [and] to promote basic economic and social rights'.[35] Despite concerns that establishing priorities would diminish the perceived importance of the other rights outlined, Carter decided to focus the greatest attention on 'governmental violations of the integrity of the person'. He was determined to use all available diplomatic tools to further these objectives, including direct diplomatic pressure; joint ventures with international organizations such as UN agencies, non-governmental organizations, and allied foreign governments; along with official public statements and symbolic acts. Preferential treatment in terms of economic and political benefits would be afforded governments with good or improving human rights records, while financial assistance and other aid would be denied governments with poor or deteriorating records.[36]

Nonetheless, although the human rights effort would affect all areas of foreign policy, the Carter administration would be careful not to let it infringe upon the national interest. Vance believed it was imperative for the policy to be 'flexible and pragmatic in dealing with specific cases that might affect our national security, and that we had to avoid rigidity'.[37] Carter agreed that Americans could not 'conduct our foreign policy by rigid moral maxims'.[38] As PRM 28 stated: 'There are clearly other major objectives of US foreign policy that are of equal – and in some situations greater – importance.' Fundamentally, the human rights objective could not be allowed to obstruct the commitment to 'protect and advance US national security'. Specifically, the administration would not permit questions of human rights to compromise efforts to limit strategic arms; to preserve the strength and unity of NATO; to seek peace in the Middle East; to normalize relations with China; or to control the spread of nuclear weapons. It was fully acknowledged among Carter and his advisers that: 'There will clearly be situations in which efforts to achieve our human rights goals will have to be modified, delayed or curtailed in deference to other important objectives.' This did not mean, however, that human rights would remain a 'marginal objective' as it had in earlier administrations. On the contrary: 'Even when other objectives outweigh the human rights factor, our policies should, nevertheless, be implemented in a manner that promotes human rights to the extent possible.'[39]

Even when national security or other objectives were not at stake, the human rights policy would have to be applied delicately, not only to be effective but also to ensure that its implementation remained consistent with American values and principles. There did exist the possibility of a particularly problematic contradiction, however. How could a US administration demand all nation states respect human rights while also claiming it would not attempt to impose its will on other peoples? Administration officials were aware that, particularly in the case of promoting civil and political liberties, there was a definite 'need … for caution to avoid giving our policy a parochial cast that appears to export American-style democracy'. The authors of PRM 28 state categorically: 'we do not seek to change governments [or] remake societies. Our experience in Vietnam and elsewhere have taught us the limits of our power to influence the internal workings of other nations.'[40] The President reiterated this point in December 1977: 'We have no wish to tell other nations what political or social systems they should have.'[41] The administration acknowledged that due consideration would have to be given to cultural differences when applying the human rights policy. For example, 'in many societies departures from generally recognized norms of human rights may be dictated by adherence to age-old social and religious traditions.' Failure to respect such cultural differences could seriously undermine the effectiveness and legitimacy of the human rights policy. The administration would have to 'constantly reassess our own standards to ensure that we are not confusing truly objectionable conduct with unfamiliar traditional patterns of relationship or conduct'.[42]

Perhaps more fundamental than the potential to clash with cultural norms was the contradiction of pursuing human rights through punishing the domestic functions of sovereign foreign nations. This contradiction was certainly not lost on the Soviet authorities, who claimed that what they did within their own borders was of no concern to the United States. The Carter administration had no right, according to the Kremlin, to impose its view of human rights on the Soviet government, and thereby criticize the internal policies of a sovereign state. In a letter written to Carter at the time of his inauguration, Soviet leader Leonid Brezhnev had commented that both governments should continue their policies of 'noninterference in the internal affairs of the other side'.[43] Both privately and publicly, Carter countered by reminding the Soviets that they were signatories to the UN Charter, the Universal Declaration of Human Rights, and the Final Act of the Helsinki agreements on security and cooperation in Europe; therefore, the US had the right to demand that the Soviet Union live up to its commitments.[44] Nonetheless, the administration went to great lengths to insist that the human rights policy would not interfere with attempts to further détente and achieve the second treaty on strategic arms limitations (SALT II). Carter saw 'no relationship' between human rights and the SALT negotiations.[45]

The limits of American power to advance global human rights were recognized in private policy discussions. It was acknowledged in PRM 28 that 'our expectations must be realistic' and that the administration 'must concentrate on encouraging the maximum possible *evolutionary* improvement'.[46] The timeframe for the fulfilment of human rights objectives was essentially unending, with expectations for visible improvements varying from country to country. Carter and his advisers believed, though, that the policy should not be regarded as a failure if changes came only very slowly or unevenly. Carter claimed to 'understand fully the limits of moral suasion. We have no illusion that changes will come easily or soon'.[47] What was needed was a 'slow, careful, methodical but persistent expression of our concerns about human rights violations'.[48]

The human rights policy was, nonetheless, heavily criticized. There were objections that the administration failed to effectively use economic sanctions or pressure to protect human rights abroad. The administration did abstain or vote against various loan proposals in international financial institutions on the grounds of human rights abuses, but Carter's delegations did not pressure their voting partners to follow suit and in each case the loans were approved. As David Forsythe argues, the administration could, therefore, 'go on record as voting a concern for human rights without really interfering with international financial institutions' programs'.[49] The administration also opposed comprehensive economic embargoes on nations such as Uganda and South Africa which it criticized for human rights abuses, and 'most-favored nation' status was extended to China and Hungary despite their poor human rights records.[50]

Many of the results of the human rights policy were also relatively intangible and, consequently, success was difficult to gauge. A Congressional Research Service study in 1981 found the policy had 'mitigated brutality only at the margins'.[51] Both supporters and opponents of the policy accused the administration of inconsistency. Carter took a case-by-case approach which meant that human rights abuses appeared to go unchecked in many parts of the world. In some cases there were fears that taking a strong moral stance against another country's internal behaviour would actually cause that government to become more rather than less repressive in order to quell disquiet and opposition strengthened by the promise of American support.

Criticisms from the political right were particularly harsh. Jeane Kirkpatrick, Georgetown University political scientist and member of the conservative American Enterprise Institute, wrote a searing indictment of Carter's foreign policy that received widespread attention. She accused the administration of applying 'double standards' in its human rights policy in a manner that was a 'wholesale contradiction of its own principles'. Kirkpatrick found particular fault in Carter's criticisms of governments friendly to the US (even though they were right-wing dictatorships) and his apparent leniency towards others that should be considered unfriendly or enemies.[52] Joshua Muravchik has also condemned Carter because he 'relentlessly debased' the notion of human rights by 'applying it to America's allies to whom no knowledgeable person, of whatever political stripe, would find it applicable'.[53] That Muravchik includes Somoza's Nicaragua and the Shah's Iran among these allies may suggest otherwise but such criticisms of double standards were widespread. Despite the criticisms of Kirkpatrick and others, the Carter administration did ignore or downgrade concerns about human rights to give substantial aid and support to US-friendly dictatorships in Zaire, Indonesia and elsewhere. These inconsistencies were criticized by the political left which also aired disquiet over the welcoming to the White House of leaders such as President Ceauşescu of Romania and Deng Xiaoping of China despite the human rights abuses in their countries.[54]

At best, then, the human rights policy should be considered problematic, at worst a failure. The question of whether it helped to restore a moral centre to foreign policy and contributed to a renewed confidence and belief in the exceptional US role in the world will be further examined at the end of this chapter. It is also necessary, though, to explore whether adopting such a policy was based on a genuine dedication to basic American cultural beliefs or whether it was a cynical, manipulative tactic to win election to the White House and then maintain public approval.

The archival record shows that Carter's advisers did create strategies for securing public and Congressional approval for the administration's foreign policy. In a memo to the President in June 1977, Chief of Staff Hamilton Jordan argued that: 'a comprehensive and well coordinated domestic political strategy [will be required] if our policies are to gain the understanding and support of the American people and the Congress.' The public, Jordan observed, had a limited understanding of most foreign policy issues. The administration, therefore, would have the task of explaining the complexities of the many challenges the US faced abroad through a coordinated public education programme. This should not be considered as entirely a hindrance, however, as it 'provides us an opportunity to present these issues to the public in a politically advantageous way'. Taking the initiative on complex foreign policy issues would, according to Jordan, be 'critical to the political success of these policies'. Finally, once foreign policy goals had been established it would be crucial that specific 'political strategies in support of those goals be developed and implemented'.[55]

It should not be surprising that such recommendations were made or that such strategies existed. All organizations, political or otherwise, are likely to be more effective in fulfilling their goals if they follow coordinated strategies. Jordan was obviously aware, though, that such suggestions within the administration could be regarded as cynical and manipulative, given Carter's public assurances that his presidency would be as open and honest as possible. Jordan reassured the President that due to the 'highly sensitive subject matter' he had typed this confidential 'eyes only' memo himself and that the only other copy was locked away in his office safe.[56] The fact that strategies for securing public and political support existed does not mean, however, that Carter's foreign policy style was adopted purely because it was considered to be politically appealing. It was noted earlier that one of the officially recognized advantages of adopting the human rights policy was that it would encourage widespread domestic approval from both the Congress and the public, because it reflected popular moral and ethical values. While Carter recognized the political value of basing his foreign policy on traditional American values and principles, however, he was also philosophically committed to those values. In his autobiography, *Why Not The Best?*, written in 1975, Carter had espoused his beliefs on the appropriate basis for policy making:

> A nation's domestic and foreign policies actions should be derived from the same standards of ethics, honesty, and morality which are characteristic of the individual citizens of the nation. The people of this country are inherently unselfish, open, honest, decent, competent, and compassionate. Our government should be the same, in all its actions and attitudes.[57]

He concluded: 'There is no legitimate reason why government should not represent the highest possible common ideals and characteristics of the people who form and support it.'[58] Those who worked closely with Carter in his administration confirm that he truly believed in these values and principles and the need to restore the moral fibre to all national and international US policy.

Vance describes Carter as an 'obviously highly intelligent' man who had 'firm principles' and who 'grasped the necessity of basing his leadership and policies on the support and common sense of the American people'.[59] Rick Hertzberg, who became the president's chief speechwriter in May 1979, claims that: 'Carter did not have a political ideology. He had a set of moral precepts, he had a moral ideology.'[60] Brzezinski has noted well the complex nature of Carter's character:

> He deeply believed in human rights and that commitment remained constant during his Administration. At the same time, he sensed, I think, that the issue was an appealing one, for it drew a sharp contrast between himself and the policies of Nixon and Kissinger.[61]

This commitment to human rights, Brzezinski suggests, reflected Carter's religious beliefs. Brzezinski had wondered whether Carter's 'proclaimed religious convictions were real or simply politically expedient' as he was 'shrewd' and 'rather deliberate'. He soon became convinced, however, that Carter did have a 'deep religiosity' that made him a 'man of genuine conviction' with a 'genuine dedication to principle'. Brzezinski argues that: 'Carter's personal philosophy was the point of departure for the foreign policy priorities of the new Administration.' The new President had a 'determination to make US foreign policy more humane and moral'. Brzezinski was convinced that Carter 'genuinely believed that as President he could shape a more decent world'.[62]

What appealed most to Brzezinski about Carter, though, was that he 'would be reasonably tough and realistic in foreign policy ... [while] ... being guided by certain basic principles'.[63] This mirrored Brzezinski's own belief that 'power should be a means for attaining morally desirable ends'.

Although Brzezinski admits he placed greater emphasis than the president on power, he shared Carter's belief that the 'philosophical assumptions' upon which the US had been founded were 'America's strength'.[64] Vance has also noted that, at least until he resigned in 1980, he 'agreed philosophically' with Carter about how the US should approach foreign policy.[65]

It is clear that Carter was genuinely committed to fundamental values and principles upon which he believed US foreign policy must be based, and that his closest advisers agreed with him. He did, however, recognize that strategic, economic, political, and ideological concerns were of an equal and sometimes greater concern, but each of these were in turn informed by the values and principles that Americans hold dear. As he explains in his memoirs:

> I was familiar with the widely accepted arguments that we had to choose between idealism and realism, or between morality and the exertion of power; but I rejected those claims. To me, the demonstration of American idealism was a practical and realistic approach to foreign affairs, and moral principles were the best foundation for the exertion of American power and influence.[66]

To a great extent, then, Jimmy Carter embraced the belief in American exceptionalism. He believed the US was the 'greatest nation on earth' and that it was the nation best qualified to help the rest of the world conform to universal standards of basic natural rights, both by example and by peaceful, benign intervention. But how successful was Carter in pursuing a foreign policy that was consistent with traditional American values? And did he succeed in reviving American self-confidence in the power, prestige, and special destiny of their nation?

The Panama Canal Treaties

Carter believed the signing of the Panama Canal Treaties on September 7, 1977 reflected the US dedication to the rights of self-government and the desire not to subjugate other peoples. Although public opinion polls and congressional will opposed relinquishing control of the Canal, Carter entered office determined to bring fourteen years of fruitless negotiation to an end. He sought to rectify what he regarded as the injustice of the 1903 treaty which had granted the US in perpetuity rights to the Canal Zone in ways the Panamanians believed impinged on their sovereignty.[67] Carter believed the issue of the Panama Canal had become 'a litmus test throughout the world, indicating how the United States, as a superpower, would treat a small and relatively defenseless nation'.[68] An internal White House memo agreed that: 'Failure to act on the new treaties would make our rhetoric sound hollow, and would severely damage a central part of the Carter Administration's foreign policy.'[69]

The agreements the Carter administration reached with the Panamanian government of General Omar Torrijos established joint control of the Canal Zone, with Panama gradually acquiring complete control by 2000. Carter believed he had demonstrated that his dedication to principle would not undermine US national interests. The administration ensured through negotiation that the US would always have access to the canal and could not be held to ransom by Panama over access rights. Had Carter not acted, he believed, the Panamanians might have seized the canal by force, thus drawing the US into a potentially costly conflict in order to maintain the right to use it.[70]

Carter had to overcome considerable public and congressional opposition to the treaties in order to secure their ratification. Opinion polls showed the most common objection to be that the US should not 'give away our canal'. With his sights firmly set on the White House, former California governor Ronald Reagan gave the rallying cry: 'We bought it, we paid for it, it's ours, and we aren't going to give it away to some tinhorn dictator!'[71] The earliest administration analysis made clear, however, that the public was considerably more willing to support the new treaties once their content was fully known.[72] The administration undertook a sustained campaign to raise public awareness and support for the treaties. Support grew dramatically when people understood that there would not be negative implications for American national security, particularly when it became clear that the US retained the right to intervene militarily to protect the canal in the future.[73] Following one of the longest and most intensive debates ever conducted on a treaty, the Senate finally authorized ratification of the two Panama Canal Treaties on March 16 and April 18, 1978, both by a vote of 68 to 32, just one vote above the required two-thirds majority, with all 100 senators voting.

Carter's success in winning Senate support for ratification had come at some political cost. Many of those senators who had voted for the treaties failed to retain their seats at their next election and the administration was criticized for using up political clout it could have utilized for other, perhaps more important issues.[74] Nevertheless, ratification had proved that, despite his lack of Washington experience, Carter was capable of rallying public opinion and forming coalitions in the Congress. He had proved effective in tackling and resolving a contentious foreign policy issue. Above all for Carter, the US had 'proven our commitment to freedom and human rights... [and demonstrated] that, in a showdown, a great democracy will practice what it preaches'.[75] As he declared at the signing ceremony, the treaties 'mark the commitment of the United States to the belief that fairness, and not force, should lie at the heart of our dealings with the nations of the world'.[76]

Although the signing and ratification of the Panama Canal Treaties was a great foreign policy success it did not herald the beginning of a hoped-for new era of benign, non-colonial and non-paternalistic relationships between the US and developing countries. Carter had hoped that the treaties would earn the administration enough goodwill in Latin America for other long-term and developing problems to be resolved. He also believed the region could become a showcase for the human rights focus of his foreign policy. Yet despite Carter's efforts, human rights violations were not reduced in the region, relations with Cuba were not normalized, and in Nicaragua and El Salvador renewed Cold War fears saw the administration put in place policies that supported anti-communist forces at the expense of human rights.[77]

China, Cambodia and the Middle East

Carter's other main foreign policy successes came in diplomatic relations with China and the Middle East. Both successes can be regarded as examples of Carter's preference for cooperation rather than confrontation in foreign policy. On December 15, 1978, Carter announced a joint US–Chinese communiqué stating that diplomatic relations between the two countries would be normalized on January 1, 1979. By giving full diplomatic recognition to the People's Republic of China, Carter was building on the groundwork laid by President Nixon. He shared some of the strategic concerns that had motivated his predecessor, but Carter also saw normalization as being consistent with his view that the US should seek peaceful, cooperative relations with all nations and establish a foreign policy agenda that was not dominated by US–Soviet relations.[78] Yet as PRM 28 had suggested would be necessary, normal relations with China had been won at the expense of human rights considerations. Several critics of the decision deplored what they called the American abandonment of its traditional allies on Taiwan. The improvement of human rights in the People's Republic had also not been a requirement of the normalization agreement. Indeed, the administration attempted to deflect criticisms that not enough pressure was being placed on the Chinese to improve their human rights record. In a letter to House Speaker Thomas P. (Tip) O'Neill, for example, Carter emphasized: 'We have recently had discussions with senior Chinese officials and firmly believe that Chinese statements and the marked increase in emigration reflect a policy of the Government of China favoring freer emigration.'[79]

In 1979, it became clearer still that the Carter administration valued the strategic relationship with China more than it valued a consistent human rights policy. In late December 1978, Vietnamese forces invaded Cambodia to depose the Khmer Rouge government led by Pol Pot. The Carter administration had characterized Pol Pot's regime as 'the worst violator of human rights in the world today'.[80] Yet the administration shared the Chinese perspective on the Vietnamese action regarding it, in Brzezinski's words, as 'a Soviet-sponsored aggression designed to strengthen Vietnam as a base for Soviet operations in Southeast Asia'. Carter and Brzezinski did not raise objections when Deng Xiaoping informed them that China would teach the Vietnamese a lesson with a limited invasion of Vietnam. The subsequent action met with only mild American condemnation as the administration adopted what Brzezinski called 'a slight tilt in favor of the Chinese'.[81] This 'slight tilt' saw the US refuse to recognize the new Cambodian government installed by the Vietnamese. The Carter administration then voted in favour of the Khmer Rouge retaining Cambodia's seat at the UN and encouraged China and Thailand to provide the remnants of Pol Pot's Democratic Kampuchean regime (DK) with aid to fight against the Vietnamese occupation. As Brzezinski said: 'I encouraged the Chinese to support Pol Pot. I encouraged the Thai to help the D.K. The question was how to help the Cambodian people. Pol Pot was an abomination. We could never support him but China could.'[82] The importance of the strategic relationship with China clearly outweighed human rights considerations as the Carter administration authorized indirect support to Pol Pot's forces even as it followed the example of the Ford administration by admitting into the US thousands more refugees from Southeast Asia.

Carter's tireless pursuit of peace in the Middle East also raised questions about consistency in the human rights policy. Carter's part in negotiating peace between Israel and Egypt and his contributions towards a comprehensive Middle East peace settlement are often remembered as the greatest achievements of his administration. For Carter, peace between Egypt and Israel became something of a personal crusade. Although he knew little about the area before becoming President, he soon developed an unwavering belief that the US had an invaluable role to play in brokering peace in the region. There were clear strategic, economic and political reasons for the US to seek peace in the Middle East, not least the concerns over oil supplies and the American relationship with Israel. Throughout the negotiations, however, Carter and his team insisted that they were negotiating for the sake of peace itself rather than any specific US interests. Carter's personal interventions did bring about agreements at the unprecedented Camp David talks in September 1978 that led to a peace treaty between Egypt and Israel the following March.[83]

The greatest dilemma of the Middle East peace process, however, was the Palestinian issue. Carter recognized that his human rights focus required the administration to seek a positive solution to the plight of the hundreds of thousands of Palestinian refugees from Israel and the territories it had occupied. Carter regarded the 'continued deprivation of Palestinian rights' as being 'contrary to the basic moral and ethical principles' of the US. In his opinion, it was 'imperative that the United States work to obtain for these people the right to vote, the right to assemble and to debate issues that affected their lives, the right to own property without fear of it being confiscated and the right to be free of military rule'.[84] The strategic and political relationship with Israel, however, also demanded that the US continue its commitment not to recognize the Palestine Liberation Organization (PLO) until the organization renounced its insistence that Israel be destroyed. Since the PLO was recognized by the majority of nations as the legitimate representative of the Palestinian people, its exclusion from the peace process undermined efforts to resolve the Palestinian issue, despite the endeavours of Egyptian President Anwar Sadat. The Israeli Prime Minister Menachem Begin categorically opposed the establishment of a Palestinian state and fought tenaciously against the Palestinians being provided with too great a degree of self-determination. In his determination to secure peace between Israel and Egypt, Carter allowed for two documents to emerge from Camp David: one that provided the framework for an Egyptian–Israeli peace treaty and the other that established guidelines for dealing with the Palestinian issue. While the first document led to a formal peace, progress was slower on the second document as Israel continued its occupation of the West Bank. As Gaddis Smith concludes, Carter 'left it up to subordinates to continue unproductive negotiations over the status of the Palestinians'.[85] Camp David continues to be widely regarded as one of Carter's greatest triumphs. Yet the administration had failed in its own objective of securing a solution to the Palestianian problem. Carter's human rights policy had again been superseded, this time by the strategic and political benefits of securing peace between Egypt and Israel.

The crisis of confidence

By June 1979, it was becoming increasingly obvious to Carter's advisers that public confidence in the American way of life had not been revived despite the administration's best efforts. The popularity of Carter's human rights policy and public support for his foreign policy successes over the Panama Canal, the Middle East and China seemed to have had little positive effect on the apparent mood of the country. The psychological wounds left by Vietnam, Watergate and the other traumas of the late 1960s and early 1970s had not been healed. Indeed, Carter's public opinion specialist Patrick Caddell presented the president with alarming poll summaries which, according to Caddell, indicated 'a rapid disintegration of optimism and efficacy in the country'. Caddell observed that levels of pessimism about the future of the nation and the effectiveness and trustworthiness of government were considerably higher than they had been even at the apex of the Watergate scandal and the defeat in Vietnam.[86] Public confidence had ebbed away further as the worsening energy crisis caused rising fuel prices and long queues at gasoline stations. The energy crisis was accompanied by increased inflation and unemployment as the country fell into a period of so-called 'stagflation'. The nation's independent truckers also went on a crippling strike. Caddell believed what he called an 'increasing malaise' in the nation had not been caused by these recent developments, but that a profound long-term pessimism, rooted in the Vietnam–Watergate trauma, had been deepened during the Carter presidency.[87]

A year earlier Anthony Lake had recommended that the president use his commencement speech to the graduates of the US Naval Academy in Annapolis to 'address the anxiety among Americans that we have lost our preeminent position in the world – to speak to *the crisis of national confidence*'.[88] On that occasion Vance's advice was followed instead and the president's speech focused on the nature of US–Soviet relations.[89] By the time Carter finally addressed the crisis the following year, as Caddell's analysis demonstrated, it had become even more acute. On July 5, 1979, Carter was scheduled to make his fifth national address on the urgency of tackling the nation's energy problems, a task he had frequently characterized as the 'moral equivalent of war'.[90] The day before he was due to speak, Carter abruptly cancelled the speech. He decided instead to spend what amounted to ten days at Camp David meeting over a hundred and fifty Americans representing diverse groups from throughout society. He sought advice and insights on the state of the nation and what needed to be done to raise the public mood and improve American life. Finally, on July 15, Carter emerged with what he considers one of the best and most important speeches of his presidency.

In his memoirs, Carter writes that Caddell's reading of the opinion polls caused him to cancel his original energy speech. The archival record reveals, however, that Carter's speechwriting staff were also firmly opposed to the address on energy. On June 29, 1979, in an urgent memo sent to the president's assistant for communications Jerry Rafshoon and chief speechwriter Rick Hertzberg, the president's main speechwriters warned that 'the mood of the country is grim'. They stated emphatically: 'We strongly advise against another televised energy speech.' The public wanted action, not more words. Any new speech on energy had to abandon the themes of the last two years and offer a fresh approach that must be 'both specific and visionary'. Energy did need addressing, but only once it was clear what the administration was going to do to solve the crisis. Whenever the next energy speech was delivered, the speechwriters cautioned, it 'may be our last chance to reach the American people'.[91]

On July 15, 1979, Carter did reach out to the American people with his much-anticipated address to the nation on 'Energy and National Goals', watched on television by sixty-five million people – double the audience his most recent speeches had attracted.[92] Carter had always dedicated himself to being frank and honest in public life. He now felt it was imperative to give an honest account of what he considered the 'moral and spiritual crisis' that had gripped the nation. He declared that the US and its people were threatened by 'a crisis of confidence'. This fundamental problem was greater than any other currently faced by the nation: 'It is a crisis that strikes at the very heart and soul and spirit of our national will. We can see this crisis in the growing doubt about the meaning of our own lives and in the loss of unity of purpose for our Nation.' This confidence was at the very root of what it was to be an American. Confidence in American values and principles, in progress and the promise of a better future, was an essential element of all Americans' personal and national make-up. Carter reminded Americans that this was not a myth but a cultural reality:

> The confidence that we have always had as a people is not simply some romantic dream or proverb in a dusty book that we read just on the Fourth of July. It is the idea which founded our Nation and has guided our development as a people. ... Confidence has defined our course and has served as a link between generations.

Although he did not identify it as such, Carter was talking about the loss of faith in the belief in American exceptionalism. The 'shocks and tragedy' of recent years had gradually eroded the traditional belief in the exceptional nature of the United States causing a 'crisis of the American spirit'. On the domestic front, political assassinations had seen violence undermine democracy and Watergate had tarnished the honour of government. In foreign policy: 'We were taught that our armies were always invincible and our causes were always just, only to suffer the agony of Vietnam.' Carter admitted that: 'These wounds are still very deep. They have never been healed.' To escape from the paralysis that held the nation, Carter proclaimed, 'First of all, we must face the truth and then we can change our course.'[93]

Patrick Caddell's analysis had helped convince the president that admitting to and describing the crisis of confidence was the best way for the nation to finally come to terms with the detrimental effects of the experiences of the previous decade and a half. Yet to adopt Caddell's 'apocalyptic' approach was 'counterproductive', according to several of Carter's advisers. They did not believe such a speech would help Americans find a solution to the crisis of confidence. As Jerry Rafshoon put it to the president, the best way to 'inspire confidence' was by 'being confident'.[94] Carter, therefore, followed the advice of his public communications team and divided his speech into three phases. The first identified the crisis of confidence, but the second and third emphasized the strength and hope that remained within the US, and detailed how the energy crisis, and with it the crisis of confidence, could be solved.

Carter told the American people they were faced with two choices. One was to succumb to the crisis of confidence and witness the fragmentation and demise of the nation's social and political fabric. For Carter, though, this was a false choice that Americans could not afford to take. He reminded his audience that: 'All the traditions of our past, all the lessons of our heritage, all the promises of our future point to another path, the path of common purpose and the restoration of American values.' Carter believed that

Americans had it within themselves to conquer the crisis of confidence. To succeed they must 'tap our greatest resources – America's people, America's values, and America's confidence'. Resolving the energy crisis together as a people, Carter promised, would help Americans to revive their belief in themselves and their future and restore faith and confidence. The American people would succeed because hope was the one thing that was always abundant in the United States. 'We know the strength of America', Carter said, 'We are strong. We can regain our unity. We can regain our confidence.' Carter was using exceptionalist rhetoric to revive the American belief in exceptionalism from which he believed all Americans drew their strength. He was calling upon Americans to 'commit ourselves to a rebirth of the American spirit. Working together with our common faith we cannot fail'.[95]

The initial reaction to the speech and Carter's follow-up addresses and question-and-answer sessions was on the whole very positive. When he had cancelled his original speech and retreated to Camp David, Carter had left behind a bewildered Washington where rumours abounded that he was having a mental breakdown or was about to resign. *Time* observed that: 'Rarely had a US President seemed so strikingly mired in indecision ... The impression of incompetence is so prevalent that it has plunged Carter close to the lowest poll ratings ever reached by a President.' An ABC News–Louis Harris poll found only 25 per cent of Americans approved of Carter's handling of the presidency, one point below Richard Nixon's lowest rating prior to his resignation.[96] One week later, however, *Time* described Carter's summit at Camp David as an 'inspirational step'.[97] The American public seemed to agree, with 61 per cent of those polled claiming the July 15 speech made them 'feel optimistic'. Carter's approval rating also gained by some twelve points.[98]

People seemed to be moved by and believe in the sincerity of what Carter had said. Not everyone was convinced, however. The scholar Robert Bellah, who had been one of Patrick Caddell's major inspirations, called the speech 'pathetic' and criticized Carter for substituting 'morale boosting' for a 'serious consideration of what the options are as we move into a different world'. Bellah concluded that Carter had 'no social vision'.[99] The editors of the *New Republic* admitted that Carter's speech was 'an effective performance ... delivered with verve for a change'. However, they declared, the speech itself was 'a farcical and insulting attempt to distract us all from the fact that our standard of living has begun to decline, and [Carter and his administration] don't have a clue what to do about it'. The speech, they suggested, was nothing more than a 'pop sociology stew' filled with 'servile flatteries' designed to assure Americans that 'this crisis is no one's fault' and that 'we are all quite wonderful despite our malaise'. Carter, the *New Republic* concluded, was 'concerned only with the appearance of things'.[100] In the same volume, Ken Bode went further, concluding: 'The Carter administration simply has imploded, collapsed inwardly under the weight of its own incompetence.'

As a result of his crisis-of-confidence speech, Bode argued, Carter had 'wound up immobilizing his own government, imperiling the American dollar on the international market, and looking more than ever like a crude, erratic, unstable amateur'.[101]

In the following weeks, more and more editorials reached the same conclusion that action rather than words were needed to solve the crises Americans faced. Carter's popularity rating fell again. His address became labelled the 'national malaise speech' and was increasingly regarded as a major source for the deepening of the crisis of confidence rather than a pivotal point in reviving Americans' faith in their nation and its exceptional nature. Carter did not actually use the term 'national malaise' in his July 15 speech. He had included the word 'malaise' in earlier speeches in a different context but most analysts attribute the renaming of the speech to Carter's opponents, such as Senator Edward Kennedy.[102] There is evidence, however, that Carter *did* use the term when discussing the crisis of confidence at the Camp David summit. As *Time* magazine reported: 'Carter was serious ... and surprisingly candid about his perception of the national mood. To one group he described it as a "malaise" of confusion, pessimism and distrust.'[103] Whether or not Carter was responsible for coining the term 'national malaise' it soon became a stock phrase for critics and opponents of the administration. There was a growing sense that Carter was contributing to rather than resolving the crisis of confidence among the American people. As one labour leader complained: 'The fault is his, not ours, and asking us to say something good about America is like Gerald Ford telling us to pin on little lapel buttons and "Whip Inflation Now".'[104] The events of the next year and a half were to further undermine any positive rallying effects the speech might have had on the American people's confidence.

Hostages in Iran, Soviets in Afghanistan

On November 4, 1979, Iranian students overran the American Embassy in Tehran, seizing 52 hostages. Less than two months later, on December 27, the Soviet Union sent troops into neighbouring Afghanistan. These two events would dominate Carter's final year in office and cause the president to reassess his attempts to balance power with principle in his foreign policy.[105] In May 1980, Carter reiterated that traditional principles remained imperative in forging a foreign policy which could cope with the crises the US faced abroad: 'Unchanging American ideals are relevant to this troubling area of foreign policy and to this troubled era in which we live.' US foreign policy, he stated, must continue to promote American ideals while defending national interests:

> [American foreign policy] must be based on the primacy of certain moral principles – principles founded on the enhancement of human

rights – and on the preservation of an American military strength that is second to none. This fusion of principle and power is the only way to ensure global stability and peace while we accommodate to the inevitable and necessary reality of global change and progress.[106]

As noted earlier, the struggle to balance the responsibilities of great power status with traditional American principles in the Carter administration was often personified by the conflicting views of Brzezinski and Vance. While Vance encouraged Carter in his attempts to implement foreign policy that was consistent with ideas of American exceptionalism, Brzezinski reminded the president of the imperatives of great power relations and the utility of threatening or using force in international affairs. This tension grew ever stronger as the administration attempted to deal with the concurrent crises over Iran and Afghanistan.

The administration's attitude towards the use of force abroad was a central element of Carter's attempts to base his foreign policy on moral principles. As we have seen, the experience of Vietnam had raised doubts among some Americans over the efficacy of using military force to achieve political ends in foreign policy. Carter gave his view in July 1978: 'I think I share the opinion of the American public that we should not again become involved in a military way in the internal affairs of another country unless our own security is directly threatened.' Carter cited Vietnam as an example that military force had lost much of its utility in the modern age (though no doubt the North Vietnamese army and the National Liberation Front would have disagreed with him).[107] The reluctance to use military force was prevalent throughout most of the Executive Branch. In a speech to the Chicago Council on Foreign Relations on May 1, 1979, Vance made his opinion clear:

> In seeking to help others meet the legitimate needs of their peoples, what are the best instruments at hand? Let me state first that the use of military force is not, and should not be, a desirable American policy response to the internal politics of other nations.

According to a Policy Planning Staff member interviewed by Richard Melanson, the word 'desirable' was inserted as a compromise 'between those who wanted to simply say that the use of military force is not an appropriate instrument, and those who felt that we could not rule it out in *every* circumstance'.[108] Such an attitude dismayed Brzezinski. As he lamented in his journal following the deployment of several thousand Cuban troops to Ethiopia in 1978:

> The Defense Department ..., the JCS ..., and State ... – all of them to me seem badly bitten by the Vietnam bug and as a consequence are fearful of taking the kind of action which is necessary to convey our determination and to reassure the concerned countries in the region.[109]

Brzezinski found Vance's views on the application of military power particularly alarming: 'His deep aversion to the use of force was a most significant limitation on his stewardship in an age in which American power was being threatened on a very broad front.'[110]

Carter had tended towards Vance's opinion about the use of force but, as the presidency progressed, Brzezinski gained increasing influence. By the time of the so-called foreign policy 'shocks' of 1979 it was evident that Carter had begun to embrace Brzezinski's view. On December 12, 1979, two weeks before the Soviet invasion of Afghanistan, Carter declared:

> We've learned the mistake of military intervention in the internal affairs of another country when our own American security was not directly involved. But we must understand that not every instance of the firm application of the power of the United States is a potential Vietnam. The consensus for national strength and international involvement, already shaken and threatened, survived that divisive and tragic war.[111]

Carter's speech was a sign that, as a result of events in Iran, his view of the Vietnam syndrome was moving closer to that of Brzezinski's. Carter was attempting to send strong signals to the Iranians and potential adversaries that the US had the will to meet any challenges to its national security.

Carter's tough stance against the Iranian hostage-takers initially won him a great deal of public and congressional support. In January 1980, 66 per cent of Americans surveyed supported Carter's handling of the crisis as 'just right' and almost half agreed his strong stance had 'increased America's prestige abroad'. Nearly four-fifths of those polled also believed the crisis had 'unified the country'.[112] As the crisis wore on, however, the public became increasingly frustrated at their president's inability to free the hostages. This frustration was not helped by Carter's decision to cancel what he considered unnecessary trips and political appearances outside Washington until the hostages had been released. Although he was praised at first for showing his dedication to efforts to end the crisis, Carter's decision to remain rooted at the White House gave a growing impression that he was paralysed by a siege mentality. The so-called 'Rose Garden strategy' gradually caused observers to consider 'the isolated President to be somehow out of touch with the nation and perhaps the world'.[113]

The pressure mounted on Carter to take some action to free the hostages. Against the advice of Vance, who subsequently resigned, Carter decided to authorize an overseas military action for the only time in his administration. On April 24, 1980 an attempt to rescue the American hostages in Tehran was launched. The rescue was aborted in disaster, however, with an accidental collision between a helicopter and a C-130 transport plane causing the deaths of eight American soldiers at a landing stage in the Iranian desert.[114]

On the morning of the operation, Brzezinski wrote confidently in his journal: 'If it is a success, it will give the United States a shot in the arm, which it has badly needed for twenty years.' Like Kissinger in the earlier *Mayaguez* situation, Brzezinski believed the Iranian crisis had an importance greater than the lives of the hostages: 'I felt that in the end our national honor was at stake.'[115] Carter appears to have shared Brzezinski's view. He recognized that he and his advisers were 'responsible for the lives and safety of the captive Americans – and for the reputation of our military forces and nation'.[116] Much of the motivation for the rescue mission appears to have been a perceived need to demonstrate the American resolve to use force, particularly in light of the continued presence of Soviet troops in Afghanistan. Such action would also challenge, in this election year, the growing sense that Carter was weak and vacillating. Although political and strategic reasons called for action, Carter and his advisers were nevertheless careful to plan the mission and then present it to the Congress and the public in such a way that it appeared consistent with traditional American principles and values.

Despite Brzezinski's distaste for the supposed lessons of Vietnam, Carter went to great lengths to comply with the main elements of the Vietnam syndrome. As early in the crisis as November 10, 1979, Carter had noted in his diary that any military action designed to free the hostages must be 'quick, incisive, surgical, [with] no loss of American lives, ... minimal suffering of the Iranian people themselves, ... [and be] sure of success'.[117] As they embarked on the mission, administration officials believed it would avoid drawing the US into another Vietnam-style quagmire because it had clear, morally justifiable objectives that could be achieved swiftly using the maximum force necessary at the lowest cost possible in lives and materiel.

When Carter revealed the failure of the mission in an address to the nation, he emphasized that it had been a 'humanitarian mission'.[118] Carter had little difficulty demonstrating to the American people that his reasons for armed intervention were just, since American citizens were being held captive 'in clear violation of international law and the norms of civilized conduct among nations'.[119] Carter made clear that the mission was not planned as an act of vengeance or aggression but was expressly limited to securing the release of all hostages with the minimum loss of life and without provoking further hostility.[120] Brzezinski confirms that: 'Carter was very emphatic in insisting that every effort be made to avoid wanton killings ... [and] that we should try to limit casualties.'[121] Although Carter carefully reviewed and approved every aspect of the rescue mission, he also made it clear to his military leaders that, unlike in Vietnam, 'there would be no interference from the White House while the mission was under way'.[122] Great care was taken to ensure that the military would have enough forces to fulfil the mission swiftly, effectively, with maximum success, and with minimal casualties. Indeed, it was as a result of these considerations that the operation was aborted once the minimum required aircraft were no longer available.

The rescue mission planners, therefore, went to great lengths to ensure that the operation would not draw the administration into a wider conflict that could develop into a Vietnam-style debacle. Carter was also determined that the action should be perceived as a well-reasoned use of force that did not compromise the moral underpinnings of his foreign policy. Following the failure of the operation, even Brzezinski joined the president's attempts to present the mission as being morally acceptable. In an interview with ABC News, Brzezinski affirmed forcefully that: 'what the President ordered to be done was morally right and politically justified. ... We had a moral obligation to do what we could do to help [the hostages].'[123]

As is usually the case when the US employs force abroad, the American people initially rallied around the president. In the three hours following Carter's address to the nation on the rescue attempt, 69 per cent of the telegrams and 83 per cent of the telephone calls received by the White House were supportive of the president's action.[124] A *Newsweek*/Gallup survey found 71 per cent of the public believed 'the president was right in attempting to rescue the hostages by using military force'.[125] The White House also described congressional reaction as 'surprisingly positive [and] favorable'. Many high-ranking Democrats and Republicans expressed support for the president's action. Several Senate offices also reported that 80–85 per cent of the calls they received from constituents were supportive. Support also came from Henry Kissinger, Richard Nixon and Republican presidential hopeful George Bush. There were many strong objections raised, however. Senator Gaylord Nelson denounced the mission as 'ill-advised' and 'doomed to failure' from the outset. Representative Paul Simon claimed defence and intelligence officials had told him months earlier that any rescue attempt would fail, while Representative George Hansen concluded the abortive mission was 'typical of a series of blunders that not only got us into this but continues to keep us here and continues to embarrass us'.[126] One of the most damning assessments, however, came from *Time* magazine which concluded the mission was 'a startlingly bold but tragic gamble' that 'failed dismally'. According to *Time*:

> For Carter in particular, and for the US in general, the desert debacle was a military, diplomatic and political fiasco. A once dominant military machine, first humbled in its agonizing standoff in Viet Nam, now looked incapable of keeping its aircraft aloft even when no enemy knew they were there, and even incapable of keeping them from crashing into each other despite four months of practice for their mission.

Carter's 'image as inept' had been fully restored.[127] Public opinion soon complied with this view. Carter was already polling behind his main

Republican challenger for the White House, Ronald Reagan. But even though the president finally abandoned his 'Rose Garden strategy' and went on the campaign trail, by August his popularity rating had fallen to 21 per cent, the lowest for any president since Gallup began polling in 1936.[128] The hostage crisis and the failure to resolve it, either diplomatically or militarily, had a profound effect upon the public's confidence in their nation and specifically in the Carter administration. It mattered little whether the rescue attempt had been morally justifiable or not, its failure only added to the sense that Carter was incapable of resolving the crisis.

Meanwhile, Soviet troops continued to occupy Afghanistan. In January 1980, Carter stated that the Soviet invasion of Afghanistan was the 'greatest threat to peace since the Second World War'.[129] The Kremlin had ordered the invasion largely to prevent a pro-Soviet neighbour becoming an Islamic fundamentalist state that Moscow believed would threaten regional stability and encourage Muslim secessionist movements within the Soviet Union.[130] Whatever Moscow's true intentions, the Carter administration took the line that the Soviet Union was aggressively attempting to establish a strategic position from which to threaten the West's oil supplies from the Middle East. Carter believed the US must adopt a tough response. In his State of the Union speech on January 23, 1980, he proclaimed what would become known as the Carter Doctrine:

> Let our position be absolutely clear: An attempt by any outside force to gain control of the Persian Gulf region will be regarded as an assault on the vital interests of the United States of America, and such an assault will be repelled by any means necessary, including military force.[131]

In the case of the invasion of Afghanistan, though, military retaliation was not a serious consideration. The administration chose instead a series of economic, political and cultural sanctions including the curtailment of grain and high technology sales to the Soviet Union, a boycott of the 1980 Summer Olympics in Moscow, and instructions to the Senate to defer indefinitely the already moribund SALT II ratification process.[132] Carter's hard line towards the Soviets signalled an end to détente, but sanctions and condemnations had little effect as the Soviet Union refused to withdraw from Afghanistan. Although initial support for Carter's new stance towards the Soviet Union was extremely high, as with the Iranian hostage crisis, the longer the Soviet occupation continued the less confident the American people became in their belief that Carter could do anything about it.

The presidential election in November 1980 coincided with the first anniversary of the hostage-taking in Iran. Opinion polls indicated that the public had little confidence that the hostages would be released in the foreseeable future. Carter's failure to secure the hostages' release, his inability to change the situation in Afghanistan, combined with increasing economic problems at home, led many Americans to view the administration, by Carter's own admission, as 'impotent' in the face of national crises.[133] On November 4, 1980, Carter failed to secure a second term as president.

Conclusions

In 1978, President Carter was asked how he hoped or intended for history to remember him. He replied first that 'I helped to restore to our Nation and to its Government a sense of purpose, of idealism, of commitment and honesty'. Second, in foreign affairs, he hoped for 'peace based on strength'. This peace would come from a 'strong national defense capability' coupled with a 'strength based on what our national character is, treating other people fairly and with respect, with a total commitment to the enhancement of human rights around the world and trying to lessen the tensions that have been built up'.[134] In other words, domestically and internationally Carter sought to revive national self-confidence and resolve.

Jimmy Carter made a concerted effort to revive American faith in the traditional belief that the United States has a special role to play in human history, that theirs is an exceptional nation. In order to restore this faith, he not only adopted exceptionalist rhetoric but also attempted to model his nation's policy and conduct on the values and principles that were traditionally believed to make the US exceptional. In foreign policy in particular, Carter strove to heal the wounds of Vietnam and Watergate by returning to first principles and restoring the nation's moral compass. In many ways, Carter achieved what he set out to do. Much of his foreign policy was tailored to be consistent with his conception of traditional American national character. The human rights policy in particular gave what Americans could view as a moral centre to their dealings with foreign nations. Despite its failures and inconsistencies, the policy did have an effect on the way diplomatic relations were conducted with other governments and influenced the nature of foreign aid programmes. Negotiating the Panama Canal treaties, facilitating peace between Egypt and Israel, normalizing relations with China, and continuing arms negotiations with the Soviet Union all demonstrated that the US preferred its traditional role of peaceful cooperation with other nations. In all these ways, the Carter administration could be perceived as 'treating other people fairly and with respect'.[135] That diplomatic solutions to international disputes were preferred was further proved by Carter's proud reflection that not a single citizen had shed blood in an act of war during his administration (aside from those who lost their lives in the abortive Iranian hostage rescue).

Yet as the analysis in this chapter has shown, Carter's foreign policy was not solely or indeed primarily driven by moral considerations. In all his major foreign policy achievements concerning the Panama Canal, China and the Middle East, strategic and political concerns took precedence over human rights. In this regard, the Carter administration was perhaps not as different from its predecessors as it had hoped. In addition, although the human rights policy was popular, it was also problematic. Most Americans agreed with the principle of human rights but beyond the abstract it was difficult for the administration to nurture widespread understanding of the policy. This was not helped by the results of the policy often being intangible or difficult to gauge in the short term. The implementation of the policy also seemed inconsistent at times and sometimes hollow, as the US often lacked the resources or leverage to enforce changes in foreign countries. The inconsistencies were further complicated by the variety of interpretations within the administration of which human rights should be given priority, for what reasons and in which contexts. Such problems were further accentuated by bureaucratic barriers and conflicts between the many executive departments charged with implementing elements of the policy.

Carter's attempts to revive a sense of national resolve in foreign policy also had mixed results. The president proved himself capable of making bold, decisive and ultimately successful decisions over the Panama Canal, China and the Middle East even when public opinion was more cautious or even opposed. Despite the charges of his opponents that he had presided over the opening of a window of vulnerability in strategic strength, Carter actually authorized a significant reversal of the post-Vietnam decline in US defence spending.[136] Yet in US–Soviet relations, Carter came to be perceived as weak and naive in light of the invasion of Afghanistan. Carter seemed culpable in enabling the Soviets to expand their influence unchallenged as he had chosen to de-emphasize the importance of superpower relations and continue détente through cooperative competition. Following the invasion, Carter appeared ineffective in his efforts to punish the Soviets and cause them to reverse their actions. It is doubtful that any other president could have done anything more, however, and certainly Carter was no less effective than Eisenhower had been in response to Soviet forces invading Hungary in 1956 or Johnson in response to the Czech crisis in 1968. Yet the image of a vacillating, ineffective president persisted and was compounded, moreover, by the Iranian hostage crisis. As the crisis wore on and on, Carter seemed paralysed, hiding in the White House, unable to bring the power of the United States to bear on a relatively weak Persian Gulf state. His general unwillingness, then apparent inability, to employ effective force to secure the hostages' release, further added to the sense that this was a president crippled by doubt and lacking the courage to break free from the debilitating effects of Vietnam and Watergate. Carter was criticized for too readily accepting that there were limits to American power, an acceptance that had caused him to allegedly give away the Panama Canal and act subserviently to the Soviet Union, China and other nations. He had been right to identify a crisis of confidence in the nation, but there came a growing sense in the final year of his presidency that Carter was, if not the original source of the malaise, certainly responsible for worsening the situation.

By 1980, the American people *did* want to feel confident again about themselves, their nation, their government and their future. As president, Jimmy Carter made honest attempts to tap into traditional beliefs in order to put the US back on a moral high ground and restore a sense of exceptionalism. As his presidency progressed, however, he was perceived to lack the strength and confidence necessary to lead the US back to its supposedly rightful place as the self-styled greatest nation on earth. By the time of the 1980 election, 83 per cent of Americans agreed that Carter was 'a man of high moral principles'. However, less than a third of those polled believed that Carter was capable of translating his principles into policies that could move the nation forward. Despite his strong personal morality, only 31 per cent believed that Carter had 'strong leadership qualities'.[137] What the American people wanted and needed was someone who personified strength and confidence. To find such leadership they turned to the retired Hollywood actor and former governor of California, Ronald Reagan.

5
Ronald Reagan – 'America is Back'

When Ronald Reagan took office in January 1981, the domestic challenges of inflation, unemployment, interest rates and energy shortages dominated the American political agenda. Despite the American hostages in Iran being released as he was inaugurated, Reagan was also confronted with problems on the international scene that had contributed to his predecessor's failure to secure a second term. The Soviet occupation of Afghanistan continued and Soviet troops now seemed poised to cross the Polish border to curb the growing power of Solidarity. In the US, the Committee on the Present Danger, of which Reagan was a member, warned of an alleged window of vulnerability in US strategic strength and pressed for a more vigilant and aggressive focus on the perceived Soviet threat to American security interests. The Reagan administration was determined to meet these challenges and thereby restore American power and strength in world affairs, resolve the economic crisis at home, and renew the self-confidence of the American people. To achieve these ends Reagan would appeal, not unlike his predecessors, to the traditional belief in American exceptionalism to which he subscribed wholeheartedly.

Reagan and exceptionalism

Lou Cannon has observed that Reagan 'held an innocent and unshakable belief in the myth of American exceptionalism'.[1] This was most clearly expressed by Reagan in November 1986 when he declared that his 'fondest hope, my grandest dream' for future generations of Americans was that: 'they would always find here in America a land of hope, a light unto the nations, a shining city on a hill.'[2] Reagan was a true believer in the greatness of the United States and its special place in human history. Throughout his two-term presidency, Reagan's belief in the missionary strand of American exceptionalism informed the way he developed, conducted and presented his policies.

Reagan was perhaps better suited than any other American president as a protagonist of the belief in American exceptionalism. As noted earlier, in order to fully believe that the US is exceptionally blessed among nations it is necessary to forget or ignore a great deal of American social and historical reality. Throughout his life, Reagan had been accomplished at doing just that as he developed his own view of the world and his and America's place within it.

Reagan's view of reality had always been very malleable. He was adept at telling stories to convey understanding to whatever audience he was addressing. These stories were not necessarily true but Reagan often made them sound as if they were. As a radio sports announcer, Reagan had quite literally invented reality. He gave vividly detailed commentary of baseball games taking place 300 miles away from his studio based solely on telegraphed information about the outcome of each ball.[3] Reagan became so used to creating reality that he even convinced himself that he was involved in events that he had not witnessed or that had never actually taken place. He believed, for instance, that he had gone 'off to war' even though his World War II military service never took him outside the US. He would mythologize genuine stories and place himself in events he had only ever read about or witnessed on film. Most famously, in 1983, Reagan told Israeli Prime Minister Yitzhak Shamir, with all sincerity, that he had been among the first Americans to enter the Nazi concentration camps and had filmed what he saw there.[4] Two years earlier, Reagan had related how he had *seen* the first secret US army films of the concentration camps in April 1945 and claimed they had left an indelible mark on his consciousness.[5] For Reagan, the experience of seeing a film could readily be transformed into the experience of actually participating in the events depicted.

Reagan did not believe that making a distant or fictitious event part of his personal reality was maliciously deceptive if by doing so he could give greater resonance to a point or message he was trying to convey to an audience. As he told the audience at ceremonies celebrating 40 years of Voice of America in 1982, Reagan believed that the truth was the truth, but there was nothing wrong with it being 'attractively packaged'.[6] Reagan was often accused of holding simplistic views and lacking a firm grasp of the detail of policy and issues. Certainly at times this was true, but Reagan was also adept at refining the presentation of complex ideas and programmes in ways that would make them as appealing as possible to the greatest number of people.[7] It is no surprise, then, that Reagan attempted to tap into the national consciousness by utilizing and appealing to the belief in American exceptionalism. This rhetorical device was made all the more powerful and effective for Reagan because he actually shared those beliefs.

Another of Reagan's characteristics also disposed him towards the role of true believer in exceptionalism: his optimism. Reagan exhibited an apparently undying faith that being optimistic about things eventually enables a person to transcend any problem. He had an excess of self-belief and was convinced that the root of America's strength lay in its people's traditional optimism. When this optimism is high then the United States and its people are capable of achieving anything. Reagan would overcome problems through motivation, believing that if something could be said repeatedly it would become true. Each problem the US faced under Reagan, be it economic recovery or nuclear disarmament, was to him what Wills has termed 'a truth waiting to happen' that could somehow be willed into existence.[8] American exceptionalism is also a truth waiting to happen. Americans know their society is not perfect but they believe wholeheartedly that it could be – eventually. Americans repeatedly assert that theirs is the 'greatest nation on earth' even if this can never be shown to be an objective truth. That it cannot be proved is irrelevant. By believing in America's exceptionalism, Americans strive to make that belief a reality. President Reagan, his foreign policy, and particularly the way it was presented to the public, cannot fully make sense unless explored in the context of this belief in American exceptionalism.

Reagan and the 'national malaise'

Reagan had learned during the Great Depression that when times are hard, Americans want to be told they have nothing to fear; they need to be addressed with confidence, not told how bad things are. In the 1980 presidential campaign, Reagan challenged what he perceived as President Carter's counterproductive pessimism about the power of the US and the attitude of the American people. 'I find no national malaise', Reagan declared. 'I find nothing wrong with the American people. ... all of us recognize that these people [e.g. President Carter] who keep talking about the age of limits are really talking about their own limitations, not America's.'[9] Ronald Reagan, that great believer in 'healthy-mindedness', saw himself and a revival in traditional American optimism as the antidote to the gloom-and-doom merchants of post-Watergate and post-Vietnam America.[10] American voters appeared to agree with him in 1980 and again in 1984.

Not unlike Presidents Ford and Carter before him, Reagan took to the White House calling for an 'era of national renewal'. In his first Inaugural Address, Reagan proclaimed: 'It is time for us to realize that we're too great a nation to limit ourselves to small dreams. We're not, as some would have us believe, doomed to an inevitable decline.' The emphasis was very much on optimism. Americans, Reagan said, 'have every right to dream heroic dreams'. The crises confronting the US at home and abroad could be overcome by nothing more than 'our best effort and our willingness to believe in ourselves and to believe in our capacity to perform great deeds'. There was no reason why this could not be achieved, Reagan said, because after all: 'We are Americans.'[11]

Reagan agreed with his predecessor that confidence was the answer to America's problems. But where Carter had lamented the lack of confidence among Americans, Reagan celebrated the *abundance* of confidence among the people. He assured them time and again that because of that confidence and optimism, Americans had always been capable of greater things than other peoples on earth and there was no reason why they should not be so again. There were, in fact, many things that Reagan said about the strength and potential of the US that Carter had said before him. In March 1981, Reagan declared: 'There is, in America, a greatness and a tremendous heritage of idealism which is a reservoir of strength and goodness. It is ours if we will but tap it.'[12] In his so-called 'malaise speech', Carter had said much the same when he told Americans all they had to do to conquer the crisis of confidence was to 'tap our greatest resources – America's people, America's values and America's confidence'.[13] Reagan's advantage, though, was that unlike Carter he did not have to acknowledge that a crisis of confidence existed. Instead, Reagan could focus on moving on from that crisis by doing essentially what Carter had prescribed: drawing on the strength of traditional American optimism. Reagan declared that: 'the era of self-doubt is over. We've stopped looking at our warts and rediscovered how much there is to love in this blessed land.'[14] By the time of his first State of the Union speech on January 26, 1982, Reagan could assert that the 'defeatism' of a year earlier had been replaced by a 'New Beginning' that ushered in the 'era of American renewal' he had promised. 'Don't let anyone tell you,' he said, 'that America's best days are behind her, that the American spirit has been vanquished. We've seen it triumph too often in our lives to stop believing in it now.'[15] According to Reagan, belief and optimism were all Americans needed to triumph over adversity. As he told a crowd at Mount Vernon, Virginia, in February 1982: 'The only limits [to what Americans can achieve] are your imagination and your determination.'[16]

The theme of 'forging a new beginning for America' would be repeated publicly throughout Reagan's first term.[17] The message was no different behind the closed doors of the administration. On March 30, 1981, Reagan told a group of new presidential appointees at a private breakfast meeting that: 'Our job is nothing less than revitalizing America.... The effort we make in the next four years will determine whether or not America is to remain a great Nation.'[18] Although Reagan is much criticized for allowing his advisers too much freedom to develop policy and to stage-manage his presidency, the root ideas and style of the Reagan presidency were very much his own. Reagan was not simply an actor playing the Great Communicator. He was a Great Persuader, tailoring the tone and language of his public persona to convey to the public a set of ideas about the US and its place in the world that he had promoted on speaking circuits for decades.[19] These were ideas rooted firmly in the belief in American exceptionalism.

Reagan's vision of the United States and its role in the world

Reagan's view of the United States was one of undying pride and admiration. He was ardently and unashamedly patriotic. For instance, where his Republican predecessor Gerald Ford had attempted to play down the symbolic trappings of the presidency, Reagan emphasized them. He frequently called upon assembled groups to burst into patriotic song, as on January 27, 1981 when he enthusiastically encouraged the American hostages, freed from Iran on the day of his inauguration, to join him in a rendition of 'God Bless America'.[20] On many occasions, Reagan espoused his belief that the US and the American people had been singled out by God to perform a special role in human history: 'I've always believed that this land was set aside in an uncommon way, that a divine plan placed this great continent between the oceans to be found by a people from every corner of the Earth who had a special love of faith, freedom, and peace.'[21]

As well as expressing his own belief in the special character of the United States, Reagan often drew upon the canon of American exceptionalism. He evoked the spirit of the American revolution by quoting Thomas Paine in his campaign to revive American self-confidence and the failing economy. Americans could make their future whatever they wanted it to be, Reagan said, so long as they remembered: 'We have it in our power to begin the world over again.'[22] He used flattering passages from Alexis de Tocqueville to affirm the greatness of the US, such as the Frenchman's description of America as 'a land of wonders'.[23] In November 1982, Reagan recalled that: 'One of the first challenges ever given any American came from John Winthrop... "We shall be a city upon a hill. The eyes of all people are upon us".'[24] The rhetoric of the United States as a city on a hill was central to much of Reagan's vision of the role the US should play in the world. In his first Inaugural Address, he promised that the US 'will again be the exemplar of freedom and a beacon of hope for those who do not now have freedom'.[25] Throughout his presidency, Reagan spoke of the US as being a beacon to the world. It was an American responsibility to bring 'truth to light in a world groping in the darkness of repression and lies'.[26] Reagan and his speechwriters were encouraged to use such language by his National Security staff. For example, in a memo suggesting themes for the 1982 State of the Union address, senior staff member Henry Nau advised the President to proclaim that the objective of his administration was to make the US a ' "city on a hill," a proud reinvigorated American society, a bastion for the free world and a beacon for those who still seek freedom and progress'. The American people, Nau suggested, would 'applaud' such goals.[27] Accepting Nau's advice was not difficult for Reagan, as he believed the US did provide an example the rest of the world would do well to follow.

Reagan regarded the US as a benign force in the world that did not pose a threat to anybody. As he told the UN General Assembly on June 17, 1982,

Americans were 'never the aggressors' in the wars they fought but were a 'force for peace' in the world. Unlike other great nations in history and unlike her potential adversaries in the contemporary world, Reagan claimed: 'America has no territorial ambitions. We occupy no countries, and we have built no walls to lock our people in. Our commitment to self-determination, freedom, and peace is the very soul of America.'[28] In a personal letter written during his recuperation from the failed assassination attempt in 1981, Reagan tried to convince Leonid Brezhnev that the US had nothing but benign intentions toward the Soviet Union and the rest of the world. Reagan denied that the US had 'imperialistic designs' that made it a threat to Soviet security. He argued that at the end of the Second World War, the US could have used its nuclear monopoly and military and industrial superiority to dominate the world. Instead, Americans followed a different course that Reagan claimed was 'unique in all the history of mankind'. The US had 'used our power and wealth to rebuild the war-ravaged economies of the world, including those nations who had been our enemies'. No one, Reagan concluded, could seriously argue that the US 'is guilty of imperialism or attempts to impose it's [sic] will on other countries by use of force'.[29]

Reagan believed wholeheartedly that the US had a special, historic mission to fulfil. He saw it as the noble, selfless leader of the march of human progress towards greater freedom and democracy for all people. He denied that this was a role Americans had sought arrogantly for themselves. 'We preach no manifest destiny', he declared. Yet in almost the same breath, Reagan claimed the US had 'a destiny and a duty, a duty to preserve and hold in sacred trust mankind's age-old aspirations of peace and freedom and a better life for generations to come'.[30] According to Reagan, there was 'no higher mission' for the US than to 'build a lasting peace that enshrines liberty, democracy, and dignity for individuals everywhere'.[31] For Reagan, as for so many other Americans, it was impossible to regard American insistence on the adoption of free markets and democracy throughout the world as being anything but a benevolent wish. The US, in Reagan's view, was merely encouraging self-determination for all peoples. Yet he dismissed the possibility that any peoples in the world might actually choose to live under a system that ran contrary to American ideals. As we shall see, Reagan could not accept that the people of Nicaragua or El Salvador might prefer to live under left-wing governments practising socialism, or at the very least be allowed to determine their own future without any interference from foreign powers, including the United States. Like most purveyors of American exceptionalism, Reagan also chose to overlook the blemishes on America's historical record where the US had failed to live up to its own high values and principles. For Reagan it was an 'undeniable truth' that the US was a successful experiment in human progress to which the whole world looked for inspiration and leadership in its hopes for a free and peaceful world.[32]

This view of the exceptional nature of the United States and its appropriate role in the world greatly affected Reagan's foreign policy.

Reagan's foreign policy

Reagan freely admitted upon taking office that his administration's first priority was to restore the failing US economy. This task was the focus of Reagan's first year in office to such an extent that he did not deliver what can be considered a major foreign policy address until May 1982. In June 1981, Reagan told a press conference: 'I don't necessarily believe that you must, to have a foreign policy, stand up and make a wide declaration that this is your foreign policy.'[33]

Internal disputes over the form, nature, and control of foreign and defence policy dogged Reagan's administration from the outset making a mockery of Secretary of State Alexander Haig's recommendation that the administration should speak with a single voice on foreign policy.[34] Haig clearly believed that voice should be his own. He had been Richard Nixon's Chief of Staff and harboured his own presidential ambitions.[35] Haig's volatile temperament and insistence that foreign policy making should be primarily his domain made for a tempestuous relationship with other members of the administration and shocked Reagan at times.[36] Haig frequently clashed with Secretary of Defense Caspar W. Weinberger who was a long-term supporter and confidant of Reagan. He was much more of an ideologue than Haig, ardently promoted Reagan's vision, and disagreed with the Secretary of State on a number of fundamental issues. Reagan was served by no less than six National Security Advisors. The second of these, William Clark, another close associate of Reagan's, had been appointed Undersecretary of State and was moved to National Security Advisor (NSA) largely to act as a buffer between Haig and Weinberger.[37]

The conflict between Defense and State continued and in many ways intensified after George P. Shultz replaced Haig in June 1982. Shultz was a far more calm and reflective character than Haig and had worked closely with Weinberger before, so Reagan was convinced the appointment would bring harmony to his foreign policy team. But Shultz was a pragmatist where Weinberger was an ideologue and they had a long history of disagreeing with each other. As Cannon puts it, they 'resembled an old couple who air ancient grievances in public, oblivious to the impact their feuding has on others'.[38] They were to quarrel over many an issue in the Reagan administration, not least, as we shall see, the appropriate application of American military force.

Despite the disputes within the foreign policy bureaucracy and the lack of a programmatic speech from the president, the administration did forge a foreign policy agenda in the opening weeks of the first term. As Haig confirms: 'In fact we were getting things done. In those early days, all of the issues that have preoccupied the Administration in foreign affairs ever since were identified.'[39] The main objective of Reagan's foreign policy was to restore the United States' national pride and strength. He sought to overcome the perceived weakness of US power in world affairs, halt the apparent gains being made by America's international adversaries, and restore the faith of the public at home and abroad in the will and ability of the United States to lead the defence of American and Western interests. To achieve these ends, the Reagan administration set out its goals as follows: (1) stop apologizing for American power and begin to stand tall and speak positively and confidently about the role of the US in the world; (2) revive the American economy in order to give stability and security to national and world markets; (3) return superpower relations to the centre of US foreign policy and treat the Soviet Union in realistic terms; (4) redress the perceived strategic imbalance through a concerted arms build-up; (5) restore faith and pride in the US military by redefining the Vietnam War and restoring the willingness to employ force abroad; and (6) promote US-backed democracy as a viable alternative to Soviet-sponsored Marxist-Leninism in the developing world.

Despite dedicating most of his first year in office to his economic recovery programme, Reagan did establish that the cornerstone of his foreign policy would be to achieve peace and security for the US from a position of strength that he believed had been lacking in recent years. It was not until 1982, though, that Reagan finally began to outline the grand scheme of his foreign policy in public. Significantly, he did so in terms that reflected his view of the US as a nation with a special role to play in the world. On May 9, 1982, Reagan made explicit that East–West relations lay at the centre of his foreign policy and identified the main elements of his Soviet policy. A month later he chose an address to the British Parliament to convey his vision of the central purpose of US foreign policy. Reagan declared: 'Around the world today, the democratic revolution is gathering new strength.' It was the duty of the US and her allies to let one objective guide their foreign policy: 'to foster the infrastructure of democracy'. This was not, Reagan believed, 'cultural imperialism' but was rather 'providing the means for genuine self-determination and protection for diversity'. Reagan was confident in the result of his long term plan: 'the march of freedom and democracy ... will leave Marxism-Leninism on the ash-heap of history.' Military strength was necessary, Reagan said, but this victory would not be won through war but through 'a test of wills and ideas, a trial of spiritual resolve, the values we hold, the beliefs we cherish, the ideals to which we are dedicated'.[40]

The key to Reagan's 'crusade for freedom'[41] was a faith in the enduring power of traditional American values and principles that he believed were shared and sought after by all the people of the world. The day after his Westminster speech, Reagan told the West German Bundestag that he was a great believer in the 'moral power' of Western civilization and its principles.

If the US and her allies stayed true to those values and allowed their policies to be guided by their ideals, he was optimistic they could meet the Soviet challenge and establish 'a lasting policy that will keep the peace'.[42] Reagan reiterated this message at home in his 1983 State of the Union address. He argued that the US had become the world's leading nation due to the values and freedoms enshrined in the Bill of Rights. These values were, Reagan said, the 'bedrock of our strength'. The US was now moving forward again, he believed, because it had cast off years of cynicism to 'rediscover' and apply those values as a 'cornerstone of a comprehensive strategy for peace with freedom'.[43] One month later, Reagan again affirmed his belief that the US had re-established itself at the forefront of international affairs by utilizing the strength of its basic principles: 'By wedding the timeless truths and values Americans have always cherished to the realities of today's world, we have forged the beginnings of a fundamentally new direction in American foreign policy.'[44]

Jimmy Carter, of course, also believed he had taken US foreign policy in a fundamentally new direction by basing it more fully on traditional American values and principles. How could his successor make apparently the same claim? In earlier chapters, we have seen that the values and principles Americans refer to as being traditionally at the root of their society are rather amorphous. Debates continue about the precise nature of those values: what are they? what do they mean? do they amount to a coherent ideology? are they mutually exclusive? do their meanings change over time and according to circumstance? It should be no wonder, then, that they can be interpreted in many different ways and utilized by public officials in order to justify or achieve radically different ends. The same is true, as has been argued throughout this book, of the belief in American exceptionalism. Carter believed the US had lost its way and had acted immorally in the Vietnam War and at home in the Watergate affair. It had ceased to conduct itself in an exceptional manner. Carter called upon traditional American values and principles in an attempt to reassert morality as the central guiding force in US foreign policy. He was convinced the US needed to measure its actions against specific standards of morality. Reagan's take on the matter was rather different. Reagan believed so thoroughly that American principles of freedom and democracy are inherently moral that he could not understand how any action in the pursuit of these goals could be conceived as anything but moral. Any aspect of US foreign policy could, therefore, be justified simply by declaring it as morally furthering the cause of freedom and democracy. Carter tried to get what he considered a fallen United States to redeem itself through conducting itself morally; an approach which required the nation to accept certain limits to what Americans could rightfully do. Reagan, on the other hand, denied that any redemption was necessary: the United States had always been great and it always would be so long as its people continued to believe in themselves and the inherent good of their society. For Reagan, then, there was no reason for the United States to limit its actions, because the US was morally superior to all other nations so whatever it did was for the good of the world.

Self-doubt had no place in the US, according to Reagan, because Americans were always on the side of right. So when Reagan cited John Winthrop it was not as a reminder of the colonial settler's warning that Americans must live up to the high standards they set for themselves, otherwise they would suffer the consternation of the world. It was to remind Americans that their land had always been a special place that had been founded as an example for humankind and that it was their duty 'to hold true to that dream of Joseph [sic] Winthrop'. The Americans of the 1980s, Reagan declared, must ensure that future generations would say of them: 'that we did act worthy of ourselves, that we did protect and pass on lovingly that shining city on a hill.' Such an end would be assured if Americans were true to themselves and their heritage. They should, therefore, 'go on the offensive' and 'foster the hope of liberty throughout the world'. Reagan was convinced that the task of the United States, because it is an exceptional nation, was to 'present to the world not just an America that's militarily strong, but an America that is morally powerful, an America that has a creed, a cause, a vision of a future time when all peoples have the right to self-government and personal freedom'.[45]

Reagan's military build-up

While Reagan did not make a major speech detailing the full breadth of his foreign policy during his first year in office, he did address the central element of his defence policy.[46] Reagan, Haig and Weinberger were agreed that restoring the military strength of the US must be the number one priority of the administration's foreign and defence policy.[47] Reagan believed, and never tired of repeating, that a 'decade of neglect' in US strategic forces coupled with a massive Soviet arms build-up had opened a 'window of vulnerability' in the United States' nuclear deterrent. Reagan was far from alone in being convinced that the US had allowed itself to fall into a weakened strategic position. Stansfield Turner, director of the CIA under President Carter, reflected the conventional wisdom: 'in the last several years all of the best studies have shown that the balance of strategic nuclear capabilities has been tipping in favor of the Soviet Union.'[48] The CIA's Office of Soviet Analysis (SOVA) provided evidence that Soviet military spending was increasing at 'an enormous rate' of 4–5 per cent per year in the late 1970s and early 1980s. By 1983, however, much to the chagrin of the Reagan administration, SOVA admitted it had been wrong and that in fact the increase had only been 1.3 per cent per year from 1976, that Soviet weapons procurement had 'remained flat', and that there had actually been a decrease of 40 per cent on offensive strategic weapons spending. By 1985,

SOVA was also scaling down its projections of the size of Soviet strategic forces since actual weapons output was much lower than earlier estimates suggested.[49] Whatever the realities of Soviet strategic strength, in 1981 public and elite opinion combined in what Lou Cannon has characterized as 'a consensus rare in American peacetime history [favouring] huge increases in military spending'.[50] On October 2, 1981, Reagan announced his programme to 'revitalize' US strategic forces through the deployment of new weapons including the MX missile, B-1 bombers, and cruise missiles, and the modernization of existing forces such as Trident submarines.[51]

Between 1980 and 1985, defence spending increased by 53 per cent, the largest and most rapid rise in US peacetime history.[52] This increase had begun during President Carter's last year in office. Indeed, most of Reagan's arms build-up, aside from the restoration of the B-1 bomber programme, was actually inherited from the Carter administration. But it was the Reagan administration that was given and took the credit for restoring US strategic strength. It was also, therefore, Reagan who prompted strong reactions from the burgeoning peace movement in Europe, especially in Britain and West Germany where cruise missiles were to be based, and the nuclear freeze movement within the United States. In the Soviet Union, Reagan became characterized as a dangerous warmonger. On June 7, 1981, the Soviet Armed Forces newspaper, *Krasnaia Zvezda* (*Red Star*) editorialized:

> The unprecedented appropriations for military purposes appear particularly sinister against the background of the blasphemous and reckless statements of the present American leaders that 'there are more important things than peace' and that it is supposedly 'possible to win' a nuclear war.

Following the announcement of Reagan's strategic weapons programme, *Pravda* concluded that Reagan was 'actively preparing for such a war'.[53]

The commonplace caricature in the Soviet and Western European press of Reagan as a gun-toting cowboy, his itchy finger poised over the nuclear trigger, was certainly encouraged by the cavalier attitude often displayed by Reagan and his advisers toward the possibility of fighting and indeed winning a nuclear war. Reagan showed he could contemplate a limited nuclear exchange when he told a group of news editors in October 1981: 'I could see where you could have the exchange of tactical weapons against troops in the field without it bringing either one of the major powers to pushing the button.'[54] The following month, Haig suggested that a nuclear warning shot might be part of NATO's contingency plans in the event of Soviet aggression in Europe. Reagan argued, rather unconvincingly, at a press conference on November 10, 1981 that his own comments in October had been nothing more than hypothetical musings. Alarmingly, he also admitted that he did not know and had not been able to find out whether NATO strategy included Haig's warning-shot contingency.[55] There is little wonder that the arms build-up and its attendant posturing raised such widespread alarm.

The administration was not oblivious, it seems, to the unease its comments on nuclear strategy were causing. A week after his fumbling performance of November 10, Reagan addressed the National Press Club on his nuclear weapons policy. He stated categorically that: 'No NATO weapons, conventional or nuclear, will ever be used in Europe except in response to attack.' He then argued through the rationale behind his arms build-up in what was the beginning of a long campaign to convey to the American public his vision of the future of American strategic policy. Reagan's argument was that the ultimate aim of the US was to bring peace to the world. Reagan agreed with his advisers and pressure groups such as the Committee on the Present Danger that the only way to achieve peace was through strength. Reagan claimed there was 'no higher priority' in his mind than to achieve substantial arms control agreements with the Soviet Union. He argued that the only way the US could secure successful negotiations with the Soviets, however, was from a position of strength. Therefore, Reagan considered that correcting the strategic imbalance through a massive arms build-up was a prerequisite for ending the arms race. He then proposed what became known as the 'zero option' that would eventually form the basis of the 1987 INF Treaty: that the US would cancel its deployment of Pershing II and ground-launched cruise missiles in Europe if the Soviet Union would dismantle its SS-20, SS-4 and SS-5 missiles.[56]

According to critics, to consider the use of nuclear weapons was not only immoral but also an 'ugly embrace of barbarism' and certainly not the exemplary action of a nation supposedly dedicated to peace and without the desire for conquest or aggression.[57] To follow such a policy seemed to contradict Reagan's own perception of his nation and its role in the world. Many people are confused by the apparent turnaround in Reagan's approach to nuclear weapons from the aggressive sabre-rattler of his first term to dedicated arms reductionist in his second term. A closer examination of the evidence reveals, perhaps surprisingly, that Reagan had always abhorred the idea of nuclear war, even in his most belligerent moments.

Reagan claims he came to office with a 'decided prejudice' against the policy of mutually assured destruction (MAD) which formed the core of nuclear deterrence between the US and the Soviet Union. He believed it to be quite literally 'madness' and was convinced there 'had to be some way to remove this threat of annihilation and give the world a greater chance of survival'.[58] Following his comments about the feasibility of limited nuclear war, Reagan frequently made clear that he in fact believed 'a nuclear war cannot be won and must never be fought', whether limited or otherwise.[59] To Reagan, nuclear weapons were 'monstrous' and 'inhumane' and he had no greater wish or priority than 'reducing and ultimately removing the threat of nuclear war and seeking the stability for true peace'.[60] Reagan claimed he agreed with the objectives of anti-nuclear protesters but not with their methods. He was convinced that the Soviet Union would only agree to negotiate reductions in strategic arms if the US was in a position of strength.

Reagan was so obsessed with eradicating the nuclear threat that he embraced the controversial idea of developing a space-based defence system that could provide an impenetrable shield against nuclear attack. Reagan believed this technology, once it was shared with the Soviet Union, would make nuclear weapons obsolete. It was an idea fraught with difficulty, not least that almost nobody in the scientific community believed a fail-safe system could ever be developed. Yet although Reagan was aware that deployment would be many years if not decades away, the Strategic Defense Initiative (SDI or 'Star Wars' as it was dubbed by the media) became his most treasured project. Reagan never faltered in his dedicated promotion of the idea and its eventual feasibility, because it would fulfil his 'deepest hope' that 'someday our children and our grandchildren could live in a world free of the constant threat of nuclear war'.[61]

SDI, whether plausible or not, fitted perfectly within Reagan's view of the world and his belief in American exceptionalism. Reagan was convinced that Americans are capable of absolutely anything so long as they believe in themselves enough. He thought there was no problem so big that given enough time and resources an American could not solve it. To Reagan, the US led the world in technological and scientific progress and boasted the foremost minds. Coupled with the pioneer spirit and the highest in human ingenuity, anything was possible. Reagan argued there had been no weapon in history for which a defence had not been developed eventually. The US had given the world nuclear weapons. Reagan saw no reason why Americans could not now invent an effective defence to make those weapons obsolete. SDI was an inherently American idea: in Reagan's view it would not serve narrow self-interest but would ensure the survival of all humankind. It was to him the ultimate action of an altruistic nation with an altruistic foreign policy. According to Reagan, it would be a system designed not to bring domination and conquest but, in the finest spirit of America, would guarantee that freedom and liberty could flourish free from the fear of extinction. That SDI lived more in Reagan's imagination than in reality did not really matter to him. As with so many other aspects of Reagan's and America's beliefs system, it was a truth waiting to happen.

SDI did, however, have far-reaching effects beyond the research and development laboratory. Far from assuring an end to the possibility of nuclear war, Reagan's scheme for a defensive shield actually heightened the threat. The Soviet Union and other critics perceived that the US president was trying to upset the strategic balance between East and West that formed the basis of deterrence policy. If the US could deploy a system that would shield its cities and missile silos from attack then it would no longer be deterred from launching a first-strike against the Soviet Union. Such a possibility might even convince the Soviet leadership to order a preemptive nuclear strike before SDI became operational rather than being held hostage by a strategically superior United States. Soviet leader Mikhail Gorbachev referred to SDI as 'an instrument for ensuring domination'.[62] Reagan, of course, did not agree. In a handwritten letter, he assured Gorbachev 'the truth is that the United States has no intention of using its strategic defense program to gain any advantage, & there is no development underway to create space-based offensive weapons. Our goal is to eliminate any possibility of a first strike from either side'.[63] Nevertheless, the Soviet view persisted and SDI provided a major obstacle to arms reduction negotiations and threatened to move the arms race into defensive as well as offensive areas. It has been argued, of course, that SDI was central to a 'squeeze' strategy deliberately designed to overburden the Soviet economy and hasten the downfall of communism.[64] Such claims, however, fail to consider the extent to which internal conditions and developments led to Soviet reforms and how the consequences of global interdependence affected the Soviet economy. In fact, Raymond Garthoff has argued, the longer the 1980s went on the less worried the Soviet Union became about the threat of SDI as it became increasingly apparent that deployment was highly unlikely. There was no need to increase defence spending to meet a threat that did not exist. Indeed, Soviet defence spending did remain 'roughly constant' between 1985 and 1988.[65] If anything, any squeeze strategy that was pursued through SDI simply had the effect of consolidating the attempts of Soviet hardliners to resist Gorbachev's reforms.[66]

Reagan and the evil empire

Another major facet of Reagan's campaign to restore American pride and strength was his rhetorical assault on the Soviet Union during his first term. The president set the tone at his very first news conference on January 29, 1981. He claimed that the Soviet leadership:

> have openly and publicly declared that the only morality they recognize is what will further their cause, meaning they reserve unto themselves the right to commit any crime, to lie, to cheat, in order to attain [their goal of worldwide Communist revolution].

Americans, Reagan proclaimed, 'operate on a different set of standards'.[67] This rhetorically anti-Soviet approach was maintained by Reagan through-out most of his first term. His efforts to rebuild American confidence in the strength and morality of their own system would be aided by a frequent comparison with what he regarded as the morally and spiritually (and indeed economically) bankrupt Soviet system. Reagan described the Soviets as cruel, inhumane, aggressive and exploitative. They were the new imperialists who could only keep their people from fleeing their system by building walls of concrete and barbed wire. By comparison, Reagan insisted, Americans were lovers of freedom and individuality who respected the rights and dignity of all humans, encouraging and helping them to live their lives to the fullness of their potential.

Reagan's anti-Soviet rhetoric reached its peak when he addressed the Annual Convention of the National Association of Evangelicals in Orlando, Florida, on March 8, 1983. Reagan famously referred to the Soviet Union as 'the focus of evil in the modern world'. He urged his audience and all Americans to never forget or ignore 'the aggressive impulses of an evil empire' as they considered whether to support his defence build-up. No American, he said, could afford to remove themselves 'from the struggle between right and wrong and good and evil'.[68]

Reagan concluded in his Orlando speech that the struggle between the US and the Soviet Union would not be settled by armed conflict but by a 'test of moral will and strength'.[69] Nevertheless, the president's characterization of the Soviets as an 'evil empire' led many in the US and Europe to fear that war between the superpowers was becoming increasingly inevitable. Reagan, however, repeatedly denied that this was the case. He told Henry Brandon of the *Sunday Times* that all he was doing in the Orlando speech and at other times was showing 'a recognition and a willingness to face up to' the differences between the US and the Soviet Union. He was simply being 'realistic' about the nature of the Soviets, but he continued to believe that 'peace is achievable'.[70] Reagan refused to accept that his 'evil empire' speech had in any way intensified the Cold War. He even told another group of reporters: 'I didn't think there were many polemics in that particular message.'[71] Reagan believed he was simply 'telling it as it is'. He felt particularly vindicated after the Soviet Union shot down a South Korean civilian passenger plane in September 1983. He told the nation: 'I hope the Soviets' recent behavior will dispel any lingering doubts about what kind of regime we're dealing with.'[72] He continued to push the point throughout 1983 and remained convinced that 'telling the truth about the Soviet empire' should never be considered 'an act of belligerence on our part'. It was imperative, Reagan believed, that Americans:

> continue to remind the world that self-delusion in the face of unpleasant facts is folly, that whatever the imperfections of the democratic nations, the struggle now going on in the world is essentially the struggle between freedom and totalitarianism, between what is right and what is wrong.[73]

In a December 1983 interview, Reagan yet again stated that he believed the Soviet Union was 'a source of evil'.[74] The relentlessness of Reagan's Soviet rhetoric was soon to change, however. In a national address broadcast throughout the world on January 16, 1984, Reagan signalled the beginnings of a change of tack towards the Soviet Union. He announced: 'I believe that 1984 finds the United States in the strongest position in years to establish a constructive and realistic working relationship with the Soviet Union.' Reagan proclaimed that the superpowers 'must do more to find areas of mutual interest and then build on them'. He proposed that the two governments strive to reduce and then eliminate the use of force in international disputes; to reduce nuclear and conventional weapons throughout the world; and to establish a better working relationship based on 'greater cooperation and understanding'. The US would approach these tasks through the guiding principles of 'realism, strength, and dialog'. Reagan admitted to having openly expressed his views on the Soviet Union but said this was no different to the way in which the Soviet leaders expressed their views on the Western system. Such public criticisms did not mean, however, that 'we can't deal with each other'. Reagan's new Soviet policy, then, would be based on 'credible deterrence, peaceful competition, and constructive cooperation'.[75] It was a turning point in the Reagan administration's relationship with the Soviet Union that, with the coming to power of Mikhail Gorbachev, would eventually lead to a thawing in superpower relations.

The reasons for the Reagan administration's sudden move towards a more conciliatory approach to the Soviet Union during his second term have been a matter of much debate. The conventional wisdom is that the Reagan administration was mostly reactive to the changes within the Soviet Union. Reagan's January 1984 speech, however, was given over a year before Gorbachev came to power. Why, then, did Reagan himself begin to thaw the Cold War by reversing his administration's hardline approach to the Soviet Union and begin to actively seek more congenial relations? In 1983, Richard Wirthlin, Reagan's pollster, drew the president's attention to the fact that growing numbers of Americans were uneasy with the ferocity of Reagan's denunciations of the Soviet Union. Nancy Reagan was also advising her husband to tone down what she considered his dangerous, confrontational stance towards the Soviets.[76] With the 1984 presidential election campaign beginning to get under way, it could be concluded that Reagan softened his anti-Soviet rhetoric in an attempt to placate fears among the electorate. In her study of Reagan's Soviet policy reversal, however, Beth Fischer shows that poll data indicate in fact that Reagan's hardline policy was becoming increasingly popular during 1983. There was no need, therefore, for Reagan to change his Soviet policy in order to secure greater electoral support. Alternatively, it is argued that Secretary of State Shultz, who had replaced Haig when he resigned in June 1982, and newly appointed National Security Advisor Robert C. McFarlane influenced the president's decision. They did both counsel a more conciliatory approach to Soviet relations but, as Fischer argues, neither had enough dominance in the policy making process to force such a sudden and sweeping change as declared in Reagan's speech. Fischer argues convincingly that Reagan himself took control of US–Soviet policy in late 1983 and initiated the policy reversal. According to Fischer, Reagan's long-held abhorrence of nuclear weapons was primed by three events in late 1983: the Soviet shooting down of the South Korean airliner, his viewing of the nuclear holocaust film *The Day After*, and a Pentagon briefing on US nuclear war plans. With his fear of nuclear war heightened by these events, Reagan was shocked to discover that Moscow had almost mistaken the NATO military exercise 'Able Archer' in November 1983 for preparation for an actual nuclear attack. The Soviet reaction made Reagan realize that his hard line was perceived as threatening in Moscow and was, despite his assurances to the contrary, aggravating the chances of a nuclear confrontation. Reagan, therefore, initiated a reversal in his Soviet policy not because his view of the Kremlin or communism had changed but because he feared that continuing with his hardline approach would cause a nuclear war.[77] If Fischer is correct then the question remains why, if his fear of nuclear war was so great, Reagan authorized such a massive military build-up, shunned arms control talks, and discussed the possibilities of limited nuclear war during the first three years of his presidency.

Reagan certainly did not confirm publicly that he was seeking improved US–Soviet relations because he had become convinced his hardline approach would inevitably lead to nuclear war. On the day he announced his new Soviet policy, Reagan told the *Washington Post* that he did not regret his 'evil empire' rhetoric. He believed 'it was necessary for them to know that we were looking at them realistically'. He thought the significance of the rhetoric had 'been overplayed and exaggerated' and that the US was certainly not in 'great danger' as a result. In fact, he told the *Post*'s reporters, he believed the US was now safer from war than it had been three years previously, thanks to his arms build-up and the renewed confidence of the American people.[78]

In an internal document of talking points prepared within the NSC for Robert McFarlane there is again little indication that Reagan had adopted his new stance due to his shock that 'Able Archer' had almost caused a nuclear confrontation. It is noted that the administration seeks the 'avoidance of war and reduction of existing levels of arms' but it is also specified that:

> Despite harsh rhetoric from both sides, [the] Soviet–American relationship is quite stable today and danger of war is actually lower than in the past. There have been no near-confrontations with Moscow, similar to Cuban Missiles Crisis, the 1973 dispute in the Mid-East or the tension created after the invasion of Afghanistan.

The memo offers an alternative to Fischer's thesis about why the administration was now adopting a more conciliatory approach. It emphasizes that the president 'spoke from a position of improved American self-confidence. Economic recovery in full swing, stronger cohesion, demonstrated willingness of US to undertake defense modernization programs and to employ military power when challenged'. The problem with détente in its later years, according to the Reagan administration, was that the US had adopted a position of relative weakness in its relationship with the Soviet Union. After three years in office, the Reagan administration now perceived that it had restored the US to a position of strength in the world from which it could again work towards a more cooperative relationship with a Soviet Union which it no longer regarded as holding a strategic or political advantage. Not surprisingly, given how bellicose Reagan and his advisers had been of late, the Soviet leadership was not convinced by the new American overtures. As the NSC memo indicates, however, the negative response from Moscow worked well from the administration's point of view as it increased the perception that the US was now making initiatives from a position of strength rather than reacting to Soviet demands and threats: 'When the Kremlin demonstrates a willingness to join us in this search for an improved relationship, we will be prepared to suggest specific initiatives that will contribute to more positive ties.'[79] Such evidence does not discount Fischer's thesis on the Soviet policy reversal but it does suggest that the administration's perception of US power relative to the Soviet Union played an important role in the adoption of a more conciliatory approach.

A further aspect of Reagan's attempt to illustrate the superiority of Western, and particularly American, values was his rather prophetic assertion that although militarily the Soviet Union was a massive force that must be met in kind, economically the Soviet system was on the point of collapse. Long before it was accepted conventional wisdom, Reagan was arguing that the 'last pages' of communism's 'bizarre chapter in human history ... are even now being written'.[80] Reagan was convinced that putting military strength before the needs of its people would eventually 'undermine the foundations of the Soviet system'.[81] He saw in the Soviet Union 'a great revolutionary crisis ... where the demands of the economic order are conflicting directly with those of the political order'. Reagan declared that the Soviet experiment was in 'decay' and the 'dimensions of this failure are astounding'. The Soviet leadership was starving its people of food and manufactured goods to maintain an aggressive war machine and running 'against the tide of history by denying human freedom and human dignity to its citizens'.[82] It was inevitable to Reagan that the Soviet system would fail and that, by contrast, the benign values championed by the US would flourish to the benefit of all humankind. Despite these realizations, though, as noted earlier there is little if no evidence that the administration deliberately contrived a 'squeeze' strategy to break the Soviet Union and 'win' the Cold War. Indeed, if such a strategy had been adopted surely it would have been better to keep 'squeezing' in 1984 and after rather than negotiating and beginning to improve relations.

Reagan and the memory of Vietnam

A further integral part of Reagan's campaign to revive American self-confidence was his attempt to redefine the way Americans felt about the Vietnam War and particularly the role of America's fighting men in that conflict. As early as his first Inaugural Address, Reagan included Vietnam in a list of places where American heroes had fallen to preserve the principles of their nation.[83] Then Reagan declared that Sunday April 26, 1981 would be a National Day of Recognition for Veterans of the Vietnam Era. He acknowledged that the period of the war had been 'a time of trial for our Nation'. As a result, 'full recognition of the Nation's debt of gratitude' to Vietnam veterans was 'long overdue'. Reagan made clear that: 'No one should doubt the nobility of the effort they made.'[84] He would frequently repeat his contention that Vietnam had been 'a noble cause' in which Americans fought as bravely and as righteously as at any other time in American history. The only difference in Vietnam was that not all Americans back home supported the military's effort and that US forces 'were not allowed to win'.[85]

The rehabilitation of the Vietnam veteran and Reagan's redefining of the war itself reached its apex with the dedicating of the Vietnam Veterans Memorial on the Mall in Washington, DC, on November 13, 1982. Two days previously, on Veterans Day, Reagan stated that: 'Nothing is more important to the soul of America than remembering and honoring those who gave of themselves so that we might enjoy the fruits of peace and liberty.' In that spirit, the 'long overdue' tribute of the Vietnam Veterans Memorial would be dedicated. Reagan reinforced his belief that: 'It's time that Vietnam veterans take their rightful place in our history along with other American heroes who put their lives on the line for their country.' Reagan admitted: 'Certainly, mistakes were made … [but] the cause for which our Vietnam veterans fought was an honorable one.' Dedicating the Memorial, or The Wall as it soon became known, would enable Americans to 'put behind us the ingratitude and injustice of the past' along with the 'divisiveness' that Vietnam had spawned.[86]

Presidents Ford and Carter had each attempted to move the US forward from the Vietnam era and heal the perceived wounds American society had suffered during the period. As we have seen, neither of them was fully successful. Reagan took an approach different from either of his predecessors. In keeping with his natural optimism, Reagan succeeded to a great extent in redefining the way most Americans felt and thought about Vietnam. In Reagan's view the war was not, as Carter had given the impression, a total disaster that Americans should feel nothing but guilt about. Reagan encouraged Americans to believe they had acted honourably in going to the aid of the South Vietnamese and that, had it not been for the failures and weaknesses of government bureaucracy, Americans would have achieved their objectives in the war. In Reagan's view of the events, Vietnam had not shown that there was anything wrong with American ideals and principles.

It had merely revealed that those who controlled the federal government were not up to the task of maintaining those principles. Reagan was able, in a sense, to redefine the Vietnam experience as a victory. It was not a victory in political and military terms (even though, as Reagan emphasized, US forces were never beaten on the battlefield in Vietnam), but a victory of the American spirit. Conveniently ignoring My Lai, Kent State, and other controversial episodes from the era, as well as denying alternative explanations for the American defeat, Reagan dwelt upon the personal efforts of those fighting the war and concluded that, although the conflict was not without its mistakes, the public could be proud of the way most Americans dedicated themselves selflessly to the cause, as they had whenever duty called from the Revolution onwards. Americans could put Vietnam behind them, Reagan contended, by embracing it as a noble part of their history. After years of being shunned by the wider society, most veterans of the war felt that largely thanks to Reagan's efforts they were finally accepted as courageous patriots regardless of whether or not the war itself was justified. According to veteran and writer Robert Timberg, Reagan was 'a one-man welcome home parade'.[87]

Despite his rhetoric, however, Reagan did not lay to rest the ghosts of Vietnam. Through his rehabilitation of the Vietnam veteran and his willingness to talk about the war, Reagan did contribute to a process of coming to terms with the Vietnam War that occupied much of American thought and popular culture throughout the 1980s and early 1990s. But in his determination to finally put Vietnam behind Americans, Reagan offered an unrealistic reinterpretation of the war that diminished the importance and significance of many of the debates over the meaning and consequences of Vietnam and its effects on American society. As Arnold Isaacs has observed: 'The real war in Vietnam was...more complicated and more ambiguous than Ronald Reagan ever seemed to understand. And so was the task of vanquishing Vietnam's legacy.'[88]

Reagan and the use of force

The most enduring legacy of the Vietnam War in terms of foreign policy, of course, is the debate over the appropriate use of American military force in international relations. Like both the previous post-Vietnam administrations, Reagan and his advisers found this issue to be most perplexing. Reagan was determined to overcome the apparent limits to American action in world affairs. In order to succeed in his efforts to restore the strength of the United States as a superpower, he believed it was necessary to demonstrate that the US had not lost the will to stand up for its interests and principles. He did not want to give the impression that the US would rush to arms upon any provocation but he was determined that allies and adversaries alike should understand that, if necessary, the US was willing to employ force to achieve its objectives.

Reagan made his intentions clear from the very beginning of his presidency. In his first Inaugural Address he warned: 'Our reluctance for conflict should not be misjudged as a failure of will. When action is required to preserve our national security, we will act.'[89] Reagan was careful to maintain that unlike many of its potential adversaries the US was an exceptional nation that did not resort to war lightly. Reagan gave a typically revised version of the historical record:

> Americans resort to force only when we must. We have never been aggressors. We have always struggled to defend freedom and democracy. We have no territorial ambitions. We occupy no countries.[90]

This did not mean, however, that the US would no longer take up arms against aggressors. On the contrary, so Reagan believed, the reinvigorated United States was ready and willing to meet any challenge anywhere in the world with force if necessary. Reagan emphasized that if any lesson had been learned from Vietnam it was that 'we must never again send our young men to fight and die in conflicts that our leaders are not prepared to win'.[91] To Reagan, this last point was very clear. He believed the military had gone to Vietnam with one arm tied behind its back and had consequently been unable to achieve victory. In the future, Reagan was determined, whenever the US committed force to a situation it would do so with adequate strength and resolve to achieve its objectives. There appeared to be little disagreement within the administration that this should be the case whenever force was employed. There were, however, major differences, particularly between the State Department and the Pentagon, over the circumstances under which it was acceptable to use force in the first place.

Secretary of State Haig agreed with Reagan that under Ford, and especially under Carter, 'the fear of "another Vietnam" paralyzed the will of the US government'.[92] Haig believed the US had earned a reputation for 'strategic passivity' that could not 'be wished away by rhetoric'. The US needed to demonstrate through 'prudent and successful actions' that it remained capable of defending its national security interests.[93] Such actions must include the effective threat and use of force because, as Haig told his Senate confirmation hearing, 'some things are worse than war'.[94] Haig believed a lesson of Vietnam was that sufficient force must be employed with enough resolve to ensure victory. He also believed that the use of force should be considered as a viable option when developing policy responses to international situations. As he wrote in his 1984 memoirs: 'If an objective is worth pursuing, then it must be pursued with enough resources to force the issue early.'[95]

The Department of Defense and the Joint Chiefs of Staff were far more reluctant to employ the force at their disposal. The military had been badly damaged by its experiences in the Vietnam War. The armed services had suffered great losses in a war that, according to the military, had been limited by the whims and desires of bureaucrats and politicians who lacked the will and commitment to get the job done. Military leaders were left wary of being again placed in a position where they would be asked to sacrifice lives and materiel for ill-defined or unpopular objectives. They were tired of being what they regarded as the pawns in White House and State Department games that often had bloody consequences. Many of them believed, as did General Colin L. Powell, who would be Reagan's National Security Advisor during his last year in office, that in war: politicians must set a clear set of objectives; the military should then be left to achieve those objectives with whatever force they deem necessary; and no conflict should be fought without assurances that the people believe the sacrifice is justified and worthy of their support.[96] In Secretary of Defense Caspar Weinberger, the military found a civilian leader who shared their apprehensions about the use of force. Weinberger claimed to have learned from Vietnam, and indeed Korea, that objectives must be clarified before forces are committed to a situation. He was also convinced that 'it was a terrible mistake for Government to commit soldiers to battle without any intention of support-ing them sufficiently to enable them to win, and indeed without any inten-tion to win at all'. Any conflict must be entered with 'all the resources and will to win' that the US possessed. Weinberger believed that securing and maintaining public support was also essential if any commitment of force were to be successful. The public would 'have to be convinced that our national interests required, indeed demanded, that we go to war'. Without such assurances, Weinberger did not believe force should be employed.[97]

When George Shultz became secretary of state he entered what he came to describe as 'a battle royal' with Weinberger over when it was appropriate to use military force.[98] Shultz shared Reagan's concerns about what the pres-ident called 'the Vietnam problem'. He believed the fear of becoming mired in 'another Vietnam' had the US 'tied in knots'. The time had come, Shultz decided, to throw off the constraints imposed by Vietnam and return the use of force to what he perceived as its rightful place as a viable option in foreign affairs. Shultz made clear his views in a speech on October 25, 1984, while addressing the US response to international terrorism:

> We cannot allow ourselves to become the Hamlet of nations, worrying endlessly over whether and how to respond. A great nation with global responsibilities cannot afford to be hamstrung by confusion and indeci-siveness. ... We must reach a consensus in this country that our responses should go beyond passive defense to consider means of active prevention, preemption, and retaliation.

Shultz's belief that his words reflected the president's views on the use of force seemed confirmed when White House spokesperson Larry Speakes announced that the speech 'was administration policy from top to bottom'.[99] Weinberger, however, had other ideas.

During the summer of 1984, Weinberger had drawn up what he called 'six major tests to be applied when we are weighing the use of US combat forces abroad'. These had been circulated in draft form among Reagan's national security team and Weinberger wanted to make them public. According to his then Senior Military Assistant, Colin Powell, Weinberger was dissuaded from doing so by White House 'political operatives' until after the presidential election.[100] On November 28, 1984, Weinberger announced his six tests in an address to the National Press Club in Washington, DC. According to Weinberger, the US should only commit troops to combat abroad if:

(1)   an interest vital to the US or her allies is at stake
(2)   the political will to win and the strength of the force used is sufficient to ensure victory
(3)   political and military objectives are clearly defined and attainable
(4)   the objectives and size of forces committed are continually reassessed and adjusted if necessary
(5)   congressional and public support is assured
(6)   the decision to use force is a last resort.

These six criteria became known as the Weinberger Doctrine.[101] It was the first time, at least publicly, that a high-ranking public official had attempted to codify the lessons on the use of force learned from the American experience in Vietnam.

Powell believed the Weinberger Doctrine provided 'a practical guide' to committing forces to combat that he would himself use to advise presidents in the future. He was concerned, however, that such an explicit public proclamation of the Pentagon's decision making criteria could invite adversaries to seek loopholes through which they could challenge US interests unhindered.[102] Shultz was far more critical, concluding that the Weinberger Doctrine was 'the Vietnam syndrome in spades, carried to an absurd level, and a complete abdication of the duties of leadership'. Shultz believed Weinberger's tests were only suitable for deciding whether to enter full-scale conventional war with an armed adversary but would forbid any lesser actions designed to combat 'the wide variety of complex, unclear, gray-area dangers facing us in the contemporary world'. Shultz maintained that diplomacy was most effective in solving international disputes when 'force – or the threat of force – was a credible part of the equation'. To follow the Weinberger Doctrine, according to Shultz, would be to weaken the power and influence the US could exert in world affairs.[103]

William Safire of the *New York Times* wrote that Weinberger and Shultz were engaged in a 'battle for Ronald Reagan's strategic soul'.[104] This battle continued throughout the administration. When and why force was authorized by Reagan raises important questions about the nature of the administration's foreign policy. Did Reagan's use of force confirm his rhetorical claim that US strength and resolve in foreign affairs had been restored? Or does the record show that, in actual fact, force was only employed in limited form under very specific conditions? If the latter is true then it is clear that the US continued, under Reagan, to be preoccupied with avoiding another Vietnam and to be wary of acting in ways inconsistent with the belief that the US is an exceptional, benign nation. To answer these questions we must look at the administration's use or threat of force in policies towards Central America, Lebanon, Grenada, the Soviet Union, and Libya and international terrorism.

Central America

The small Central American nations of El Salvador and Nicaragua had been governed by elites since the 1930s. In Nicaragua, the corrupt Somoza government, which the Carter administration had condemned for its human rights abuses, was finally overthrown by the Sandinista movement in July 1979. Carter initially extended diplomatic recognition and humanitarian aid to the new government but withdrew support in light of the Nicaraguan backing of a leftist insurgency in El Salvador. An oligarchy had kept tight control of El Salvador since 1932. Following a coup in October 1979, the Carter administration hoped a moderate middle way had been found, but repression and death squads continued to dominate El Salvadoran politics. The *Frente Farabundo Martí de Liberación Nacional* (FMLN) led a campaign of guerrilla warfare against the El Salvadoran government with arms acquired from the Nicaraguan Sandinistas. Despite the perception in Washington, Nicaragua did not become a fully fledged communist country.[105] The Sandinistas allowed some 60 per cent of the economy to remain under private ownership. Lacking American support, they did seek aid from Cuba and the Soviet Union but also received economic help from Canada, Japan and Western Europe.[106] The Reagan administration also overemphasized the Soviet links to the FMLN. Indeed, in 1981, the *Wall Street Journal* quipped it had 'found only one instance of outright Soviet aid to the rebels – an airplane ticket from Moscow to Vietnam for one guerrilla'.[107]

According to Gaddis Smith, none of the major architects of Reagan's Central American policy 'knew very much about the region, nor did they consider such knowledge relevant or necessary'.[108] Haig believed that 'a determined show of American will and power' could stem what he regarded as the expanding influence of the Soviet Union and its Cuban pawn in Central America. Haig was particularly enthusiastic for the prospects of success in bolstering the El Salvadoran government in their struggle with the FMLN.[109] In private, he told Reagan: 'Mr. President, this is one you can win.'[110] Yet Reagan's policy towards El Salvador, and his opposition to the

Sandinista government in Nicaragua, was restrained by the limits on American action imposed by the lessons of Vietnam.

Reagan emphasized how imperative he believed it was for the US to help Central America overcome 'externally supported aggression'. He told the Congress that the 'political and strategic stakes' were the same in El Salvador and Nicaragua as they had been in Greece and Turkey in 1947. Reagan believed the American response must be as 'appropriate and successful' as the Truman Doctrine had been to those earlier crises. The US, Reagan concluded, could not afford to 'stand by passively while the people of Central America are delivered to totalitarianism'. But Reagan was also very careful to allay fears that the US would be dragged into another Vietnam-style quagmire. He insisted: 'there is no thought of sending combat troops to Central America.'[111] According to Reagan: 'there is no comparison whatsoever in this situation and Vietnam.'[112]

The American experience in Vietnam, however, was a major determinant of how the Reagan administration approached its Central American policy making. Haig believed that one lesson of Vietnam was that any foreign involvement must avoid 'incrementalism'. By his own admission, however, Haig was 'virtually alone' in his belief that the US should give massive economic and military aid to El Salvador while also treating the problem 'at its source' by bringing the full economic, political and military strength of the US to bear on Cuba.[113] Weinberger claims that Haig advised the President to actually invade Cuba and overthrow Castro's regime as the only way to eliminate the spread of communism in Central America. Weinberger opposed any such action, insisting that the American public would not support an invasion.[114] The Secretary of Defense was supported in his views by the rest of the NSC members, apart from Haig who is critical of Weinberger for 'insistently rais[ing] the spectre of Vietnam'. Reagan disliked upsetting any of his advisers and appeared sympathetic to Haig's views, but he followed the majority advice within the NSC and ordered what Haig describes as 'a low-key treatment of El Salvador as a local problem and sought to cure it through limited amounts of military and economic aid'.[115]

However, US support for the El Salvador government, and later for the *Contra* rebels in Nicaragua, *did* bear a marked resemblance to early efforts to support the government of South Vietnam in the 1950s and early 1960s. Large sums of military, economic and humanitarian aid were complemented with American advisers who trained the El Salvadoran armed forces and the *Contras*. It is true that US combat troops were not deployed to fight in either country, so to that extent Reagan was correct in saying that the US was not involving itself in another Vietnam. But Haig's fears of incremental escalation were justified and Reagan's Central American policy might well have embroiled the US in another intractable small-scale conflict had it not been for increasing congressional and public unease that led to the cutting of funds for the administration's efforts aside from humanitarian aid. In the case of Nicaragua, of course, policy then went underground, leading to the ignominy of the Iran-Contra affair; but more of that later.

Lebanon

The legacy of the Vietnam War also cast its shadow over the first major deployment of armed forces by the Reagan administration. From August 25 to September 10, 1982, and again from September 29, 1982 to February 26, 1984, US Marines were deployed as part of a multinational peacekeeping force (MNF) in the Lebanese capital of Beirut. The Palestine Liberation Organization (PLO), with the support of Syria, had established its headquarters in Beirut during the Lebanese civil war and used it as a base for attacking Israeli targets. On June 6, 1982, Israel launched a full-scale invasion of Lebanon to root out the PLO. The Israelis occupied southern Lebanon, laid siege to Beirut and cut off supply lines to the PLO from the Syrians, who occupied eastern Lebanon.[116]

After West Beirut had suffered weeks of shelling and bombing, the US, along with France and Italy, deployed the MNF in Lebanon with what Reagan considered two clear objectives: to facilitate the safe departure of all members and operatives of the PLO from Lebanese territory and to restore the authority and sovereignty of the Lebanese government. To further assuage fears that US involvement would lead to a long, inconclusive and costly commitment, Reagan assured reporters and the Congress that in 'no case' would US troops stay longer than 30 days.[117]

The initial deployment of Marines lived up to expectations as they successfully oversaw the withdrawal of the PLO and the restoration of Lebanese control of Beirut within the allotted time period. The MNF soon returned, however, following the assassination of the Lebanese president-elect and a massacre of Palestinian refugees that exposed the continuing instability of a country still occupied by Israeli and Syrian forces and the many warring Lebanese factions.[118] This time, the US-led MNF had three main objectives: to provide an 'interposition force' to prevent further bloodshed; to facilitate the restoration of a strong and stable central government; and to preside over the withdrawal of all foreign forces from Lebanon. The deployment would again be in a noncombatant role and for a 'limited time', although Reagan did not specify the expected duration of the mission.[119]

Initially, the violence subsided, but it soon returned, culminating in the suicide bombing of the American and the French barracks in the early hours of October 23, 1983. The bombs took the lives of 241 US Marines and 58 French paratroopers.[120] Reagan reacted angrily to the bombings but insisted that withdrawing US forces from Lebanon could not be considered as an option 'while their mission still remains'.[121] In what Cannon describes as an 'extraordinary triumph of optimism over reality', Reagan argued that the MNF was attacked 'precisely because it is doing the job it was sent to do in

Beirut. It is accomplishing its mission'.[122] Despite mounting pressure from the public, the media, the Congress and within his own administration, Reagan continued to believe that the MNF was achieving its goals and that the US could not abandon the people of Lebanon.[123] He told the nation that Americans could not and would not 'turn our backs on friends' and 'cut and run' from Beirut.[124] On February 6, 1984, Reagan stated: 'The commitment of the United States to the unity, independence, and sovereignty of Lebanon remains firm and unwavering.'[125] Yet the very next day, Reagan announced the 'redeployment of the marines from Beirut airport to their ships off-shore'.[126] He refused to accept, however, that the 'redeployment' was actually a withdrawal. Reagan was convinced that the US was continuing to fulfil its 'moral obligation' to the Lebanese people. The offshore deployment, coupled with the authority to use naval gunfire and air support against hostile positions, was, Reagan argued, the way 'to use our diplomatic and military resources to the best advantage'.[127] Regardless of Reagan's perception, significant US involvement in Lebanon ended before any of the three stated objectives of the MNF had been achieved.

No matter what Reagan may have concluded, the American experience in Lebanon demonstrated that the limits to American will and power exposed by the Vietnam War still existed. The American public would not have accepted a full-scale intervention to drive foreign forces from Lebanon and restore law and order between the warring indigenous factions. The Reagan administration, therefore, could only affect the situation in Lebanon in a limited way. The initial deployment illustrated that the US could make effective contributions to military missions with clearly defined objectives that were morally justifiable and readily attainable given the size and strength of the force employed, even though on this occasion those accomplishments had collapsed as soon as the US withdrew. With the second deployment, however, Reagan managed to make the mistakes of Vietnam despite trying to apply its lessons. He authorized a relatively small, low-key deployment in order to minimize the chances of the US becoming involved in an intractable long-term commitment, yet he failed to define US objectives narrowly or clearly enough so that they could credibly be achieved by the force deployed. This rather schizophrenic approach resulted from Reagan's desire to please all his advisers rather than decisively resolving conflicts within his cabinet. While Shultz, the NSC staff, and the State Department convinced Reagan that the interests at stake in Lebanon warranted a US 'presence', Weinberger and the Pentagon made clear their reluctance to commit US troops to a situation that might embroil them in an interminable conflict.[128] The resulting noncombatant, limited-term force lacked operational effectiveness and was dangerously vulnerable in the volatile environment of Beirut. The whole American involvement in Lebanon exposed the continuing limits to US power: the Reagan administration had neither the will nor the ability to end the fighting and resolve the situation; the forces on the ground were unable to defend or protect themselves adequately against terrorist attack; the American public and their representatives in Congress were unwilling to give continued support to a military campaign that was reaping no tangible rewards at the expense of too many American lives, particularly in a distant nation of which they had little knowledge or understanding; and potential adversaries throughout the world were shown that killing large numbers of Americans would encourage the US to withdraw from a situation rather than suffer greater casualties. Reagan's actions in Lebanon failed to give much authenticity to his claims that the US was once more a strong, confident and powerful nation. Yet the debacle in Lebanon had few negative effects on the public standing of the administration, largely, thanks to some rather fortuitous events closer to home in the Caribbean.

Grenada

On October 25, 1983, two days after the barracks in Lebanon were bombed, US forces invaded the small Caribbean island of Grenada in what Reagan characterized as a 'rescue mission'. The successful intervention demonstrated, according to administration officials, that Reagan's claims that American will and resolve had been restored were not simply empty words. Shultz believed the Grenada invasion sent a message around the world that 'Ronald Reagan is capable of action beyond rhetoric'.[129] The American response in Grenada, the administration contended, would show other nations that the US was willing to use force to achieve its objectives. Reagan and his advisers believed it would demonstrate to the Soviet Union in particular that the US would not stand by and allow communist revolution to spread throughout the western hemisphere unchallenged. Yet the intervention was a low-risk, limited objective action that Reagan and his advisers knew could be conducted swiftly and with little cost, under conditions likely to ensure public support.

Grenada is the southernmost of the Windward Islands north of Trinidad and Tobago, measures only 21 miles long by 12 miles wide (about the size of Martha's Vineyard or the Isle of Wight), and has a population of around 100,000. After gaining independence from Britain in 1974, it was ruled by an anti-communist government led by the corrupt and bizarre Eric Gairy, who was renowned for frequently warning the UN General Assembly of the threat of extraterrestrial invasion! In March 1979, the opposition New Jewel Movement (NJM) led by a populist nationalist Maurice Bishop took control of the island in a coup. Bishop's deputy prime minister, Bernard Coard, was a Marxist who encouraged an opening of relations with Cuba. The Carter administration denied Grenada aid and publicly denounced Bishop's government. Relations worsened once Reagan became president and in mid-1982 Bishop signed an economic aid agreement with the Soviet Union. Then on October 12, 1983, Coard led a coup and imprisoned Bishop and his loyal cabinet ministers. A week later Bishop and his four ministers were freed by a crowd of supporters only to be recaptured and shot by Coard's troops along with several of the crowd members. Coard then imposed a shoot-on-sight curfew.[130]

Reagan believed wholeheartedly that American intervention in Grenada on October 25 was justified. He believed not only that vital American interests were at stake but that the US had a duty to assist other regional states in seeking to restore stability and freedom to Grenada, where what he described as 'a brutal group of leftist thugs' had overthrown the government, murdered its leaders and many of its supporters, imprisoned the governor general, and imposed a 'shoot-to-kill' curfew. American interests were directly at stake because some one thousand US citizens, most of them attending St George's University Medical School, were residents of Grenada. With the shoot-on-sight curfew in effect, the administration argued the students were in 'life-threatening danger', or at least vulnerable to seizure as hostages.[131] As Reagan declared in his October 27 address to the nation: 'I believe our government has a responsibility to go to the aid of its citizens, if their right to life and liberty is threatened. The nightmare of our hostages in Iran must never be repeated.'[132]

The administration also argued that American security was threatened in strategic terms by developments in Grenada. As early as April 8, 1982, Reagan had raised concern about the 'overturn of Westminister [sic] parliamentary democracy in Grenada'. He warned other East Caribbean states that Grenada 'now bears the Soviet and Cuban trademark, which means that it will attempt to spread the virus among its neighbors'.[133] On March 23, 1983, evoking memories of the Cuban missile crisis, Reagan used aerial reconnaissance photographs to reveal to the American public the full extent of the apparent threat posed by developments on Grenada:

> On the small island of Grenada, ... the Cubans, with Soviet financing and backing, are in the process of building an airfield with a 10,000-foot runway. Grenada doesn't even have an air force. Who is it intended for? ... The rapid buildup of Grenada's military potential is unrelated to any conceivable threat to this island country of under 110,000 people and totally at odds with the pattern of other eastern Caribbean states, most of which are unarmed.
>
> The Soviet-Cuban militarization of Grenada, in short, can only be seen as power projection into the region.[134]

These developments had taken place under the leadership of Maurice Bishop but when his regime was violently overthrown the Reagan administration had concluded that the threat of Soviet-sponsored communist expansion from Grenada was ever more likely.

Not all Americans agreed with the administration's assessment of the situation, however. Two days after Reagan's speech in March, Rev. Herbert

Daughtry, president of the North Carolina based African Peoples' Christian Organization, wrote a letter to Reagan in which he claimed he had evidence that there was nothing sinister about the new international airport in Grenada. Daughtry related how a group of '17 youth and 6 adult chaperons' from his organization spent ten days in Grenada on a work-study and recreation visit:

> Many of the youth toured the airport construction site. It was not a top secret construction site. Our youth have the same photographs you have, taken with simple inexpensive photographic equipment. Why then, Sir, was it necessary to use complicated aerial equipment when the construction site is accessible to all who want to visit it?[135]

Needless to say, the administration did not heed the advice of Daughtry or others who questioned Reagan's policy. Indeed, in the wake of the American intervention, Reagan claimed his concerns about the communist presence on Grenada were vindicated:

> We had to assume that several hundred Cubans working on the airport could be military reserves. Well, as it turned out, the number was much larger, and they were a military force. Six hundred of them have been taken prisoner, and we have discovered a complete base with weapons and communications equipment, which makes it clear a Cuban occupation of the island had been planned.... Grenada, we were told, was a friendly island paradise for tourism. Well, it wasn't. It was a Soviet-Cuban colony, being readied as a major military bastion to export terror and undermine democracy. We got there just in time.[136]

The Reagan administration further justified its intervention in Grenada by stressing that its actions were legitimate because they were conducted in conjunction with members of the Organization of Eastern Caribbean States (OECS). Reagan made clear that the US was answering a formal request for military assistance from the OECS whose members had voted for a 'collective security force' to restore order to Grenada.[137] Such support, though minimal in size, was important to Reagan and his advisers as it enabled them to deflect criticism that the US was acting as a self-interested, domineering superpower imposing its will on weaker neighbours.

That force should be employed to achieve US objectives seems not, on this occasion, to have aroused much conflict within the administration. Shultz suggests in his memoirs that Weinberger and the Joint Chiefs exhibited their usual reluctance to resort to military intervention, at least until a suitably long period of preparation had been undertaken.[138] However, it is clear that Reagan made his decision to intervene within hours of learning of the situation in Grenada, and Weinberger, in his own account, shows little indication that he and Chairman of the JCS, General John Vessey, advised against the use of force.[139] This willingness to resort to force reflects the belief within the administration that Grenada offered a model example of the conditions under which the US could effectively employ military options.

Reagan emphasized that US objectives in Grenada were clear, compelling and attainable. Those objectives were: 'to protect our own citizens, to facilitate the evacuation of those who want to leave, and to help in the restoration of democratic institutions in Grenada.'[140] Reagan and his advisers were unanimous in their belief that the military should be allowed to employ whatever degree of force they deemed necessary for the successful completion of their mission and that the Joint Chiefs should have full control over the operation. In fact, both Shultz and Weinberger went out of their way to ensure a more than adequate degree of force was applied. Shultz recalls that he told Reagan to: 'call Jack Vessey back and ask him what the numbers of troops were that would be required for this operation. "After he has told you, Mr. President, I suggest that you tell him to double it".'[141] Weinberger gave the Joint Chiefs similar instructions to 'double whatever CINCLANT [Commander in Chief, Atlantic Forces] says he needs'.[142] Consequently, over three thousand US troops were involved in the intervention, including Army Rangers and paratroopers, Navy, Marine, and Air Force personnel. American forces outnumbered the resistance they met by more than three to one.[143]

Administration officials were confident that intervention would not lead to an inconclusive, prolonged, Vietnam-style conflict. Vessey reported to Weinberger prior to the mission that there was 'a good degree of certainty that we would be able to free the American students very quickly'.[144] Reagan was determined that American forces would not remain in Grenada for an extended period of time. When he announced the deployment, he stressed: 'We want to be out as quickly as possible.'[145] Reagan assured the Congress that the deployment of US troops was a 'temporary' measure: 'Our forces will remain only so long as their presence is required.'[146]

This intention to leave Grenada as soon as the administration's limited objectives had been achieved not only served to quell fears of another Vietnam but also gave apparent confirmation of the exceptional nature of the United States. Reagan was able to use the Grenada intervention as an example of the benign intentions of the US towards the rest of the world. He denied, for example, that there could be any comparison between American actions in Grenada and Soviet action in Afghanistan.[147] In his mind, Grenada proved Reagan's frequent assertion that: 'America seeks no new territory, nor do we wish to dominate others.' The mission to rid Grenada of its 'leftist thugs' demonstrated clearly to Reagan that: 'We commit our resources and risk the lives of those in our Armed Forces to rescue others from bloodshed and turmoil and to prevent humankind from drowning in a sea of tyranny.'[148] The Reagan administration claimed it had no intention of seizing control of Grenada and imposing American authority. As soon as the island was secured and law and order restored, the Grenadians would be left to determine their own future free from foreign pressure. In accordance with American plans, the island was secured rapidly. Within a day the medical school had been secured, the airport captured, and within a few days the island was cleared of Cubans and 'other resistance'.[149] Governmental authority and law and order were soon restored to the island with a free election following on December 19, 1983. As Weinberger recalls:

> Four days before the election, to the considerable amazement of many of our critics ..., the American forces simply left. By December 15, 1983, less than two months after they went in, United States combat forces had all been withdrawn from Grenada. We left behind only training, police, medical and support elements.[150]

The intervention appeared a resounding success. All US objectives had been achieved rapidly with minimal cost in lives and materiel. Reagan had insisted that a 'top priority' of the operation be 'to minimize risk, to avoid casualties to our men and also the Grenadian forces as much as humanly possible'.[151] By the end of the mission, American casualties totalled only 18 killed, 93 wounded and 16 missing, with 45 Grenadians also losing their lives.[152] Reagan believed that US armed forces in Grenada were 'heroes of freedom' who had 'conducted themselves in the finest tradition of the military'. They had 'rescued' the US citizens on the island and 'liberated' the Grenadians themselves.[153] Following a fact-finding mission for the Senate Committee on Armed Services, Senator John Tower reached conclusions similar to the president's. Tower reported that he had found 'overwhelming support from Grenadians for the incursion' which he claimed they referred to as a 'liberation, not an invasion'.[154]

Public opinion polls conducted in the immediate aftermath of the intervention showed a high approval rating for the action in Grenada. A November 1983 ABC News-*Washington Post* poll, for example, showed a margin of 71 to 22 per cent in favour of the Grenada intervention. The public appeared responsive to Reagan's rationale for becoming involved in the island's affairs. A CBS News-*New York Times* poll found 50 per cent of those polled believed the US had intervened 'mainly to protect the Americans living there', while 35 per cent felt the intervention was conducted primarily to 'overthrow a Marxist government'. Polls also indicate, however, that the public was more concerned that the administration should avoid allowing Grenada to turn into another Vietnam than they were dedicated to the cause of ensuring a democratic future for the Grenadians. A Gallup-*Newsweek* poll found that by a 'five to four margin' respondents believed: 'American troops should leave Grenada "as soon as the safety of Americans is assured" rather than wait until "a democratic government is capable of running the country".'[155] The popularity of the Grenada intervention appears, therefore, to rest more on a sense of relief that military force was used without the US becoming entangled in a complex, long-term commitment, than representing a full restoration of confidence in the strength and certainty of American power. The administration viewed the planning and execution of the Grenada intervention as clear evidence that the US was once more conducting itself in an exemplary manner. Shultz was proud to conclude that: 'Our effort in Grenada wasn't an immoral imperialist intervention.' Indeed, to Shultz the intervention was 'a shot heard around the world by usurpers and despots of every ideology'. Along with British action in the Falklands War, Shultz believed that Grenada sent the 'sharp and clear' message that 'some Western democracies were again ready to use the military strength they had harbored and built up over the years in defense of their principles and interests'.[156] Yet despite this belief and the popularity of the intervention in the US, the American action was not received so well abroad.

The most striking criticism came from Reagan's closest foreign ally, British Prime Minister Margaret Thatcher, whose government roundly opposed the US intervention, not least because Grenada was a member of the British Commonwealth with the Queen as its Head of State. Thatcher clearly did not share Shultz's comparison between the American action in Grenada and her own government's war over the Falkland Islands. In a last minute communiqué before the invasion began she told Reagan she was 'deeply disturbed' by his plan of action and was strongly against military action. She relates in her memoirs how she believed Washington had exaggerated the threat from Grenada and that the coup 'morally objectionable as it was, was a change in degree rather than in kind'. When Reagan proceeded with the invasion, the prime minister 'felt dismayed and let down by what had happened'.[157] Thatcher made her feelings plain on the BBC World Service on October 30, 1983:

> We in the Western countries, the Western democracies, use our force to defend our way of life. We do not use it to walk into independent sovereign territories. ... If you're going to pronounce a new law that wherever communism reigns against the will of the people, even though it's happened internally, there the USA shall enter, then we are going to have really terrible wars in the world.[158]

Thatcher's sentiments were echoed in stronger terms by reaction in Moscow. *Pravda* criticized the Reagan administration's 'ongoing recklessness' and its 'militarist policy'. Moscow Radio condemned Reagan for showing openly that 'his administration is prepared to use any means to overthrow governments it doesn't approve of'.[159] Reagan himself had given the Soviet Union the ammunition to accuse him of hypocrisy over the Grenada intervention. In an official letter to Brezhnev on April 24, 1981, Reagan had chastised the Soviet Union for bestowing upon itself 'special rights and, indeed, duties, to preserve a particular form of government in other countries'. Reagan told Brezhnev firmly that: 'Claims of special "rights," however defined, cannot be used to justify the threat of force to infringe upon the sovereign rights of any country to determine its own political, economic and social institutions.'[160] Reagan and his advisers would no doubt argue the Grenadians had already lost their sovereign rights to Soviet and Cuban interference and that US action aimed to return those rights. However, Reagan's admonishment of Soviet behaviour in 1981 could readily be directed at his own administration's actions in Grenada. The administration, of course, claimed its actions were legitimate because they were conducted as part of a collective action with members of the OECS. Yet it was the Reagan administration that defined the mission's objectives, planned the operation and supplied the vast majority of the forces used. As was Reagan's way, however, he was able to ignore the realities of the invasion and convince the American people that the action in Grenada was legitimate, justifiable, and showed the world that the US was once again 'a beacon of hope for all those who long for freedom and a better world'.[161]

The claim of Reagan, Shultz and others that Grenada proved US power and resolve had been restored is also highly questionable. The intervention was a strictly limited operation in which overwhelming force was employed against substantially weaker opposition. That the US achieved its objectives should come as no surprise. Although the intervention did illustrate the willingness of the Reagan administration to employ military force, it did not prove that the US would readily resort to force again to meet future threats. There was little in the Grenada action to indicate that the limits to American power and resolve exposed by the Vietnam War had been overcome. Reagan and his advisers, including Weinberger and the Joint Chiefs, supported the use of force in Grenada precisely because they believed the situation could be resolved swiftly, conclusively and with few American losses. The public supported the effort for the same reasons. The success of the mission did not mean that the administration would exercise military options to deal with all future threats to American security. On the contrary, if anything it made it ever more likely that force would only be applied if conditions similar to those in the Grenada situation existed – that is, objectives were clear and attainable; a swift, low-risk victory was expected; and no long-term commitment of troops was necessary. The battle between Shultz and Weinberger, therefore, was not solved by the Grenada intervention. Shultz believed the intervention had proved that the use of force must not be left only to a last resort but applied whenever it is the option most likely to efficiently achieve US objectives. The threat and use of force had to be recognized as 'legitimate instruments of foreign policy'.[162] For Weinberger, Grenada provided 'the complete model for future similar activities' where the United States could achieve 'our political objectives at minimum cost, in the shortest possible time'. The Grenada mission did not change Weinberger's general attitude towards the use of force, however, and met with his support only because it satisfied the conditions under which he believed combat troops should be committed to a situation.[163] President Reagan also remained cautious about the actual use of force even though Grenada strengthened his belief that the US 'must not and will not be intimidated by anyone, anywhere'.[164] He assured a reporter on November 3, 1983 that the success in Grenada did not mean that the US would now apply military force elsewhere because: 'I can't foresee any situation that has exactly the same things that this one had.'[165]

Libya and terrorism

That the use of force remained an element of policy applied only under the strictest conditions is further illustrated by the administration's handling of the threat of international terrorism. As early as January 27, 1981, Reagan warned terrorists throughout the world: 'when the rules of international behavior are violated, our policy will be one of swift and effective retribution.'[166] In the aftermath of the deaths of the US Marines in Lebanon, Reagan promised that the United States would be at the forefront of international efforts to curb terrorism.[167] Yet the administration found itself relatively powerless to prevent or respond to the acts of terrorism being increasingly perpetrated throughout the globe. Commercial airliners were hijacked, cruise liners seized, airports attacked, and hostages taken by a host of terrorist groups without serious repercussions despite Reagan's insistence that such activity would never be condoned or tolerated.[168]

The only time Reagan's anti-terrorism policy culminated in an aggressive response was with the bombing of Libya on April 14, 1986. Next to the Grenada intervention, the attack on Libya was the only other major use of force employed by the Reagan administration. Weinberger claims that the Libya bombing demonstrated Reagan's 'strong resolution and determination to use America's newly regained military power'. Yet the bombing was only carried out because, like the Grenada intervention, it was a low-risk, limited action that could be swiftly and effectively executed. As Weinberger admits, his tests for determining whether force should be used 'seemed to me to be fulfilled by the President's decision to use our military in Libya'.[169]

On April 5, 1986, a bomb had exploded at a West Berlin discotheque, killing an American serviceman and a Turkish woman and wounding some 230 others including 50 US military personnel. Reagan assured the public that US intelligence had gathered irrefutable evidence that the bomb was planted by Libyan operatives under the direct orders of Libyan President Colonel Muammar Gaddafi. A few days earlier, Gaddafi had formally called upon Arabs everywhere to attack anything American, claiming a state of war existed between his country and the United States. Since 1981, the US had been in dispute with Libya over the jurisdiction of the Gulf of Sidra, recognized by all but Tripoli as international waters. In August 1981, two Libyan fighters were shot down after opening fire on US planes in the area. Tensions had remained high ever since with the Reagan administration convinced of Gaddafi's involvement in many acts of terrorism against the US and its allies, but until the West Berlin bombing nothing could be proved. The Reagan administration considered the bombing to be an attack upon the US and therefore justified the bombing of Libyan military targets associated with the training of terrorists as a retaliatory strike made in self-defence, consistent with Article 51 of the UN Charter. The attack was also considered a response to an obvious threat to American security interests. The administration believed a punitive attack on Libya was necessary to protect the lives of American citizens travelling or living abroad against state-sponsored terrorism. The action was given added legitimacy by the support of Margaret Thatcher who authorized the use of British airspace so that American F-111 bombers could be deployed from their British base.[170] The French government, however, refused overflight permission for the bombers and led a chorus of European critics following the operation. French President François Mitterand commented: 'I don't believe that you stop terrorism by killing 150 Libyans who have done nothing.'[171] As Geir Lundestad observes, many Europeans regarded as 'too emotional' Reagan's policy towards Libya and other 'enemies' such as Nicaragua. Actions such as the bombing of Tripoli were thought to reflect 'a certain itch to get even with rulers who had certainly offended America, but who did not really threaten its vital interests'.[172]

The objective of the mission was to deal a heavy blow to the Libyan capacity for supporting terrorism and to send a message to Gaddafi that any further sponsorship of terrorist acts against the US or its allies would not go unpunished. Reagan insisted the targets in Libya were 'carefully chosen, both for their direct linkage to Libyan support of terrorist activities and for the purpose of minimizing collateral damage and injury to innocent civilians'.[173] The administration was determined to maximize the strength of the message sent to Gaddafi while remaining true to its claim to be a benign nation that did not resort to force lightly.

The attack was regarded by the administration as a great success that again confirmed the US had restored its reputation as a powerful nation willing to defend its interests with force if necessary. Shultz believes that: 'Seldom in military history ... had a punch been so clearly telegraphed.'[174] The bombing raid was completed in about half an hour, with the loss of only one F-111 (out of more than forty that had flown from their base in England) and its two crew members. Despite facing criticism for off-target bombs that destroyed civilian buildings, causing injuries and deaths, the administration celebrated the substantial damage it claimed to have inflicted on all its main targets. Larry Speakes proclaimed the mission a great success because it made clear that 'terrorism cannot be supported without incurring a heavy price'. He claimed the action would 'deter future terrorist attacks' and 'send a clear message that we will no longer tolerate death of innocent Americans and others'. He concluded that this message had been 'heard and understood' by Gaddafi.[175] Shultz claims this assumption proved largely correct: 'Qaddafi, after twitching feverishly with a flurry of vengeful responses, quieted down and retreated into the desert.'[176] Robert Rotberg agrees that in 'subtle ways' the bombing did curb Gaddafi's 'adventurism' in Chad, the Sudan, and other parts of North Africa.[177] International terrorism, however, did not abate and Libya itself would again be implicated in the December 1988 destruction of Pan Am Flight 103 over Lockerbie.

The American public was as enthusiastic about the Libya bombing as it had been towards the intervention in Grenada. A *Newsweek*-Gallup poll found 71 per cent of respondents approved of the military action while only 21 per cent disapproved.[178] Reagan's approval rating leapt six points to 68 per cent in the month following the raid, the highest of his tenure and a level of popularity unprecedented for a mid-term president.[179] Even more telling though is that, in light of the Libya bombing, 62 per cent of those polled believed Reagan 'makes wise use of military forces to solve foreign-policy problems' while only 26 per cent held that Reagan was 'too quick to employ US forces'.[180]

The Reagan administration seemed to gauge well the circumstances under which it was acceptable to use force to pursue its objectives. At the symbolic level, Reagan's attitude towards the use of military force did help restore a great deal of American self-confidence, but most Americans remained overtly cautious about future deployments of force. Polling conducted by the Chicago Council on Foreign Relations in October and November 1986, a few months after the bombing of Tripoli, indicates that the American public remained 'generally opposed to using troops overseas'. The Council found that Americans were 'somewhat more willing to use troops overseas in selected circumstances'. In fact, a majority of those polled favoured deploying troops only if the Soviet Union invaded Western Europe (68 per cent) or Japan (53 per cent). A small plurality of 45 per cent favoured the use of troops if the Nicaraguan government permitted the Soviets to build a missile base on their territory, compared with 42 per cent who disapproved. In all other circumstances, however, including the case of North Korea invading South Korea, a sizeable majority opposed committing US troops. The Council also found that there was a strong correlation between attitudes towards the Vietnam War and willingness to use troops overseas. In 1986, a majority of the public maintained that the Vietnam War had been 'a thoroughly misguided effort' and these people were less willing, in every circumstance, to commit troops overseas than those who defended the Vietnam War as just.[181]

In the case of both Grenada and Libya, the Reagan administration had employed force decisively but neither example offered a major test of American resolve. At most these were convenient opportunities for the administration to support its rhetoric with action, without risking great losses or becoming involved in complex and prolonged hostilities. With his rhetoric, Reagan promoted the image of a United States standing tall, ready and willing to meet any challenge anywhere in the world with all the power and resources of the greatest nation on earth. In reality, the limits to American power, revealed by the defeat in Vietnam, continued to restrain the reach and effectiveness of American influence on international affairs. The perceived lessons of the Vietnam War determined when and how the apparently renewed will and resolve of the US could be applied to international situations. This gap between rhetoric and reality can be seen most clearly in the Reagan administration's policy towards the Soviet Union.

Rhetoric vs reality I: Reagan and the Soviets

We have seen how Ronald Reagan took a strong rhetorical stance against the Soviet Union. He believed this approach demonstrated the renewed strength and resolve of the United States. As he told the Veterans of Foreign Wars in August 1983: 'For too long our nation had been moot [*sic*] to the injustices of totalitarianism. So we began speaking out ... for freedom and democracy and the values that all of us share in our hearts.'[182] Yet despite his May 1982 claim that all Soviet aggression 'will meet a firm Western response', Reagan's words were far stronger than his actions towards the Soviet Union.[183]

Although Reagan came to office criticizing the Carter administration for being too weak and accommodating in its Soviet policy, within a few months he had overturned many of the sanctions his predecessor had imposed on the Soviet Union. Most obviously, on April 24, 1981, Reagan ended the grain embargo imposed after the Soviet invasion of Afghanistan, claiming it hurt American farmers more than it did the Kremlin. The Reagan administration found itself relatively powerless to influence Soviet action not only in Afghanistan but also in Poland. In response to the early 1980s crisis in the latter country, for instance, Reagan was able only to impose limited sanctions and organize symbolic acts such as national candlelit vigils.[184] But the gap between Reagan's vociferous anti-Soviet rhetoric and his actual Soviet policy can be seen most clearly in his response to the shooting down of Korean Airlines Flight 007 over Soviet airspace on September 1, 1983.

Reagan condemned the killing of 269 civilians aboard the South Korean jumbo jet as a 'horrifying act of violence' and an 'appalling and wanton misdeed'.[185] Reagan believed this 'barbaric act' was a 'crime against humanity' and questioned the nature of Soviet civilization and whether they valued human life as much as other nations.[186] In an address to the nation he had largely written himself, Reagan laboured home the point that he had been right to call the Soviet Union an evil empire. He said that by shooting down a defenceless airliner the Soviet Union had launched an attack

> against the world and the moral precepts which guide human relations among people everywhere. It was an act of barbarism, born of a society

which wantonly disregards individual rights and the value of human life and seeks constantly to expand and dominate other nations.[187]

But despite the ferocity of Reagan's verbal condemnations, the US was notably restrained in the action it took in response.

Reagan was careful to tell the nation that it 'would be easy to think in terms of vengeance, but that is not a proper answer'.[188] It was not the proper answer partly because the administration saw an opportunity to firmly take the moral high ground. It was also the case, though, that short of risking full-scale war there was very little that could be done that involved wielding the full power of the United States. As Carter had found when the Soviet Union occupied Afghanistan and Johnson had realized when Soviet tanks rolled into Prague, the United States' ability to respond effectively to what were regarded as aggressive Soviet acts was severely limited. No amount of strong rhetoric from the Reagan administration could change this fundamental fact of the Cold War. In his response to the shooting down of KAL 007, Reagan told the nation: 'We can start preparing ourselves for what John F. Kennedy called a long twilight struggle' with the Soviet Union.[189] But that struggle would not and could not involve the use of America's military might to force the Soviets to change their ways. Reagan himself recognized, in fact, that his actions must be more reserved than his rhetoric. In a private meeting with his foreign policy advisers, Reagan made clear that he did not believe the US should overreact to the Soviet action: 'The world will react to this. It's important that we do not do anything that jeopardizes the long-term relationship with the Soviet Union.'[190] It is clear from this statement that even when his public rhetoric was at its most vociferous, privately Reagan was aware that a more conciliatory approach to the Soviet Union was required. The US, therefore, resorted to formal condemnations and demands for a full explanation and apology from the Soviet government; the suspension of all Aeroflot activity in the United States; the encouraging of other nations to suspend flights to the Soviet Union; and symbolic acts such as declaring a national day of mourning for KAL 007's victims. But the administration refused to suspend arms talks with the Soviet Union or break off other diplomatic activity and claimed the 'most effective, lasting action' would be to simply 'go forward with America's program to remain strong'.[191]

As with so much of his foreign policy, Reagan talked tough with the Soviet Union, particularly during his first term, but this did not mean that US actions were also more belligerent than in previous administrations. As the case of KAL 007 shows, the Reagan administration was just as constrained by the unthinkable threat of actual war with the Soviet Union and, therefore, maintained open diplomatic channels no matter how tense the rhetorical sparring between the White House and the Kremlin became. Reagan's anti-Soviet rhetoric was part of his illusion-making. By openly criticizing the Soviet Union, Reagan was able to accentuate the positive elements of US society and culture and, therefore, help bolster American confidence. But standing tall did not mean the US was prepared to use its military might directly against the Soviet Union. The limits on American power remained, even though, through his rhetoric, Reagan seemed able to resurrect much of America's self-image.

Rhetoric vs reality II: Reagan and exceptionalism

Reagan was particularly adept at portraying the US as an exceptional nation that was once again conducting itself in accordance with the finest traditions of its fundamental values and principles. He claimed: 'We've tried to bring a new honesty and moral purposefulness to our foreign policy.'[192] The reality of American actions during his administration, however, did not always live up to the high standards of his rhetoric. This inconsistency can be best illustrated by returning to Reagan's policies towards El Salvador and Nicaragua.

Reagan appealed to the American belief in exceptionalism by describing those whose cause he supported in Central America as 'freedom fighters'. In a radio address in August 1984, Reagan attempted to clarify the administration's policy towards Central America:

> We support the elected Government of El Salvador against Communist-backed guerrillas who would take over the country by force. And we oppose the unelected Government of Nicaragua, which supports those guerrillas with weapons and ammunition. Now that, of course, puts us in sympathy with those Nicaraguans who are trying to restore the democratic promises made during the revolution, the so-called *contras*.[193]

Reagan not only referred to the *contras* as freedom fighters, but also compared them to America's own revolutionaries who 200 years earlier had struggled for 'freedom, democracy, independence, and liberation from tyranny'.[194] Reagan claimed it was the duty of the US to support the cause of the *contras* because they 'are the moral equal of our Founding Fathers'.[195] To turn away would be 'to betray our centuries-old dedication to supporting those who struggle for freedom'.[196] In what became known as the Reagan Doctrine, the President argued that 'we must not break faith with those who are risking their lives – on every continent, from Afghanistan to Nicaragua – to defy Soviet-supported aggression and secure rights which have been ours from birth'.[197]

Reagan, therefore, counselled support for the *contras* because he claimed they were fighting for the same values and principles upon which the United States was founded. In 1986, however, *contra* leader Enrique Bermúdez admitted that the *contras'* objectives were not to 'foster democratic reforms' but to 'heighten repression'.[198] The previous year, American lawyer Reed Brody had uncovered over 200 abuses committed by *contras* between 1982 and 1985 including 'assassination, torture, rape, kidnapping and mutilation of civilians'. In March 1985, the human rights group Americas Watch also condemned the *contras* for 'the deliberate use of terror'. Any civilians who helped the Sandinistas were considered combatants by the *contras* and, therefore, legitimate targets.[199] Reagan's 'freedom fighters' were certainly far from beyond reproach and the comparison with the Founding Fathers seemed to critics wholly inappropriate.

In support of the *contras'* cause, Reagan also authorized activities that were inconsistent with the values and principles for which he claimed they were fighting. Although Reagan and his advisers denied it, supporting the *contras* was tantamount to advocating the overthrow of a legitimate government that the US itself had recognized under the previous administration. Such an approach appeared hypocritical when the administration was also condemning guerrilla groups in El Salvador for attempting to fulfil a comparable goal. Yet such policies were consistent with the influential distinctions identified by Reagan's Ambassador to the UN, Jeane Kirkpatrick, which allowed support for anti-communist authoritarian regimes such as that in El Salvador while finding opposition to totalitarian communist regimes morally acceptable.[200] Reagan coupled this rationale with his belief that all US action must be, by definition, moral because the United States was the most moral nation on earth. Using these beliefs as a starting point, Reagan was able to accept any action that furthered his Central American objectives as being morally justifiable – even acts that broke federal or international law. That the Reagan administration was capable of such unexceptional behaviour became most apparent in late March and early April 1984 when the Nicaraguan government complained formally to the UN and the World Court that the US had conducted illegal acts of war including the mining of Nicaraguan harbours.

In its final judgment on June 27, 1986, the World Court cited the US for violating international law. The court ruled that the Reagan administration

> by training, arming, equipping, financing and supplying the contra forces or otherwise encouraging, supporting and aiding military and paramilitary activities in and against Nicaragua, has acted, against the Republic of Nicaragua, in breach of its obligation under customary international law not to intervene in the affairs of another State.

The court condemned a series of specific US actions, including the covert mining of the harbours and the imposition of a trade embargo, and called upon the US to 'immediately cease and refrain from all such acts'. The court also ruled that the US was 'under obligation to make reparation' to Nicaragua for all 'injury' incurred.[201]

The Reagan administration ignored the ruling, having already refused to recognize the World Court's jurisdiction over its activities in Central

America, and boycotting the proceedings. The administration argued that its activities in support of the *contras* were justified as self-defence in response to Nicaraguan support for the rebels in El Salvador. The majority on the World Court were not the only ones, however, to disagree with the administration's argument. The mining of Nicaraguan harbours met with particularly strong opposition at home and abroad. The covert action, carried out by the CIA under Reagan's approval, was roundly condemned within both the House and the Senate. Even Reagan's conservative ally, Barry Goldwater, heavily criticized the administration for 'violating international law' and perpetrating 'an act of war'. The *New York Times* compared the action to the torpedoing of neutral shipping by German U-boats in the Second World War and called it 'Illegal, Deceptive and Dumb'. Shultz, who had earlier opposed such action and claims not to have known of its eventual execution, concludes the 'mining episode was a political disaster for the administration'.[202]

Contrary to Reagan's rhetoric, the conduct of the administration's policy towards Central America can be regarded as inconsistent with the belief that the US is an exceptional nation. As the Iran-Contra affair came to light in late 1986, it became apparent that the gap between what the Reagan administration said and what it actually did was far wider than imagined. The complex web of intrigue surrounding the sale of arms to Iran in exchange for hostages and the subsequent diversion of illegal funds to the *contras* has been explored well elsewhere.[203] The important point to make here is that the revelations threw substantial doubt over Reagan's claims that the US could stand proud, that its strength and prestige in the world were once more assured, and that the American people could trust their leaders to conduct policy consistent with their traditional values and principles. By agreeing to trade arms for hostages with Iran, Reagan had misled the American people and broken his solemn promise that 'America will never make concessions to terrorists – to do so would only invite more terrorism'.[204] By diverting money to the *contras*, whether with or without the president's knowledge, the administration had ignored the will of the Congress and the wishes of the American public in an effort to pursue its objectives in Central America. Much of the dishonesty, immorality and corruption that had characterized the Vietnam and Watergate era was resurrected by the Iran-Contra affair. Reagan had often said that deeds mattered more than words. As his popularity rating plummeted in the wake of the Iran-Contra revelations it appeared that he was right. In December 1986, 71 per cent of the respondents to a Harris poll felt let down by the president. Most tellingly, the number of Americans who believed Reagan could 'continue to inspire confidence' fell from 66 per cent to 43 per cent. Writing in the *Washington Post*, Lou Cannon summed up the depth of public disappointment in Reagan's involvement in Iran-Contra: 'The betrayal seemed greater because the betrayer was Reagan, who had spent 50 years insinuating himself into the national consciousness as a believable character who was America's best version of itself.'[205] Ronald Reagan, the president who perhaps more than any other embodied the belief in American exceptionalism, had shown himself to be just as fallible as the nation that he led.

Conclusions

It is clear that Reagan was a true believer in the missionary strand of American exceptionalism. The belief that the United States has a special role to play in human history is central to his own personal beliefs system and, therefore, provided the framework within which most of his policy making was conducted. It is no surprise, then, to find that he frequently couched his administration's policies and actions in terms that were consistent with the belief in exceptionalism and appealed to the public's own faith in that belief. A larger question also needs to be answered, however. Did Ronald Reagan succeed in restoring American confidence and so revive the public's faith in American exceptionalism?

At least at the rhetorical level, Reagan enabled Americans to speak confidently about themselves again. In his own pronouncements, Reagan measured the degree to which he considered Americans had recovered from the self-doubt he believed had paralysed the nation prior to his election. In 1981, he spoke of the crisis of confidence in the US as a 'temporary aberration' from which the American people had recovered and were now undergoing a 'spiritual renewal'.[206] In 1982, despite the deep recession, Reagan believed many Americans had regained their confidence that things would get better again.[207] By 1983, Reagan could claim that 'America is on the mend'.[208] He was convinced that: 'Even with all our recent economic hardships, I believe a feeling of optimism is entering our national consciousness ... and that an era of unity and national renewal is upon us.'[209] Then in 1984, the rallying cry of the Reagan administration was 'America is back'. In his State of the Union address, Reagan declared: 'America is back, standing tall, looking to the eighties with courage, confidence and hope.' Reagan believed the US was once again the greatest nation on earth and that 'America's new strength, confidence, and purpose are carrying hope and opportunity far from our shores'.[210] Reagan celebrated what he called the 'new patriotism' at every given opportunity, most grandly at the 1984 Summer Olympics in Los Angeles and again at the rededication of the Statue of Liberty in 1986. Such events symbolized, for Reagan, the success of his attempts to revive public faith in 'the values, the principles, and ideas that made America great'.[211] Upon leaving office in January 1989, Reagan believed he had helped restore America's 'morale', and left the country 'More prosperous, more secure, and happier than it was eight years ago'.[212] Yet, as was so often the case with Reagan's rhetoric, his optimism concealed a more complex reality. As Jerry Hagstrom observes in his assessment of post-Reagan America: 'For every Reagan success, there was a great failure.'[213]

On the domestic front, Reagan had fulfilled his first priority by reviving the American economy. Reagan left office celebrating 72 straight months of economic growth dating back to January 1983 – the longest peacetime economic recovery cycle of the century. Unemployment was the lowest it had been for a decade and a half and inflation was down two-thirds from its highest point under Carter. Reagan had presided over the creation of 19 million new jobs, a technological boom, and unprecedented prosperity that saw the ranks of the multi-millionaires swell to over a hundred thousand. But despite appearances, all was not well with the American dream. Eighties prosperity had come at a heavy price. Budget and trade deficits soared, not least as a result of Reagan's massive defence build-up, and the US was transformed from the world's largest creditor to a net international debtor nation for the first time since the Second World War. By late 1987, US foreign debt had reached \$368 billion. The prosperity of the Reagan era also failed to benefit the American population as a whole. Indeed, income and wealth inequality grew ever wider during the Reagan presidency. The nation's wealth became increasingly concentrated among the richest Americans. In 1986, the top 10 per cent of households controlled 68 per cent of US family net worth while the top half of 1 per cent of households accounted for 26.9 per cent. In terms of average after-tax family income, these households fared phenomenally well under Reagan with the top 10 per cent gaining 24.4 per cent between 1977 and 1987 while the top 1 per cent gained a staggering 74.2 per cent. But official government figures showed that all other Americans made relative losses in family income during the Reagan years with the lowest 10 per cent faring worst with a fall of some 14.8 per cent. The Reagan boom did benefit the most affluent fifth of Americans, but it was at the expense of the remaining 80 per cent of the population.[214] The Reagan administration also demonstrated an unwillingness or inability to deal effectively with growing societal problems such as crime, homelessness, racial tension, drugs, AIDS, and other issues such as health, education and the environment.

In foreign policy, as we have seen, substantial questions remained over the appropriate application of American power in international affairs and the use of military force in particular. Reagan had shown a willingness to employ force but only under very specific conditions. No amount of rhetoric could overcome the fact that genuine limits to the scope and effectiveness of American power still existed.

One of Reagan's greatest triumphs appears to have been his success in negotiating the first ever reductions in nuclear arms with the Soviet Union and, through his anti-communist policies, allegedly providing the impetus for the end of the Cold War. As discussed above, this latter point is highly debatable. Although the 1987 INF Treaty was a laudable, landmark agreement, which laid the groundwork for further reductions in nuclear arsenals,

Reagan's defence policy and his approach to superpower relations is not unproblematic.

Reagan played a dangerous game during his first term in office. His bellicose statements about the Soviet Union came at a time of great instability in Moscow as the leadership of the Communist Party passed shakily from one generation to another and, as Reagan himself noted, the Soviet economy suffered great strain. Although Reagan insists his rhetoric did not worsen the Cold War or make an actual war more likely, the opportunities for misunderstandings and disagreements to escalate to armed confrontation were greatly increased by his bravado and arms build-up. The war scare that swept Europe in late 1983 was certainly a genuine response to increasingly strained tensions, as the Soviets shot down KAL 007, the Americans invaded Grenada, the deployment of cruise missiles began in Western Europe, and the Soviets walked out of arms negotiations in Geneva. Reagan was risking a great deal in order to reassert American strength and moral superiority.

Reagan did, of course, change his attitude towards the Soviet Union by the time of his second term. That he believed Gorbachev to be a different kind of Soviet leader was certainly a factor. Reagan's reluctance to meet with a Soviet leader disappeared almost as soon as Gorbachev came to power. Yet Reagan offered to have talks with Gorbachev before the new Soviet leader had the chance to prove his character. As we have seen, it was not simply Reagan's fondness for Gorbachev that caused his change of tack towards the Soviet Union. It appears that the war scares and his overwhelming personal desire to end the nuclear threat caused Reagan to tone down his rhetoric. Also, by 1984 he believed the US had regained its position of strength in the world and could now afford to negotiate with the Soviet Union without appearing weak.

Despite the successes of his second term, Reagan's Soviet policy was not without its costs. Reagan had insisted that achieving renewed strategic strength relative to the Soviet Union was essential before fruitful negotiations were possible. But this approach actually weakened the US position in the world due to the detrimental long-term economic effects of Reagan's arms build-up and the attendant budget deficits and mounting national debt. Reagan's rhetoric and posturing not only came close to irreparably damaging relations with the Soviet Union but also strained relations within the Western Alliance. Finally, his obsessive commitment to SDI nearly scuppered any chance of reaching an arms reduction agreement with the Soviet Union and could also have triggered an even more dangerous and economically damaging arms race. As with domestic policy, Reagan's successes in strategic policy and superpower relations were ambiguous and won at a heavy price.

Reagan's claim that he was pursuing a foreign policy rooted in the values and principles upon which the US was founded was also exposed as artifice by his covert war in Central America and the policy of selling arms to the pariah state of Iran in exchange for hostage releases. Such activities fed into the lingering doubts, which Reagan had strived so hard to overcome, about whether the US could still be considered an exceptional nation. For many Americans, Iran-Contra in particular exposed the gap between Reagan's rhetoric and the reality of American behaviour in the world.

Yet despite the growing economic and social inequalities, the ambiguous foreign policy successes, and the evidence of unexceptional administration behaviour, Ronald Reagan still left the White House with a final approval rating higher than any president since Franklin Roosevelt.[215] Reagan was a highly persuasive president who was able, despite all the evidence to the contrary, to convince a sizeable majority of the American public to share his belief that the US was in reality the greatest nation on earth. Theirs was a nation whose strength and morality could no longer be questioned and whose people should be confident in their own ability to achieve whatever they wanted in life. The United States, Reagan told Americans, was indeed a truly exceptional nation and a shining city on a hill. Lou Cannon concludes his study of Reagan by arguing that the president's 'greatest service was in restoring the respect of Americans for themselves and their own government after the traumas of Vietnam and Watergate, the frustration of the Iran hostage crisis and a succession of seemingly failed presidencies'.[216] The American people believed in Reagan's optimism and his vision of the greatness of their nation even when they did not approve of his specific policies or were critical of the mistakes he made. They believed Reagan because they shared his conviction that the United States has a special role to play in the world, even if they did not all agree on what that role should be. Reagan's success, or at least his continued popularity despite his policy failures, lay in his embodiment of what Americans believe to be exceptional about their nation: optimism, dedication to freedom, and hope in a better future. As Reagan said in his Farewell Address: 'as long as we remember our first principles and believe in ourselves, the future will always be ours.'[217] Reagan's greatest achievement was to make Americans feel good about themselves, no matter how illusory that feeling might have been. But could this renewed sense of confidence in America's promise survive once its greatest protagonist had left the White House?

6

George Bush – the 'Vision Thing' and the New World Order

George Herbert Walker Bush came to the White House in January 1989 determined to consolidate the achievements he believed his predecessor had made. During his presidential campaign, Bush made clear that he saw no need to 'remake society' or take the country in 'radical new directions'. No doubt eager to maintain the votes of Reagan's supporters, Bush emphasized his dedication to completing 'the mission we started in 1980' when he had become Reagan's choice for vice president. Bush would be what David Mervin has termed a 'guardian president': one who seeks to protect and preserve the status quo while recognizing the need for only marginal change.[1] Americans expected their new president, with his emphasis on prudence and caution, to be far more pragmatic and competent than they perceived Reagan to have been. Bush was more interested in the detail of policy than his predecessor and had a preference for political compromise, while Reagan had placed ideological considerations first.[2]

The 'vision thing'

The most frequently aired criticism of President Bush, however, is that he lacked vision. As argued in the previous chapter, the main reason for Reagan's personal popularity was his ability to motivate his fellow citizens to believe in themselves and in a brighter future for the United States. Americans like their leaders to tell them where the country is going to and how they are going to get there. George Bush, however, did not believe in the need to present a vision of America's future by laying out a rhetorical road map or master plan. As he declared during his campaign for the White House: 'I am a practical man. I like what's real. I'm not much for the airy and the abstract. I like what works. I am not a mystic, and I do not yearn to lead a crusade.' Bush exhibited what Mervin calls an 'extravagant lack of interest in ideas' or what the president himself pejoratively termed 'the vision thing'.[3]

Bush's problem with the 'vision thing' led many critics to accuse him of being directionless, without convictions or even consistent policy preferences, and unable to explain why or how he was doing things.[4] The contrast with Reagan's approach made the Bush administration appear even more rudderless. As Fred Barnes put it in the *New Republic*: 'Reagan was an ideological architect. Bush is a bricklayer.'[5]

Even though US presidents tend to take a pragmatic approach to actual policy, it is usual for them to articulate some kind of vision or theme for their presidency. Most candidates achieve this during their presidential campaigns, while others develop an overarching theme during their inaugural address or other speeches early in their presidency. This was certainly true of post-Watergate presidents, with Ford calling for 'a time to heal', Carter seeking to restore the nation's 'moral compass' and Reagan declaring 'an era of national renewal'. It can be argued that Bush faced a situation unlike that of his post-Vietnam predecessors. Reagan had largely succeeded in restoring American confidence. When Bush came to power there was no longer a need to call for renewal or to have an all-encompassing theme for his presidency. The US was perceived by Americans to have been restored to its place as leader of the free world and, in the face of the demise of the communist threat, that position stood largely unchallenged. Bush was the perfect leader for such a time because he was committed to maintaining the status quo. Such an argument has its supporters,[6] but the perception of the restored power and stability of the US in the post-Reagan era was also open to question. In 1989, it remained unclear whether the Cold War would come to a peaceful conclusion or whether communist regimes would violently oppose an end to their rule. Many perplexing questions faced the US and its allies, such as how post-communist states could renew or form cooperative ties with the West and how security forces and strategies could be adapted to deal with threats beyond the Cold War. On the domestic front, major doubts were being aired about the strength of the American economic recovery under Reagan, and its far-reaching consequences. A debate raged within elite and popular circles over whether the US was in relative decline as an international power as the world democratized, emphasis shifted away from military prowess as a measure of global power, and American economic dominance faced threats from Japan and Germany.[7] Americans, according to this perspective, needed a leader who could assure them that their special role in the world remained intact and who would find a way to deal with the uncertainties that were developing at home and abroad.

Given the depth of criticism that Bush lacked vision, it is perhaps surprising to find that many of his speeches did in fact contain familiar rhetorical references to the special nature of the United States. Bush's advisers and speechwriters appear to have recognized that, despite the president's admission that he was 'not comfortable with rhetoric for rhetoric's sake',[8] it was necessary to present the public with reassurances that he, like Reagan, believed the US to be a special nation with a special place in the world. In his Inaugural Address, written by Peggy Noonan who had also been responsible for Reagan's Farewell Address, Bush declared that the US was a 'proud, free nation, decent and civil, a place we cannot help but love'. Americans, he said, 'know in our hearts, not loudly and proudly but as a simple fact, that this country has meaning beyond what we see, and that our strength is a force for good'. Bush reaffirmed that 'America is never wholly herself unless she is engaged in high moral principal'. He even went so far as to rhetorically set out a purpose for his presidency. Bush said he would strive to 'make kinder the face of the nation and gentler the face of the world'. Admittedly, elsewhere in the speech, Bush's rhetoric became rather strained, mixing metaphors more incongruously than Reagan would ever have allowed. His assertion that 'a new breeze is blowing' in the world as totalitarianism was swept away and that the 'future seems a door you can walk right through into a room called tomorrow' were hardly the kind of rousing rallying cry to which Americans had become accustomed under Reagan. But the Inaugural Address does show that Bush utilized much the same traditional rhetoric that had characterized the public pronouncements of his predecessors.[9]

Throughout the early months of his presidency, Bush's speeches continued to contain phrases that reinforced the belief that the US was an exceptional nation. Bush echoed Reagan when he told the Congress in February 1989:

> There are voices who say that America's best days have passed, that we're bound by constraints, threatened by problems, surrounded by troubles which limit our ability to hope. Well, tonight I remain full of hope. We Americans have only begun on our mission of goodness and greatness.

Bush reiterated the belief that there was no challenge the US could not meet: 'Let all Americans remember that no problem of human making is too great to be overcome by human ingenuity, human energy, and the untiring hope of the human spirit.'[10]

As communism waned, Bush saw what he considered as the worldwide adoption of American principles as confirmation that the US had been reserved an exceptional place in human history. He took pride in proclaiming that: 'Never before in this century have our values of freedom, democracy, and economic opportunity been such a powerful and intellectual force around the globe.'[11] Bush believed the US should celebrate the triumph of that 'particular, peculiar, very American ideal: freedom'. Bush recognized that Americans had not created democracy but he did believe it was a 'gift' that had been granted to generations of Americans to preserve and pass on to others. It was a duty of the US, therefore, to continue to do whatever it could to 'help others attain the freedom that we cherish'.[12]

Yet although Bush used much of the same rhetoric that Reagan and other presidents had used before him, the public image that he lacked vision persisted. A major part of the problem, several commentators noted, was not in the use of words themselves but in the way Bush delivered them. Thomas Cronin observed that Bush 'is rhetorically and oratorically a handicapped man'. Robert Novak remarked that Bush 'lacks an essential weapon of politics: the ability to stir the nation with words'.[13] Particularly since the advent of radio, and even more so television, US presidents have found that much political advantage can be gained from making direct appeals to the public though national addresses. Bush did not feel comfortable with such necessities of modern day American politics. He lacked the natural ability to communicate effectively with the American people that his predecessor possessed in such abundance. Mervin sums up Bush's problem well:

> His fractured syntax, his unwillingness to take direction from media advisers, his 'hot' rather than 'cool' persona, his obvious discomfort in front of television cameras and his oratorical limitations combined to make him a less than effective communicator.[14]

This inability to convey his thoughts and priorities effectively to the American public, despite making use of familiar rhetoric, compounded the sense that Bush lacked a masterplan or indeed any firm convictions about what would be best for America's future. As we shall see, there were occasions during his presidency, particularly following the Panama invasion and during the Persian Gulf crisis, when Bush *was* able to make effective use of the bully pulpit and rally the public around his foreign policy. These were exceptions rather than the rule, however. At other times, his pragmatic, conservative, usually reactive approach to foreign and domestic policy-making tested the patience of much of the American public and Bush's critics.

The Bush foreign policy

George Bush's foreign policy was, by his own admission, characterized by prudence and caution. Upon taking office, he ordered the NSC to undertake a 90-day systemic review of US foreign and defence policy. The lengthy strategic review compounded the impression that the administration lacked initiative. The sense of inaction in the face of international developments was also not helped by the Senate rejection of Bush's initial nomination for Secretary of Defense, John Tower.[15]

The President's foreign policy team eventually comprised at its centre Secretary of State James A. Baker III, Secretary of Defense Richard Cheney, and National Security Advisor Brent Scowcroft. General Colin Powell completed the team in September 1989 when he became Chairman of the Joint Chiefs of Staff. All four men knew or had worked with each other and Bush in previous administrations and had developed close working and personal relationships.[16] By assembling a core foreign policy team who were already acquainted and clearly able to work with each other, Bush carefully avoided the kind of infighting that had disrupted the foreign and defence policy process in the Reagan, Carter and even Ford administrations. There were disagreements but they tended to be over tactics rather than fundamentals and remained private rather than leaking out into the public domain. While such arrangements made for a more harmonious foreign policy inner sanctum, they did also lead to criticisms that the decision making process was too secretive and insulated from external sources of opinion and advice.[17]

Between April and May 1989, with the strategic review completed, Bush gave a series of foreign policy speeches that outlined the priorities and objectives of his administration. There would be six central elements to the Bush foreign policy: (1) to promote democracy and the free market throughout the world; (2) to encourage the success of glasnost and perestroika in the Soviet Union; (3) to curb the proliferation of nuclear, chemical and biological weapons; (4) to 'check the ambitions of renegade regimes'; (5) to enhance the ability of America's allies to defend themselves; and (6) to encourage greater stability in the developing world. Central to American defence policy would be the maintenance of an 'effective deterrent' coupled with arms reductions that could achieve stability at the 'lowest feasible level of armaments'. Bush saw such an agenda as moving US foreign policy 'beyond containment' in a prudent manner.[18] This cautious approach was most apparent in his handling of the transformation of the Soviet Union and Eastern Europe.

The end of the Cold War

Bush was not as convinced as his predecessor that Gorbachev was leading the Soviet Union away from its communist past and towards a positive relationship with the West. It was too early, according to Bush, for the US to be entirely sure of Soviet intentions. He advocated, therefore, from the outset of his administration, a Soviet policy based on 'Prudence and common sense'.[19] The US would do whatever it could to encourage the success of Soviet reforms and the democratization of Eastern Europe but Bush would not drop America's guard before he was convinced any changes made were permanent. During a trip to Europe in July 1989, Bush would not be drawn on whether the Cold War was over or whether the West had 'won' it. He reminded reporters that there were 'big differences, still' between Western democracies and the Soviet Union. The US and her allies would 'encourage the change' but Bush was certain he would only be able to 'answer your question in maybe a few more years more definitively'.[20] Even when East German border controls were suspended and the Berlin Wall opened on November 9, 1989, he gave a muted response. Bush said he 'welcome[d] the decision' and termed it 'a good development'. He said it was 'probably' a step towards what Gorbachev was calling a common European home. When a reporter observed that the falling of the Berlin Wall was 'a great victory for our side in the big East–West battle' and asked why Bush did not seem elated, the president replied simply, 'I am not an emotional kind of guy.' Pushed further on the matter he allowed himself to admit, 'I'm very pleased.'[21]

It was hardly the stirring reaction Americans might have expected to hear from their president as the single greatest symbol of the Cold War division of Europe dramatically yet peacefully came to an end. As communist regimes lost power across Eastern Europe under the compliant gaze of the Soviet leadership, the American president remained cautious in actions and in words. House majority leader, Democrat Richard Gephardt, complained that: 'At the very time freedom and democracy are receiving standing ovations in Europe, our president is sitting politely in the audience with little to say and even less to contribute.' In the last week of November 1989, *Newsweek* agreed that 'George Bush's reaction to the stirring events in Eastern Europe this fall has been remarkably bland. Ronald Reagan would have trumpeted the triumph of democracy, gloating over the demise of the "evil empire".'[22]

Vietnam and the use of force

Given the caution with which George Bush approached foreign policy, he could be expected to be even less willing to employ military force than his post-Vietnam predecessors. Yet Bush was determined that his administration would finally move beyond the American defeat in Vietnam. In his Inaugural Address, he admitted that the Vietnam War 'cleaves us still. But, friends, that war began in earnest a quarter of a century ago, and surely the statute of limitation has been reached. This is a fact: The final lesson of Vietnam is that no great nation can long afford to be sundered by a memory.'[23] Bush believed the American ability to resolve foreign crises should not be hampered by an unwillingness to utilize the considerable power of the US military. He claimed to 'prefer the diplomatic approach' but also believed 'there is no substitute for a nation's ability to defend its ideals and interests'. Bush was convinced that 'Diplomacy and military capability are complementary' and that American efforts at solving international disputes peacefully would be enhanced if they were backed by a willingness to resort to force.[24]

Although Bush's foreign policy team did not have the divisiveness that had troubled the Carter and Reagan administrations, there were differences of opinion concerning the appropriate use of force. National Security Advisor Brent Scowcroft believed the US could 'choke on such strictures' as the Vietnam syndrome and the Weinberger Doctrine. For Scowcroft, war was a legitimate tool of foreign policy that should be threatened and applied when necessary. Secretary of Defense Dick Cheney showed no reluctance either, to consider force as a policy option.[25] Secretary of State James Baker was more cautious. In his memoirs Bush claims that Baker 'never backed away from any decision to use force or planning for it'. But Baker was determined that diplomacy should be given every possible chance to work before force was used and was concerned about entering conflicts that could see the US getting 'bogged down' as they had in Vietnam.[26]

Chairman of the Joint Chiefs of Staff Colin Powell also exhibited a cautious approach to the application of force but appeared willing to recommend military action. On September 20, 1989, at his Senate confirmation hearing for the chairmanship, Powell was asked what he thought of the Weinberger Doctrine. Powell admitted Weinberger had provided 'useful guidelines' but added 'I have never seen them to be a series of steps each one of which must be met before the Joint Chiefs of Staff will recommend the use of military force.' Powell cited Grenada and Libya as examples of how, in his recent experience, there had been: 'no hesitancy to use the armed forces as a political instrument when the mission is clear and when it is something that has been carefully thought out and considered and all the ramifications of using military forces have been considered.'[27] Although Powell may not have believed that the Weinberger Doctrine provided the definitive guide to the appropriate use of American military force, this was the first of many expressions of his own view that there were limits to American power that should be observed. Indeed, by the time Powell left his post his own views on the use of force came to be known as the Powell Doctrine.

Although Powell and Baker held reservations about when and how to apply US military force, Bush was determined that it should be considered as a viable option for resolving international crises. Yet, as the following analysis demonstrates, whenever the Bush administration authorized the use of force abroad it was within the limits that had restricted the actions of other post-Vietnam presidents.

Panama

The Bush administration's first major use of military force was in the invasion of Panama on December 20, 1989. General Manuel Noriega was head of the Panama Defense Force (PDF), the true power behind a series of Panamanian governments, and a former ally and, indeed, employee of the US government. He was now wanted by the US Justice Department on drug trafficking, money laundering and racketeering charges, and his arrest was an official foreign policy objective. In May 1989, Noriega nullified democratic elections when it became apparent that American-supported opposition candidate Guillermo Endara would defeat Noriega's puppet president.

US public opinion was incensed by television pictures showing Endara's vice-presidential candidate Guillermo Ford being physically beaten by PDF soldiers at post-election demonstrations. A *Newsweek*-Gallup poll found 71 per cent of Americans believed that it was now very important to the US that Noriega give up power. However, only 32 per cent favoured a 'US military invasion to overthrow Noriega'. The clear preference of 81 per cent of those polled was that the Bush administration should 'persuade other nations in the region to pressure Noriega to surrender'.[28] In October 1989, Bush was heavily criticized in the media and Congress for not helping an attempted coup against Noriega. As a result, the administration stepped up planning and preparation for a possible intervention to seize Noriega and overthrow the PDF.[29]

On December 16, 1989, the PDF provided what Powell describes as 'unignorable provocation'.[30] An off-duty American soldier was shot dead by members of the PDF at a roadblock in Panama City. Another serviceman and his wife who witnessed the shooting were arrested, interrogated, beaten, and threatened with sexual abuse. Two days earlier, Noriega's self-appointed legislature had declared that Panama was 'in a state of war' with the US.[31] It now appeared that the PDF was taking the declaration seriously. All the president's key foreign policy advisers agreed that the time had come to use force to remove Noriega, so Bush authorized an invasion of Panama.

The administration concluded it had clear strategic and political reasons for intervening in Panamanian affairs. The US had a duty to protect the Panama Canal and ensure the safety of the 35,000 Americans living and working in Panama (including 13,000 military personnel). The prospect of deposing a troublesome national leader was also an attractive one. The unspoken motivation was also, perhaps, that embarking on a successful military operation would go some way towards silencing critics who accused Bush of being a directionless wimp in foreign policy. When Bush announced the operation publicly, however, he emphasized not only what he regarded as legitimate strategic and political reasons for the intervention but also moral justifications.

Bush informed the Congress that the objectives of the US military action were 'to protect American lives, to defend democracy in Panama, to apprehend Noriega and bring him to trial on the drug-related charges for which he was indicted in 1988, and to ensure the integrity of the Panama Canal Treaties'.[32] In a televised address to the nation, Bush detailed Noriega's and the PDF's 'reckless threats and attacks' against Americans in Panama and claimed he ordered military action because: 'As President, I have no higher obligation than to safeguard the lives of American citizens.' Bush also emphasized that the operation would bring the 'indicted drug trafficker' Noriega to justice and restore democracy by enabling the Endara government to take up office. The US action, Bush concluded, supported the 'noble goals' of the Panamanians who desired 'democracy, peace, and the chance for a better life in dignity and freedom'.[33] Bush thus made attempts to portray the military intervention as being not only in the interests of the US but also a benevolent action designed to benefit the Panamanian people. To reinforce the administration's claims of moral justification, the original codename Blue Spoon was dropped in favour of Operation Just Cause. Powell liked the new name, not only because its 'inspirational ring' would provide a 'rousing call to arms', but also because: 'Even our severest critics would have to utter "Just Cause" while denouncing us.'[34]

Operation Just Cause achieved its objectives rapidly and with very few American casualties. A little over six hours after the mission had begun, Bush was able to inform the American public: 'Key military objectives have been achieved. Most organized resistance has been eliminated ... [and] the United States today recognizes the democratically elected government of President Endara.'[35] On January 3, 1990, the final objective was achieved when Noriega emerged from the sanctuary of the Papal Nuncio's residence, was taken into custody, and flown to face trial in the United States. Bush concluded the US had 'used its resources in a manner consistent with political, diplomatic, and moral principles'.[36]

The administration had gone to some lengths to establish whether its objectives in Panama could be justified. The Justice Department had produced a legal opinion which argued that the administration could legally seize a foreign citizen from a sovereign country if they were wanted on criminal charges in the US even if the action violated customary international law.[37] Bush also insisted to Congress that the action was legally justified in accordance with Article 51 of the UN Charter, the provisions of the Panama Canal Treaties, and his 'constitutional authority with respect to the conduct of foreign relations'.[38] But although Bush insisted he had acted in accordance with the War Powers Act, Congress was not in session at the time and, rather than being consulted about the operation in advance, members of Congress were informed only once the invasion had begun. As with previous administrations, the decision to employ force had been taken solely within the executive.[39] Many foreign governments were unmoved by Bush's attempts to justify the intervention. The Organization of American States voted 20–1 to condemn the military action and call for the immediate withdrawal of US troops. The UN General Assembly passed a similar resolution by 75 votes to 20.[40] Reaction in Panama itself, though, was far more encouraging for the administration. In a poll released by CBS on January 5, 1990, 92 per cent of Panamanians claimed to approve of the US action.[41]

American public support for the intervention was also considerable. A *Newsweek*-Gallup poll conducted on December 21, 1989, found 80 per cent of those polled believed the US was 'justified ... in sending military forces to invade Panama and overthrow Noriega', while only 13 per cent disapproved.[42] Bush's job approval rating shot up nine points to an almost unprecedented 80 per cent in January 1990. This was the second highest approval rating for any US president in polling history and the highest rating for a president at the beginning of his second year in office.[43] In February, when Bush's approval rating fell back to 73 per cent (still the second highest of his administration), Frank Newport of the Gallup organization argued that foreign policy generally, and the Panama intervention specifically, were the major factors behind the president's extraordinary popularity. The Panama intervention and Noriega's capture were considered Bush's greatest achievement up to that time by twice as many respondents (18 per cent) as for any other single issue or event. Panama, and the administration's policies towards the break-up of the Soviet bloc, were the main contributing factors to the belief of 77 per cent of the public that Bush was making great progress on handling the problem of keeping the US out of war.[44] The American public greatly favoured and supported the manner in which Bush had chosen to employ force, as it had with the similarly short and successful missions in Grenada and Libya under the Reagan administration.

Bush, like his predecessor, had been careful to employ force in a manner which would meet with the approval of the American public. As we have seen, he made efforts to establish a just cause with clear and compelling objectives. The administration was also determined to employ sufficient force to achieve those objectives swiftly and with minimal American casualties. Bush's military planners were convinced that Operation Just Cause would quickly and efficiently achieve all the administration's stated political and military objectives through the use of overwhelming force. The 13,000 US troops already stationed in Panama would be reinforced with a further 11,000 from the United States. This force, Powell and the Joint Chiefs were convinced, would be more than a match for the 16,000-member PDF of whom they believed only 3500 were combat-ready. Such odds would ensure rapid success and avoid the US becoming embroiled in a protracted conflict. Powell argued that such a mission held fewer risks than a smaller operation designed simply to capture Noriega. To use massive force was the prudent option.[45] At his first news conference after the campaign began, Bush emphasized that he made a specific decision to intervene 'with enough force – this was a recommendation of the Pentagon – to be sure that we minimize the loss of life on both sides'.[46] At the meeting where the decision was taken to intervene, Scowcroft had warned: 'There are going to be casualties. People are going to die.' Powell concurred that there would be casualties on both sides, both military and civilians, but he assured Bush: 'We will do everything we can to keep them at a minimum.'[47] American casualties during the intervention amounted to 23 dead and 324 wounded. Generally accepted official sources reported 314 Panamanian military deaths and 202 civilian deaths.[48]

The relatively low cost of the operation, its rapid and successful conclusion, and the fact that the reinforcements were soon pulled out of Panama, all contributed to widespread public approval of the operation. As with

Grenada and Libya before it, Panama had enabled the US to give the appearance of standing tall while still adhering to the requirements of the Vietnam syndrome. As Powell concludes in his memoirs:

> The lessons I absorbed from Panama confirmed all my convictions over the preceding twenty years, since the days of doubt over Vietnam. Have a clear political objective and stick to it. Use all the force necessary, and do not apologize for going in big if that is what it takes. Decisive force ends wars quickly and in the long run saves lives. Whatever threats we faced in the future, I intended to make these rules the bedrock of my military counsel.[49]

Powell's doctrine of when and how to apply military force would also be followed in the response to the greatest foreign policy crisis of the Bush administration.

The Persian Gulf War

On August 2, 1990, Iraq invaded and occupied its southern neighbour Kuwait. Iraq's President Saddam Hussein declared that Kuwait was rightfully a province of Iraq and that the Iraqi action had eradicated a remnant of nineteenth-century 'Western colonialism'. The invasion also resolved a number of more recent disputes between Iraq and Kuwait. In May, Saddam Hussein had accused Kuwait of declaring war on Iraq by attempting to drive down the price of oil. Such action would cripple the Iraqi economy, which was yet to recover from the costly war with Iran during which Kuwait had loaned Iraq $10 billion. The occupation of Kuwait would also grant Iraq control of the disputed Rumaila oilfield and provide valuable access to coastal harbours.[50]

Whatever Saddam Hussein believed his justifications to be, the international reaction to the invasion was immediate and unambiguous. The UN Security Council, no longer burdened by Cold War divisions, condemned the invasion by a unanimous vote and demanded an immediate and unconditional withdrawal of all Iraqi forces from Kuwait. This was the first of twelve UN resolutions concerning the crisis which culminated in the November 29 authorization for member states to 'use all necessary means' to implement the resolutions if Iraq did not withdraw from Kuwait on or before January 15, 1991.[51] The US led an international coalition of forces from 28 nations which were deployed initially to defend Saudi Arabia from attack. Following Iraq's failure to comply with the UN Resolutions, coalition forces launched an air campaign on January 16, 1991 to force Iraq from Kuwait. On February 24, the coalition began a ground offensive which after a mere four days of fighting resulted in a total Iraqi withdrawal from Kuwait and a temporary ceasefire.

The Bush administration gave five main strategic, political and economic reasons why the US must take steps to reverse the Iraqi invasion. First, Bush argued, the acquisition of territory by force was unacceptable international behaviour. He insisted that Iraq must not be allowed to benefit from its invasion of Kuwait because: 'Every use of force unchecked is an invitation to further aggression. Every act of aggression unpunished strikes a blow against the rule of law – and strengthens the forces of chaos and lawlessness that, ultimately, threaten us all.'[52] Second, the Iraqi action threatened the American and global economies. Iraq and Kuwait each held 10 per cent of the world's oil reserves and a further 20 per cent could be seized in Saudi Arabia. Bush's advisers agreed that oil production and pricing would be adversely affected unless something was done to curb Iraqi expansion. Baker warned ominously that an unchecked Iraq could 'strangle the global economic order, determining by fiat whether we all enter a recession or even the darkness of depression'.[53]

Third, the seizure of Kuwait would cause considerable disruption to stability in the Persian Gulf area. The CIA warned Bush that Jordan, Yemen and other Arab states would now 'probably tilt toward' Iraq. As a result, Israel was threatened and the Middle East peace process in jeopardy.[54] Fourth, Bush was concerned for the safety of American citizens living in the region. There were almost four thousand Americans in Kuwait and around five hundred in Iraq. Bush's 'constant worry' was that 'we would be presented with a hostage situation along the lines of the 1979 Tehran embassy crisis'.[55] His fears appeared realized when foreign nationals, including Americans, were detained by the Iraqis and Saddam Hussein threatened to use them as human shields to protect potential military targets. After much diplomatic activity, however, all foreign hostages were released unharmed on December 6, 1990.

Finally, the administration believed that intervention was necessary because Iraq was on the verge of acquiring a nuclear capability to add to its developing stock of other weapons of mass destruction, including chemical and biological weapons. As Iraq was perceived by the administration as an aggressive and expansionist state it could not be trusted to maintain a nuclear arsenal as merely a deterrent force. Saddam Hussein's regime had already demonstrated its willingness to use chemical weapons in the Iran–Iraq war and against the Kurdish minority within Iraq. Bush made clear: 'We are determined to knock out Saddam Hussein's nuclear bomb potential. We will also destroy his chemical weapons facilities.'[56]

The US could, therefore, draw upon a considerable range of strategic, political and economic justifications for its stance toward Iraq. However, as so many times before in US history, the Bush administration also made attempts to show that its policy was consistent with the tradition of benevolence in American foreign policy. In his August 8 address to the nation, announcing the deployment of US forces to Saudi Arabia, Bush did not merely lay out the political, strategic and economic reasons for the

American opposition to Iraq's action. The US, he argued, would reverse Iraqi aggression as a matter of moral principle: 'Standing up for our principle is an American tradition.' Bush called upon the belief in American exceptionalism, declaring: 'As I've witnessed throughout my life in both war and peace, America has never wavered when her purpose is driven by principle. And on this August day, at home and abroad, I know she will do no less.'[57]

At an NSC meeting at Camp David on August 4, Cheney expressed doubts that the American public would maintain their support for the administration's policy based solely on strategic and economic arguments. Bush was confident, however, that what he perceived as the moral dimension of the crisis would help sustain public and international support. He observed, 'Lots of people are calling [Saddam Hussein] Hitler.' King Fahd of Saudi Arabia had offered the comparison in a telephone conversation with Bush the previous day.[58] Bush took up the theme in a series of speeches in which he drew analogies between Saddam Hussein's conduct of the invasion and occupation of Kuwait with Hitler's goals and strategies in the Second World War. Many critics accused Bush of over-personalizing the conflict by demonizing Saddam Hussein and making unnecessary and inaccurate comparisons with Hitler's regime. Even officials within the administration felt uneasy about the ferocity of the president's public denunciations of the Iraqi leader. Powell in particular was disturbed by Bush's attempts to turn Saddam Hussein into the 'devil incarnate'.[59] Scowcroft also recalls in his memoirs: 'It was clear the President was becoming emotionally involved in the treatment of Kuwait. He was deeply sincere, but the impact of some of his rhetoric seemed a bit counterproductive.' Scowcroft was concerned by press charges that 'the President was turning the crisis into a personal vendetta against Saddam'.[60]

In his memoirs, Bush denies that he held 'a personal grudge against Saddam Hussein'. Instead, he argues, 'I had a deep moral objection to what he had done and was doing.' To Bush, the crisis in the Gulf *was* a case of 'good versus evil, right versus wrong', but he insisted:

> I think you can be objective about moral judgment, and I think that what [Saddam Hussein] did can be morally condemned and lead one to the proper conclusion that it was a matter of good versus evil. Saddam had become the epitome of evil in taking hostages and in his treatment of the Kuwaiti people. ... [O]ur policy was based on principle, not personalities.

As early as August 8, Bush had been told by the Kuwaiti ambassador that Iraqi troops in Kuwait were raping women, 'pillaging and plundering'. On September 22, Bush wrote in his diary that he had read 'a horrible intelligence report on the brutal dismembering and dismantling of Kuwait. Shooting citizens when they are stopped in their cars. Exporting what little food there is. Brutalizing the homes'. Bush argues in his memoirs that during this period he 'began to move from viewing Saddam's aggression exclusively as a dangerous strategic threat and an injustice to its reversal as a moral crusade'. Bush admits, 'I became very emotional about the atrocities. They really gave urgency to my desire to do something active in response.'[61] He was determined to use his public pronouncements on the crisis to help the American people understand the nature of Iraq's occupation of Kuwait and the moral imperative of reversing it. When he announced that allied military action had begun on January 16, 1991, Bush reiterated, in terms that placed responsibility squarely and singularly on the Iraqi leader that: 'Saddam Hussein [has] systematically raped, pillaged, and plundered a tiny nation, no threat to his own. He subjected the people of Kuwait to unspeakable atrocities.'[62] Bush seems to have emphasized the moral justifications for American intervention not as a manipulative tool to ensure public support but because he believed deeply that the Iraqi action was immoral and must be reversed. But by insisting that 'this was not a matter of shades of gray, or of trying to see the other side's point of view',[63] Bush ensured that his administration would view all Iraqi actions as absolutely evil and all American actions as absolutely good. Such Manicheanism was a typical expression of the belief in American exceptionalism.

While offering the American response to the crisis as evidence of the special nature of the United States, Bush was also, rather paradoxically, determined to show that his actions had full legitimacy because they were backed by the UN and a coalition of international powers. He admits in his memoirs that he was always 'prepared to deal with this crisis unilaterally if necessary'. Scowcroft agrees that the administration did not believe it required a UN mandate. In fact, he admits candidly, UN support simply 'provided an added cloak of political cover. Never did we think that without its blessing we could not or would not intervene'.[64] Nevertheless, Bush preferred to move ahead with the backing of the UN, his coalition partners, and the Congress. The support of other Arab states and the Soviet Union was necessary partly for strategic reasons, because taking action against Iraq without such backing could be more damaging to regional stability than leaving the occupation of Kuwait intact. Military and financial support from nations such as Britain, France, Germany and Japan would also deflect domestic criticism that the US was paying too high a price for international stability.

Nevertheless, debate did rage within the Congress. Non-binding resolutions supporting US objectives but urging a diplomatic solution were passed overwhelmingly in both chambers during October. Although the Congress was united in believing that Iraq must leave Kuwait, the main controversy was over whether the US should employ force to achieve that objective or give sanctions longer to work. Congress Members also debated whether they or the President had the constitutional power to authorize the use of force in the Gulf. Although political, strategic, economic and constitutional arguments dominated the debate, many of the speakers on both sides of the issue couched their arguments in familiar terms which evoked the idea of

American exceptionalism. Republican Senator Bill Roth of Delaware, for example, emphasized that the situation in the Gulf

> requires the exercise of judgment – judgment that finds its source in our history, philosophy, and cultural ties; in our religious and patriotic convictions; in our concepts of morality and our need for security. When these basic values are examined in the context of the offensive threat Saddam Hussein has taken in the Middle East, it becomes clear why our President reacted speedily and in the manner he did.

While Roth's views drew upon the missionary strand of exceptionalism, Democratic Senator Bill Bradley of New Jersey utilized the exemplar version of the same notion to argue against the use of force. He stated that: 'if America truly hopes to lead the world in a new way...we will lead by the power of our example, not just by the firepower of our military.' He concluded that the US 'can lead a changing world if we hold fast to our vision..., steadfast in our principles, patient in our will to meet any challenge,...imaginative about peaceful solutions, and conscious of our limits but limitless in our hopes.'[65] As with previous debates about the American role in the world, the language of American exceptionalism provided the basic framework for discussion on both sides of the issue. Critics also raised the spectre of Vietnam, with Republican conservative Pat Buchanan, for example, warning that the Gulf crisis 'has quagmire written all over it'.[66]

There were also anti-war demonstrations in the US, Europe and elsewhere that evoked memories of Vietnam. In the *Nation* magazine, an anti-war group called Out Now placed an advertisement that asked 'Must we trade body bags for oil? Why not Give Peace a Chance? Speak Out Now – Remember Vietnam'. In October 1990, a six-block long march in New York City was led by chants of 'Hell, no, we won't go – we won't fight for Texaco'.[67] Anti-war rallies were also held at the White House and on Capitol Hill in January 1991 as the Congress debated whether to grant Bush its approval for the use of force against Iraq. The protesters seemed unimpressed with Bush's moral arguments for intervention in the Gulf – their stark rallying cry was 'No Blood For Oil'.

Despite the protests, on January 12, following three days of debate, the House voted 250–183 and the Senate '52–47 in favour of resolutions authorizing the president to use force to implement the UN resolutions if Iraq did not fully comply by January 15. Bush admits in his memoirs that 'In truth, even had Congress not passed the resolutions I would have acted and ordered our troops into combat.' In December, Bush had confided in his diary and in a personal letter to his children that he was determined to employ force against Iraq even if it meant facing impeachment.[68]

Bush's memoirs also indicate that despite his claims to have followed the finest American traditions by continually seeking a peaceful resolution to the crisis, the president had decided very early on that force would be a necessity rather than a last resort. He admits that by the end of August he 'could not see how we were going to remove Saddam Hussein from Kuwait without using force' although he remained 'reluctant to speak publicly' of doing so.[69] Powell relates how on August 12, a mere six days after the UN imposed economic sanctions on Iraq, the president had stated in private, 'I don't know if sanctions are going to work in an acceptable time frame.' Powell had, in fact, become convinced as early as August 5 that Bush was determined to use force when he saw the President emphasize to reporters: 'This will not stand, this aggression against Kuwait.'[70] The administration perceived the crisis as a test of American resolve now that the Cold War had ended. As Bush wrote in his diary on November 28: 'we will prevail. ... Our role as a world leader will once again be reaffirmed, but if we compromise and we fail, we would be reduced to total impotence, and that is not going to happen.'[71] Bush was also determined that the administration's response to the Gulf crisis would finally enable Americans to put the experience of Vietnam behind them.

On March 1, 1991, after achieving victory against Iraq, Bush declared, 'by God, we've kicked the Vietnam syndrome once and for all.'[72] Yet, in his address to the nation announcing the end of the Gulf War, Bush himself had told Americans they could feel 'pride in our nation and the people whose strength and resolve made *victory quick, decisive, and just*'.[73] The planning and conduct of the Gulf War, far from 'kicking' the Vietnam syndrome, had been carefully designed to comply with all of its central tenets: only use force in pursuit of a just cause with compelling objectives that can be achieved swiftly and with minimal casualties.

The lengths to which Bush went to demonstrate just cause for American intervention against Iraq have already been shown. The administration also maintained clearly stated political objectives throughout the crisis. As Bush stated on August 8, 1990: 'First, we seek the immediate, unconditional, and complete withdrawal of all Iraqi forces from Kuwait. Second, Kuwait's legitimate government must be restored.'[74] Militarily, the objectives went through two phases. During Operation Desert Shield, between August 1990 and January 1991, the US and Allied forces were ordered 'to defend against an Iraqi attack on Saudi Arabia and be prepared to conduct other operations as directed'.[75] Once hostilities began, on January 16, 1991, the objective of Operation Desert Storm was to implement the UN resolutions by using force to drive Iraq out of Kuwait. Bush made it clear that: 'Our goal is not the conquest of Iraq. It is the liberation of Kuwait.'[76] As Powell concludes: 'We were fighting a limited war under a limited mandate for a limited purpose.'[77]

The decision to use force was made with careful consideration of the lessons Bush and his advisers had learned from the Vietnam conflict. The president was often very explicit about his concerns, both privately and in public. During a November 30, 1990 meeting with the congressional leadership, Bush asserted that: 'We don't need another Vietnam War. World unity is there. No hands are going to be tied behind backs. This is not a Vietnam. ... It will not be a long, drawn-out mess.'[78] According to journalist Bob Woodward, Cheney 'had come to realize what an impact the Vietnam War had had on Bush. The president had internalized the lessons – send enough force to do the job and don't tie the hands of the commanders'.[79] Powell confirms that: 'We had learned a lesson from Panama. Go in big, and end it quickly. We could not put the United States through another Vietnam.'[80] This intention was demonstrated by Bush in one of the most explicit public expressions of the Vietnam syndrome ever to be given by a US policy maker:

> Prior to ordering our forces into battle, I instructed our military com-
> manders to take every necessary step to prevail as quickly as possible, and
> with the greatest degree of protection possible for American and allied
> service men and women. I've told the American people before that this
> will not be another Vietnam, and I repeat this here tonight. Our troops
> will have the best possible support in the entire world and they will not
> be asked to fight with one hand tied behind their back. I'm hopeful that
> this fighting will not go on for long and that casualties will be held to an
> absolute minimum. ... And let me say to everyone listening or watching
> tonight: When the troops we've sent in finish their work, I am deter-
> mined to bring them home as soon as possible.[81]

The conduct of the war, therefore, embodied rather than defeated the Vietnam syndrome. General H. Norman Schwarzkopf, commander of US forces in the Gulf, was assured by Powell that 'the President and Cheney will give you anything you need to get the job done. And don't worry, you won't be jumping off until you're ready. We're not going off half-cocked'.[82] The original troop deployment to Saudi Arabia was almost doubled to around 540,000, together with 254,000 coalition troops, so that the Pentagon was confident enough force was available to achieve victory and do so swiftly. The first phase of the campaign would be limited to air attacks, turning to a ground offensive only in the final phase, in the hope of minimizing the number of US and coalition casualties. As Bush declared when the air war began: 'Our operations are designed to best protect the lives of all coalition forces by targeting Saddam's vast military arsenal.'[83]

Efforts were also made to limit civilian casualties by carefully selecting targets and conducting most of the bombing at night when civilians would be in their homes. Powell relates the extent to which efforts were made to ensure only legitimate targets were attacked: 'Lawyers got into the act. We could not complete a list of air targets until the Pentagon general counsel's office approved.'[84] Much was also made of the precision targeting of so-called 'smart bombs' and the pinpoint accuracy of cruise missiles. Television pictures taken from F-15 and F-117 cockpits of targets being hit with 'surgical' accuracy brought comparisons with popular computer games and drew attention away from the human costs of the nightly bombardments of Iraqi towns and cities. In reality, American technology was not as infallible as it appeared. *Washington Post* reporter Rick Atkinson claims that of the 167 laser-guided bombs dropped by F-117s in the first five nights of the air war, 76 were entirely off-target. 'Friendly fire' also killed 35 coalition soldiers, some of them when their transports were misidentified by US pilots. This amounted to an unusually high 23 per cent of total allied casualties. Civilians were also killed in relatively high numbers and the Soviet Union in particular criticized the bombing of targets in population centres including Baghdad. Most controversial of all was the destruction of Public Shelter Number 25 in Baghdad that the US claimed was an 'activated, recently camouflaged command-and-control center'. Whether this centre was contained somewhere within the bunker remains a matter of dispute, but the bunker did house an air raid shelter where 204 civilians were killed in their sleep, many of them children.[85]

Aside from the incidences of 'collateral damage' and 'friendly fire', the Persian Gulf War went beyond the best expectations of most US foreign policy makers. The air war lasted 38 days while the ground war took a mere four days before a ceasefire was declared. Kuwait was liberated with relative ease, the Iraqi army was routed, Saddam Hussein's ability to develop weapons of mass destruction was severely disrupted, and the perceived threats to regional and economic security diminished. Despite estimates that up to 50,000 Americans would be killed, coalition casualties were extremely low with 148 Americans and 92 coalition troops killed in action. Iraqi casualties were much higher with early estimates of around 100,000 dead, although the actual figure may be nearer 35,000.[86]

The disproportionate number of Iraqi dead was a source of some criticism at the end of Operation Desert Storm. Journalists in particular focused on the bombing and strafing of Iraqi combat units retreating from Kuwait along civilian motorways which became known as the Highway of Death or the Highway to Hell. Tony Clifton of *Newsweek* reported, 'It really looked like a medieval hell … because of the great red flames and then these weird little contorted figures.' Bob Dogrin of the *Los Angeles Times* wrote, 'Scores of soldiers lie in and around [hundreds of] vehicles, mangled and bloated in the drifting desert sands.' A US army intelligence officer, Major Bob Nugent, observed, 'Even in Vietnam, I didn't see anything like this.'[87]

Back in Washington, Powell worried that the television pictures of some fifteen hundred burning and charred vehicles were giving the impression that US forces were 'engaged in slaughter for slaughter's sake'. He recalls that he advised the president: 'We presently [hold] the moral high ground. We could lose it by fighting past the … "rational" calculation [that] would indicate the war should be ended.'[88] Before authorizing the use of force,

Bush had himself aired concerns about 'overkill' and wanted to be sure 'we are not in there pounding people' after American objectives had been achieved.[89] Baker and Scowcroft agreed that continuing the killing too long could sour the effects of victory. Bush, therefore, gave the order to cease fire after 100 hours of the ground war. He noted in his diary, 'We crushed their 43 divisions, but we stopped – we didn't just want to kill, and history will look on that kindly.'[90]

Yet the destruction of the retreating Iraqi forces was designed to fulfil a major American objective: diminishing Iraq's ability to threaten its neighbours. As Scowcroft recalls: 'If Saddam withdrew with most of his forces intact, we hadn't really won.' While the ground war was under way, Saddam Hussein proposed a ceasefire and an unopposed withdrawal which the US rejected. As Bush explains:

> I was not about to let Saddam slip out of Kuwait without any account-ability for what he had done, nor did I want to see an Iraqi 'victory' by default or even a draw. Either he gave in completely and publicly, which would be tantamount to surrender, or we would still have an opportunity to reduce any future threat by grinding his army down further.[91]

Nevertheless, some elements of the Iraqi forces slipped through the trap being closed by the coalition forces, although Powell concludes that the 'back of the Iraqi army had been broken'.[92] Lawrence Freedman and Efraim Karsh have also concluded, 'Despite the horrific images, most of the vehicles on the "highway of death" were empty, and though there were other such highways the total casualties in these attacks were probably measured in hundreds rather than thousands.'[93] Nonetheless, the bombing of retreating soldiers combined with relatively high civilian casualties raised serious questions about the morality of some of the US military assaults and cast something of a shadow over the administration's claims to be acting in the principled traditions of the exceptional nation.

Although the American public consistently approved of US objectives in the Gulf, it had been uneasy about employing military force throughout the crisis. In December 1990, a *USA Today* poll found only 42 per cent of Americans were in favour of employing force against Iraq if Baghdad failed to meet the January 15 deadline, although 80 per cent did believe the US would eventually go to war. On the day of the deadline, Gallup found 45 per cent of Americans believing the US should fight in the Gulf and 44 per cent disagreeing. Once the air war was under way, however, 75 per cent of Americans polled consistently declared support for the decision to go to war and a steady 85 per cent approved of the way Bush was handling the situation. Concerns then switched to the introduction of ground forces and the resulting prospect of greater casualties. A *Newsweek* poll taken on February 15 found 87 per cent of those surveyed supporting a continued air war while only 8 per cent believed a ground offensive should be launched 'soon'.[94] American nervousness appeared to stem from the fear that the campaign in the Gulf would be costly and protracted like the Vietnam War.

Following the rapid victory in the ground war, however, a sense of euphoria swept the US. Victory parades were held in towns and cities across the country to welcome home US troops in scenes reminiscent of the end of the Second World War. Bush's approval rating soared to 89 per cent, the highest Gallup had ever recorded for a president.[95] In a Gallup-CNN poll, 74 per cent of Americans believed the Persian Gulf War had been a 'just war'. Of all US wars, only the Second World War was thought by significantly more Americans (89 per cent) to have been fought for a just cause, while the Gulf War was placed on a par with the Revolutionary War and the First World War.[96] After victory was declared, Bush proclaimed, 'the specter of Vietnam has been buried forever in the desert sands of the Arabian peninsula.'[97] Yet, the Gulf War was a major success for the US and extremely popular precisely because it was fought in accordance with the Vietnam syndrome. As Powell concludes: 'We had given America a clear win at low casualties in a noble cause.'[98]

If further evidence were needed of the persistence of the Vietnam syndrome beyond the expulsion of Iraq from Kuwait, it was provided by the administration's decision to halt the war short of driving Saddam Hussein out of power and the refusal to renew hostilities in support of the Kurdish and Shiite uprisings in Iraq that were suppressed in the aftermath of the war. On February 15, during the air war, Bush had called upon 'the Iraqi military and the Iraqi people to take matters into their own hands – to force Saddam Hussein, the dictator, to step aside, and to comply with the United Nations resolutions and then rejoin the family of peace-loving nations'.[99] Scowcroft believes it is 'stretching the point to imagine that a routine speech in Washington would have gotten to the Iraqi malcontents and have been the motivation for the subsequent actions of the [Shias] and Kurds'.[100] Nevertheless, the media and public perception was that Bush had encouraged the uprisings in Iraq and that the US now had a moral obligation to help Saddam Hussein's opponents.

The moral crusade that Bush had portrayed the Gulf War as being now succumbed to strategic imperatives and the limits placed on American action by the Vietnam syndrome. The administration publicly justified leaving Saddam Hussein in power and following a policy of nonintervention to help the Kurds and Shias by appealing to the very same principle of state sovereignty it had declared as a justification for aiding Kuwait. The administration could find no mandate in the UN resolutions which had authorized military action to expel Iraq from Kuwait for further intervention in what was becoming an Iraqi civil war. More importantly, though, Bush and his advisers did not want such a mandate.

The administration had hoped that the Gulf War would result in the Iraqi army deposing Saddam Hussein but, as Bush and Scowcroft note in their memoirs, 'for very practical reasons there was never a promise to aid an uprising'. Although they hoped for a less threatening Iraqi leadership, for strategic reasons the US did not want to see Iraq dismantled as a state. Powell gives a clear summary of the administration's policy:

> However much we despised Saddam and what he had done, the United States had little desire to shatter his country. For the previous ten years, Iran, not Iraq, had been our Persian Gulf nemesis. We wanted Iraq to continue as a threat and a counterweight to Iran. ... In none of the meetings I attended was dismembering Iraq, conquering Baghdad, or changing the Iraqi form of government ever seriously considered.[101]

The strategic objective of maintaining stability and the balance of power in the Middle East outweighed any moral concerns for the self-determination of the Kurds or the Shias. The administration was also convinced that the international coalition assembled by Bush would not tolerate taking the war into Iraq. As Bush confirms: 'I firmly believed that we should not march into Baghdad. ... To occupy Iraq would instantly shatter our coalition, turning the whole Arab world against us, and make a broken tyrant into a latter-day Arab hero.'[102]

The persistence of the Vietnam syndrome also had its influence on the decision to stop the war short of driving Saddam Hussein from power. Bush and his advisers did not relish the prospect of becoming entangled in a long and bloody civil war that would cause increasing American casualties. As an anonymous administration official admitted:

> We decided early on if there was anything that could turn this into a Vietnam conflict it was going into densely populated areas and getting twelve soldiers a day killed by snipers. The main reason was that if we went in to overthrow [Saddam Hussein], how would we get out? If we set up a puppet government, how would we disentangle? That was the main question.[103]

To have taken the Gulf War any further would have necessitated the US and its allies conquering and occupying Iraq. Before the war began, Scowcroft had noted that the 'indefinite occupation of a hostile state and some dubious "nation-building"' was not a desirable option.[104] Any such action would almost certainly have involved larger numbers of American casualties either in the face of a sustained defence of Baghdad or the development of a guerrilla war during occupation. Another, anonymous, senior administration official confirmed in the *New York Times*: 'Frankly, there is complete agreement in this government that the American people have no stomach for a military operation to dictate the outcome of a political struggle in Iraq.'[105]

The fear of another Vietnam thus greatly influenced the decision not to continue the war beyond the stated objective of the liberation of Kuwait.

Public opinion seems to confirm that adherence to the Vietnam syndrome was not weakened by the experience in the Gulf War. A CBS News-*New York Times* poll conducted in March 1991 found that only 17 per cent of the American public believed the US should 'try to change a dictatorship to a democracy where it can', while 60 per cent believed it should 'stay out of other countries' affairs'. More than 3 to 1 of Americans polled by *Time*-CNN responded that the US should not 'fight violations of international law and aggression wherever they occur'. Most telling of all, though, was a *Newsweek* survey conducted two days after the allied victory. To the question 'Does success in the Persian Gulf war make you feel the US should be more willing to use military force in the future to help solve international problems?' only 32 per cent said yes, while 60 per cent answered no.[106]

The use of force in the post-Gulf War era: Yugoslavia and Somalia

Still further evidence that the Gulf War had failed to kick the Vietnam syndrome was offered by the Bush administration's reaction to the two major foreign policy crises the US faced in 1992: the disintegration of Yugoslavia and the humanitarian disaster in Somalia. In Yugoslavia, Bush initially sought to preserve the territorial unity and integrity of the former communist state and only belatedly recognized the independence of Slovenia, Croatia and Bosnia-Herzegovina. As war broke out between the former Yugoslav republics and news of atrocities and the refugee problem filled television screens, support grew in the US for some form of American intervention.[107]

Bush authorized humanitarian assistance for the refugees and economic sanctions against Serbia but would not contemplate intervening with force. In June 1992, Bush told reporters: 'I think prudence and caution prevents military actions.'[108] In August, Bush made it fairly obvious that the prospect of another Vietnam influenced his decision not to apply force to resolve the conflict in the Balkans: 'I do not want to see the United States bogged down in any way into some guerrilla warfare. We lived through that once.'[109] When he was asked what similarities Bush saw between the situation in Bosnia and the situation in Vietnam he replied, 'I don't see any yet. And I'm determined there won't be any.'[110] In a televised debate on October 11, with his bid for re-election a mere month away, Bush made explicit his reasons for not intervening militarily in Bosnia: 'I vowed something, because I learned something from Vietnam: I am not going to commit US forces until I know what the mission is, until the military tell me that it can be completed, until I know how they can come out.'[111] Unless he could meet those criteria, which were clearly part of the Vietnam syndrome, Bush was determined not to commit US forces to the Balkans.

The Vietnam syndrome also played a role in the administration's policy towards the war-torn East African state of Somalia. On December 4, 1992, despite having lost the presidential election to the Democratic candidate Bill Clinton, President Bush announced the deployment of US forces to lead a UN humanitarian mission to Somalia. Civil war had raged in the country since 1988. By 1992, government rule and civil society had collapsed, various factions fought for dominance throughout the country, and famine ravaged the civilian population.[112] Despite UN attempts to provide humanitarian aid, over 250,000 Somalis had starved to death by December 1992, with another one-and-a-half million deaths predicted over the next five months. Between August and December, the US had helped airlift 20,000 tons of food and medicine to Somalia but due to the fighting and the state of anarchy little of the aid was getting through to the starving population. Faced with a humanitarian disaster, the US agreed to lead Operation Restore Hope to alleviate the famine.

With no obvious strategic or economic interests at stake, Bush appealed to the belief in American exceptionalism in his justification for using force to aid the Somali people. He declared that the US had a moral duty to intervene: 'The people of Somalia, especially the children of Somalia, need our help. We're able to ease their suffering. We must help them live. We must give them hope. America must act.' He argued that the US was in a unique position of strength in the world that gave it the responsibility to act when a humanitarian disaster such as that in Somalia arose:

> In taking this action, I want to emphasize that I understand the United States alone cannot right the world's wrongs. But we also know that some crises in the world cannot be resolved without American involvement, that American action is often necessary as a catalyst for broader involvement of the community of nations. Only the United States has the global reach to place a large security force on the ground in such a distant place quickly and efficiently and thus save thousands of innocents from death.

The US would not be acting alone, Bush said, but without its leadership the situation in Somalia could not be resolved. He also stressed that American intervention was purely benevolent and in the finest tradition of the American dedication to helping others. He assured the Somalis:

> Let me be very clear: Our mission is humanitarian. ... We do not plan to dictate political outcomes. We respect your sovereignty and independence. ... We come to your country for one reason only, to enable the starving to be fed.[113]

Bush's justifications for intervention were warmly accepted by most Americans. A Gallup poll, conducted on December 4 and 5 found that

74 per cent of those surveyed approved of the decision to send US armed forces to Somalia.[114]

The question arose, however, why the US was willing to commit forces to support humanitarian efforts in Somalia when it refused to do so in Bosnia. The answer in December 1992 was that the mission to Somalia could satisfy the requirements of the Vietnam syndrome whereas the Bosnian situation could not. Bush found that the US objective was clear and attainable in Somalia: 'Our mission has a limited objective: To open the supply routes, to get food moving, and to prepare the way for a U.N. peacekeeping force to keep it moving.' He could also assure the American people that US forces had 'the authority to use whatever military action is necessary to safeguard the lives of our troops and the lives of Somalia's people'. Bush also made it absolutely clear that 'once we have created [a] secure environment, we will withdraw our troops, handing the security mission back to a regular UN peacekeeping force. ... This operation is not open-ended. We will not stay one day longer than is absolutely necessary.'[115] With the blessing of president-elect Clinton, Bush authorized the deployment of US forces to Somalia because he believed the operation would be a short, low-risk, and low-cost success.

It appears that the public agreed with their president. In the Gallup poll that showed overwhelming support for the American intervention, 59 per cent believed US involvement should be limited to 'delivering relief supplies' rather than attempting to 'bring an end to the fighting in Somalia'. Almost two-thirds (64 per cent) expressed 'at least some confidence that the US will be able to accomplish its goals with very few or no American casualties'. The poll also found that a 'majority of Americans (52 percent) are very or somewhat confident that US troops will be able to withdraw from the country within a few months, as planned'. Another poll conducted by Gallup for *Newsweek* revealed that only 15 per cent of Americans 'expect the operation to last a year or more'.[116] Despite expectations of a short, successful commitment to Somalia, however, as we shall see in the next chapter, President Clinton was to find the conflict far more complex and costly than had his predecessor.

Conclusions: George Bush and the New World Order

Despite his self-confessed problems with the 'vision thing', George Bush did utilize the familiar rhetoric of American exceptionalism in many of his public speeches and news conferences. He often did so to lesser effect than his predecessor, due to his staccato style of public speaking. There were times, however, when the president took to the bully pulpit with an enthusiasm that enabled his message to strike a chord with the American public, none more so than during his two major foreign policy crises in Panama and the Persian Gulf. Bush confided in his diary in September 1990 that he preferred working on international rather than domestic affairs. He admitted to being able to become 'fully engrossed' in international crises such as that in the Persian Gulf: 'I enjoy working all the parts of it and I get into much more detail than I do on the domestic scene.'[117]

Bush did eventually attempt to formulate overarching themes or visions for both his domestic and foreign policy. On the domestic front it was the rather nebulous notion of a 'Thousand Points of Light' which, particularly during his campaign for re-election, became a catchphrase derided by critics as being almost wholly devoid of meaning or content. In international affairs, however, Bush came to promote a vision that he called the 'New World Order'.

Although he did not use the phrase 'new world order' until the Gulf crisis, Bush had first aired some of the ideas that would form his vision during one of his earliest foreign policy speeches. On May 24, 1989, Bush claimed Americans had 'an opportunity before us to shape a new world' which would be based on 'a growing community of democracies anchoring international peace and stability, and a dynamic free-market system generating prosperity and progress on a global scale'.[118] Later that year, at the UN, Bush gave his vision a name that would fail to catch on. He spoke of a 'new world of freedom' which would be formed around a 'true community of nations built on shared interests and ideals' including the spread of democracy, global economic growth through the free market, the pursuit of environmental protection, and an end to the threats posed by weapons of mass destruction, the illegal drugs trade and terrorism. Bush believed the collective pursuit of these goals would give 'unity of purpose' to the UN and 'make the new world of freedom the common destiny we seek'.[119] A year later, Bush's vision of a new world of freedom would be transformed into what he now called the new world order.

Bush and Scowcroft relate how the phrase new world order first arose in a 'long, philosophical chat' they had about the state of the world while fishing on August 23, 1990.[120] Bush first publicly used the phrase rather casually at a news conference a week later. He remarked that the broad coalition against Iraq made him think that 'we do have a chance at a new world order'.[121] On September 11 that year, though, Bush gave greater form to his vision in an address to the Congress:

> We stand today at a unique and extraordinary moment. The crisis in the Persian Gulf, as grave as it is, also offers a rare opportunity to move toward an historic period of cooperation. Out of these troubled times ... a new world order can emerge: a new era – freer from the threat of terror, stronger in the pursuit of justice, and more secure in the quest for peace. An era in which the nations of the world, East and West, North and South, can prosper and live in harmony. A hundred generations have searched for this elusive path to peace, while a thousand wars raged across the span of human endeavor. Today that new world is struggling

to be born, a world quite different from the one we've known. A world where the rule of law supplants the rule of the jungle. A world in which nations recognize the shared responsibility for freedom and justice. A world where the strong respect the rights of the weak.[122]

A year later at the UN, Bush laid out more specifically the goals of the new world order. It would, he said, be 'characterized by the rule of law rather than the resort to force, the cooperative settlement of disputes rather than anarchy and bloodshed, and an unstinting belief in human rights'.[123]

Yet if the new world order was Bush's guiding vision for international affairs, the record of his own administration indicated that in reality his rhetoric meant very little. In the crisis with Iraq, the US had acted in concert with an international coalition under the blessing of the UN. It is clear, however, that almost from the outset the administration preferred the 'resort to force' over the 'cooperative settlement' of the dispute and that it was willing to act alone if the coalition or the UN objected. Bush's call for a world where the 'strong respect the rights of the weak' also appears rather hypocritical in light of the invasion of Panama which, after all, was roundly condemned by the UN General Assembly. The 'unstinting belief in human rights' was also set aside in favour of strategic and economic concerns in the administration's China policy, particularly after the Tiananmen Square massacre in 1989.[124]

Although Bush suggested that the UN would be the forum for the development and maintenance of the new world order, he actually regarded the United States as the nation that would dictate the form, content and direction of that order. Bush assured the UN General Assembly that the US had 'no intention of striving for a Pax Americana'. It would 'offer friendship and leadership' while seeking 'a Pax Universalis built upon shared responsibilities and aspirations'.[125] Yet in his 1991 State of the Union Address, Bush had made clear that the new world order would be dominated and defined by the United States. In a speech rich in exceptionalist rhetoric, he declared that 'American leadership is indispensable'. Bush reaffirmed that the US is a special nation with a special destiny:

[We] know why the hopes of humanity turn to us. We are Americans; we have a unique responsibility to do the hard work of freedom. And when we do, freedom works. As Americans, we know that there are times when we must step forward and accept our responsibility to lead the world away from the dark chaos of dictators, toward the brighter promise of a better day.

A new world order would be possible, Bush argued, because the US is the only nation in the world that: 'has both the moral standing and the means to back it up. We're the only nation on this Earth that could assemble the forces of peace. This is the burden of leadership and the strength that has made America the beacon of freedom in a searching world.'[126] Bush's conception of the new world order was clearly an expression of the missionary strand of American exceptionalism.

The new world order was Bush's answer to the uncertainties of the post-Cold War world. It was a vision of how the world's nations could strive collectively to achieve and then maintain international stability. Characteristically, it was a prudent, cautious vision that preferred the status quo to any rapid or drastic international change. Most importantly, though, Bush maintained that world order was only possible under US leadership, guidance and protection. For all his talk of universalism, Bush's new world order was distinctly an American idea that assumed traditional American values and principles had universal applicability – indeed, it saw the US as a redeemer nation. Bush's vision also ensured freedom of action for the United States. The US would not be subservient to the collective will of the UN but would define and follow its own priorities, preferably with but if necessary without the support of the international community. As Bush and Scowcroft admit, despite the success of the Gulf War, they remained unsure of the UN Security Council's 'usefulness in a new role of actively resisting aggression, and we opposed allowing the UN to organize and run a war. It was important to reach out to the rest of the world, but even more important to keep the strings of control tightly in our own hands'.[127]

Bush's justifications for his foreign policy decisions, particularly those involving the use of force, were also regularly couched in the language of the missionary strand of American exceptionalism. Bush emphasized the moral dimensions of the Panama and Persian Gulf crises even though ample strategic, political and economic justifications for the administration's policies also existed. Yet the moral dimension was rarely the major driving force behind policy. Without the compelling strategic and economic concerns surrounding the Iraqi invasion of Kuwait the administration would most likely have been just as unwilling to intervene as it was in Bosnia where no obvious American interests appeared to be at stake. The moral dimension certainly failed to sway Bush's policy towards China following the violent suppression of the pro-democracy movement.

In terms of direct influence, the limits imposed by the requirements of the Vietnam syndrome continued to have greater consequences for the actual conduct of foreign policy than did the belief in American exceptionalism. The administration's determination not to become embroiled in another Vietnam-style conflict largely dictated the course of policy in confronting crises in Panama, the Persian Gulf, Bosnia and Somalia. Indeed, far from 'kicking' the Vietnam syndrome, as Bush claimed, the Gulf War demonstrated how institutionalized the syndrome has become in US foreign policy making. Yet although the belief in American exceptionalism did not dictate policy, Bush nevertheless made much use of its rhetoric and couched most of his foreign policy decisions in exceptionalist language. There are also clear indications from his public pronouncements, published diary entries and his memoirs that, just like his predecessor, George Bush believes that the US is a special nation with a special destiny. Indeed, Bush ends his memoirs with a clear affirmation of his belief in American exceptionalism:

> As I look to the future, I feel strongly about the role the United States should play in the new world before us. We have the political and economic influence and strength to pursue our own goals, but as the leading democracy and beacon of liberty, and given our blessings of freedom, of resources, and of geography, we have a disproportionate responsibility to use that power in pursuit of a common good. We also have an obligation to lead. Yet our leadership does not rest solely on the economic strength and military muscle of a superpower: much of the world trusts and asks for our involvement. The United States is mostly perceived as benign, without territorial ambitions, uncomfortable with exercising our considerable power.[128]

The strong public approval for Bush's justifications for his policies towards Panama, Iraq and Somalia indicate that the American people responded well when his appeals were couched in their shared belief in American exceptionalism. Bush's ability to rally the nation around his major foreign policy actions, however, failed to be translated into support for his domestic policies. His apparent lack of understanding and concern for the country's social and economic problems contributed greatly to his inability to secure a second term in the White House. Lingering doubts remained among the American public about the relative power of their nation, especially in terms of economics. Yet Bush's success in utilizing arguments couched in the language of exceptionalism to justify some of his most important foreign policy decisions demonstrates that the belief in American exceptionalism continues to have resonance with the American public. For all his pragmatism, the belief in American exceptionalism still provided the framework for foreign policy discourse in George Bush's administration.

7
Bill Clinton and the 'Indispensable Nation'

William Jefferson Clinton defeated George Bush in the 1992 presidential election largely by focusing on the nation's troubled domestic agenda. The Democrats' rallying cry against Bush was 'It's the economy stupid!' Clinton entered the White House in January 1993 promising to focus on the domestic problems facing Americans, and particularly the failing US economy. Nonetheless, Clinton also had to address an international agenda that was much changed from that faced by other post-Vietnam presidents. With the Cold War now firmly consigned to history, scholars, analysts and practitioners alike attempted to provide a comprehensive framework through which a far more unpredictable and potentially unstable international system could be understood. During his two terms in office, President Clinton would give an increasingly greater emphasis to foreign policy and preside over more uses of military force than any of his post-Vietnam predecessors. As a result, he would face many of the same questions regarding the continuing influence of the legacy of Vietnam. He would also draw upon the belief in American exceptionalism in an attempt to pursue a foreign policy that he claimed was not divorced from 'the moral principles most Americans share'.[1]

The Clinton foreign policy

Particularly during his first term, Bill Clinton was widely criticized for lacking coherence, decisiveness and vision in his foreign policy.[2] He was accused of lurching from crisis to crisis without sufficient forethought and then improvising his way through them. His ability to see the merit in all sides of an argument and make their advocates feel he agreed with them gave the impression to his critics that he lacked leadership skills and convictions. He was thought to vacillate from view to view in an ad hoc manner that was detrimental to American interests. Critics argued in particular that Clinton had failed to 'formulate a strategic vision for the post-Cold War era'.[3]

Much of the criticism seemed rooted in the idea that the US must have a coherent foreign policy mission. The realities of the post-Cold War world may be such, however, that an overarching vision or doctrine is simply not attainable or perhaps even desirable. George Bush, as we have seen, had also struggled with the 'vision thing'. His successor had to deal with an international situation where even more of the apparent certainties of the Cold War era had disappeared. The US faced 'no predictable adversary, no familiar structure of conflict, and few external constraints' to its foreign policy.[4] As a result, Eliot Cohen of Johns Hopkins University observed: 'I honestly don't believe we'll see the equivalent of George Kennan's "X" article outlining a strategy as cohesive as containment.'[5]

The Clinton administration did, nevertheless, develop an overarching foreign policy theme during its first few months in office. Clinton and his foreign policy advisers made clear that the end of the Cold War and the renewed focus on the domestic agenda would not cause the US to step back from its international commitments. The president assured the UN that his administration 'intends to remain engaged and to lead. We cannot solve every problem, but we must and will serve as a fulcrum for change and a pivot point for peace'. At the forefront of this 'engagement' would be the policy of 'enlargement'. The 'overriding purpose' of US foreign policy, Clinton argued, 'must be to expand and strengthen the world's community of market-based democracies' and, now that the Cold War had ended, to 'enlarge the circle of nations that live under...free institutions'.[6]

The enlargement policy was formally launched in September 1993 by Clinton's National Security Advisor Anthony Lake. He argued that the US must 'engage actively in the world in order to increase our prosperity, update our security arrangements, and promote democracy abroad'. He contended that the new policy of enlargement would be the 'successor' to the doctrine of containment. There were four main components of enlargement. First, that the US would 'strengthen the community of major market democracies – including our own'. Second, the US 'should help foster and consolidate new democracies and market economies, where possible'. Third, the administration 'must counter the aggression – and support the liberalization – of states hostile to democracy and markets'. These were what Lake and others within the administration called 'backlash' or 'rogue' states such as Iraq and North Korea. Fourth, Lake argued, the US needed to 'pursue our humanitarian agenda not only by providing aid but also by working to help democracy and market economics take root in regions of greatest humanitarian concern'.[7]

John Dumbrell has argued that enlargement looked very much like 'reborn Wilsonianism: a restating of old notions about progress, American power, free markets, and liberal democracy all advancing together without contradiction'.[8] James McCormick agrees that the Clinton approach to foreign policy was 'steeped in idealism'.[9] The policies of engagement and enlargement are certainly examples of how exceptionalist assumptions underpinned much of the Clinton administration's foreign policy thinking. Both policies were supported by exceptionalist rhetoric and were themselves expressions of the missionary strand of American exceptionalism. The rationale of enlargement was based upon the assumption that American values, principles and ways of conducting politics and business had universal appeal. The administration argued that enlargement would have security, economic, political and social benefits not only for the US but also for the rest of the world. Clinton suggested that the spread of democracy and free markets was to the benefit of all because:

> Democracy is rooted in compromise, not conquest. It rewards tolerance, not hatred. Democracies rarely wage war on one another. They make more reliable partners in trade, in diplomacy, and in the stewardship of our global environment. And democracies, with the rule of law and respect for political, religious, and cultural minorities, are more responsive to their own people and to the protection of human rights.[10]

As US Ambassador to the UN, and later Secretary of State, Madeleine Albright put it, the US would 'remain engaged in the world...to protect America and build a better world'.[11]

With the policies of engagement and enlargement, therefore, Clinton and his advisers advocated a clear theme of American leadership in world affairs from early in his first term. Indeed, in a speech given by Secretary of State Warren Christopher in May 1993, reporters noted that he had used the terms 'lead' and 'leadership' 23 times.[12] Lake also argued that the US position as the 'dominant power' in the post-Cold War era meant it had a responsibility to exercise global leadership:

> The fact is, we have the world's strongest military, its largest economy, and its most dynamic multi-ethnic society. We are setting a global example in our efforts to reinvent our democratic and market institutions. Our leadership is sought and respected in every corner of the world. ... Around the world, America's power, authority, and example provide unparalleled opportunities to lead.

As Lake emphasized: 'our interests and our ideals compel us not only to be engaged but to lead.'[13]

Despite this recognition of American dominance and leadership, Clinton insisted that the policy of enlargement would not be 'some crusade to force our way of life and doing things on others'.[14] Albright argued that American 'leadership' rested on a 'solid foundation of principles and values' or what she called 'enlightened self-interest'.[15] Lake was also adamant that enlargement did not mean the US would 'seek to expand the reach of our institutions by force, subversion, or repression'. American efforts at 'fostering democracy and markets' would, he claimed, be entirely benign.[16]

Nonetheless, the leadership theme indicated that the administration, drawing on the long tradition of exceptionalist belief, perceived the US as holding an elevated position within world affairs. Clinton claimed that the US 'occupies a unique position in world affairs today'.[17] In fact, he frequently suggested that it was the world's 'only indispensable nation'. George Bush had also claimed in his 1991 State of the Union address that US leadership in the world was 'indispensable', but Clinton made the phrase his own at the suggestion of Albright. On August 5, 1996, he declared: 'The fact is America remains the indispensable nation. ... America, and only America, can make a difference between war and peace, between freedom and repression, between hope and fear' in the world.[18] In his Second Inaugural Address in 1997, Clinton reaffirmed that 'America stands alone as the world's indispensable nation', a claim firmly within the tradition of the missionary strand of American exceptionalism.[19]

US foreign policy under Clinton would have the dual purpose, then, of enabling domestic renewal and maintaining the US role as a global power. The administration line was that continued engagement internationally was in the national interest but also that American leadership brought with it responsibilities that the US must uphold in its traditionally benign manner. The administration emphasized the necessity of maintaining US credibility in world affairs and also the redemptive nature of such engagement. The Clinton White House continued the age-old theme that US actions globally would bring benefits to the whole world. As Siobhán McEvoy-Levy has observed, the administration 'evoked the ideas of American exceptionalism and responsibility and linked the preservation of American power and prestige with the maintenance of American credibility'.[20]

Initially, both domestic and international economic interests were at the centre of this attempt to preserve American power. In early 1995, Warren Christopher stated: 'I make no apologies for putting economics at the top of our foreign policy agenda.'[21] The administration had scored major victories with its economic foreign policy in 1993 and 1994 with congressional approval of the North American Free Trade Agreement (NAFTA) and the Uruguay Round of the General Agreement on Tariffs and Trade (GATT). Indeed, the economic facets of enlargement at times clashed with and usually outweighed the administration's avowed dedication to democracy promotion.[22] On announcing the policy of enlargement, Lake had admitted this would sometimes be the case: 'Other American interests at times will require us to befriend and even defend non-democratic states for mutually beneficial reasons.'[23] Despite his earlier criticisms of the Bush administration's policy, for example, Clinton downgraded concerns over human rights and democracy in order to support the return of China to Most Favored Nation trading status. The administration admitted, however, that economic interests alone could not 'constitute a successful and popular foreign policy doctrine'.[24] Clinton also had to deal with the diplomatic and strategic challenges in foreign affairs that are the focus of this chapter. As Martin Walker observes, 'George Bush had bequeathed his successor a series of unresolved crises and vague commitments' around the world in places such as Somalia, Iraq, and Bosnia.[25] The Clinton administration, therefore, had to face the same questions of when and how the 'indispensable nation' should intervene internationally that had haunted all post-Vietnam presidencies.

Vietnam and the use of force

The Vietnam War actually became a major issue in the 1992 presidential campaign. The Bush campaign charged Clinton with having dodged the draft during the war by joining an ROTC (Reserve Officer Training Corps) programme from which he later withdrew to take up a low draft lottery number. He was also accused of having organized anti-war protests while he was studying as a Rhodes scholar at Oxford University.[26] The political furore was tempered somewhat by Clinton's choice of Vietnam veteran Al Gore as his running mate and also by Bush's Vice President Dan Quayle whose own record on the issue was suspect. In the presidential election debates, Clinton nevertheless responded forcefully to Bush: 'You were wrong to attack my patriotism. I was opposed to the war, but I loved my country.'[27] The extent of his protests against the war do seem to have been overstated and, as Martin Walker concludes, 'Clinton's rebellion was a tame one for those times, neither radical nor violent, and located squarely within the political mainstream.'[28] Clinton was, though, the first president from the Vietnam generation. His election campaign represented 'in an acute and highly visible way the coming together of a new American establishment', much of which was drawn from 'the respectable wing' of the anti-Vietnam war movement now grown 'older and wiser'.[29] How would a president who had opposed the Vietnam War be influenced by its continuing legacy?

Clinton was in fact determined, in common with many of his predecessors, to move on from the Vietnam War. During the election campaign he declared: 'If I win, it will finally close the book on Vietnam.'[30] Once in office, Clinton succeeded in moving reconciliation efforts with Vietnam along further than any previous president. On February 3, 1994, he announced that the US trade embargo on Vietnam would be ended.[31] Clinton went still further on July 11, 1995. Just over twenty years after the fall of Saigon, he announced the full normalization of relations between the US and Vietnam. He declared that this step would help the US 'to move forward on an issue that has separated Americans from one another for too long now'. In words reminiscent of many of his post-Vietnam predecessors, Clinton told Americans:

> This moment offers us the opportunity to bind up our own wounds. They have resisted time for too long. We can now move on to common ground. Whatever divided us before, let us consign to the past. Let this

moment, in the words of the Scripture, be a time to heal and a time to build.[32]

In November 2000, in a further act of reconciliation, Clinton became the first US president to visit the Socialist Republic of Vietnam. At a state dinner in Hanoi, he reminded those present that 'the history we leave behind is painful and hard. We must not forget it, but we must not be controlled by it. The past is only what precedes the future, not what determines it'.[33] Yet despite all Clinton's efforts to move beyond the Vietnam War, its legacy remained a clear and important influence on one major aspect of his policy making: the appropriate use of American military force.

In his First Inaugural Address, Clinton had asserted, 'When our vital interests are challenged or the will and conscience of the international community is defied, we will act, with peaceful diplomacy whenever possible, with force when necessary.'[34] Indeed, in the first few months of the administration, Clinton and his foreign policy team spoke frequently of 'assertive multilateralism', suggesting that the US would readily intervene in Somalia-style operations in coalition with allies. It seemed the administration might be attempting to move beyond the Powell Doctrine to redefine the appropriate use of force.[35] By September 1993, however, with questions being raised about the ongoing commitment to Somalia, the administration moved away from the policy of assertive multilateralism and back towards a more constrained view of when to use force.

On September 23, 1993, Madeleine Albright aired her views on whether the US should employ force internationally: 'Diplomacy will always be America's first choice, and the possibilities for diplomatic achievements today are ample. But history teaches us that there will be times when words are not enough, when diplomacy is not enough.' To ensure its national security, she argued, the US must possess 'both the capacity to use force effectively and the will to do so when necessary. When neither our ability to fight nor our resolve to fight are in doubt, we can be most certain not only of defeating those who threaten us but of deterring those who are tempted to take such action'. Albright emphasized the administration's resolve on the matter: 'let no one doubt that this President is willing to use force – unilaterally if necessary.'[36]

Albright acknowledged that a debate had 'raged' through previous administrations over when and how to use force. She claimed that the Clinton White House had 'wisely avoided the temptation to devise a precise list of the circumstances under which military force might be used'. Yet in the same speech, Albright laid out a set of clear criteria, consistent with the tenets of the Vietnam syndrome, by which the administration would decide whether to support the use of force in UN operations. She suggested 'certain fundamental questions' that should be answered before the UN committed to 'new obligations' including:

> Is there a real threat to international peace and security ... ? Does the proposed peace-keeping mission have clear objectives, and can its scope be clearly defined? Are the financial and human resources that will be needed to accomplish the mission available to be used for that purpose? Can an end point to UN participation be identified?[37]

Albright's speech revealed much of the substance of a long policy review that would result in a further codification of the Vietnam syndrome in US decision making over the use of force. The result of the review was Presidential Decision Directive (PDD) 25, signed by Clinton and released publicly in May 1994. The directive detailed the conditions, which were clear expressions of the Vietnam syndrome, under which the US would be prepared to commit forces to 'multilateral peace operations' in the future. In keeping with Albright's earlier announcement, the US would vote for the deployment of UN peacekeeping forces only if the 'political, economic and humanitarian consequences of inaction by the international community have been weighed and are considered acceptable'; in other words, if just cause can be shown. The US would make a significant contribution of troops only if there 'exists a determination to commit sufficient forces to achieve clearly defined objectives ... decisively' and that an 'endpoint for US participation can be identified'.[38]

The Vietnam syndrome was also clearly at the forefront of other members of the administration's views on the use of force. Anthony Lake, and Strobe Talbott, ambassador at large and later deputy secretary of state, both 'represented the Vietnam syndrome' in the administration. According to William Hyland:

> They saw the Vietnam War as a catastrophe; they not only feared another 'quagmire' but, more positively, wanted policy to represent high-minded ideals. Lake believed Vietnam had reduced the United States to 'just another nation,' tremendously powerful but 'almost as vulnerable to others as they have been to us.' To correct this deplorable state of affairs it was necessary to adopt a righteous foreign policy.[39]

In testimony before the Senate Committee on Foreign Relations in April, 1993, Warren Christopher laid out the four conditions under which he believed US military force could be used. There must be: '1. Clearly articulated objectives; 2. Probable Success; 3. Likelihood of popular and congressional support; and 4. A clear exit strategy.'[40] The Powell Doctrine itself remained influential, since initially its author was retained as Chairman of the Joint Chiefs of Staff. His successor, General John M. Shalikashvili, built on Powell's strategy, stating that the US military was 'prepared to use decisive and overwhelming force, unilaterally if necessary, to defend

America's vital interests'. He could also countenance using US forces to defend humanitarian interests but insisted that in all cases, 'the commitment of US forces must be based on the importance of the US interests involved, the potential risks to American troops, and the appropriateness of the military mission'.[41]

In Clinton's second term, his new National Security Advisor, Samuel R. 'Sandy' Berger, moved the debate over the use of force forward by advocating what he called 'Powell-Plus'. He criticized the Powell Doctrine for being too limiting and not enabling the US to use military force short of all-out war: 'Where it needs to be updated is on the question of whether or not military force can be used for more limited purposes than the decimation of the enemy. It cannot mean that we have choices between nothing and everything.' Berger thus advocated the use of force in situations where the US was 'strong enough to dominate an opponent' to achieve its objectives rather than needing to totally defeat them.[42] Yet Berger's 'Powell-Plus' was still a variation on a theme, and indeed Powell's own record demonstrated he was willing to accept limited uses of sufficient force to achieve limited objectives. The remainder of this chapter will consider how this debate within the administration was played out, by analysing the extent to which the perceived lessons of the Vietnam War continued to influence decision making. It will also address how the belief in American exceptionalism continued to influence US foreign policy, by focusing on the administration's three main interventions, in Somalia, Bosnia and Kosovo.

Somalia

Clinton had inherited the humanitarian mission to Somalia, begun during the last weeks of the Bush administration. In March 1993, however, the mission gained a political objective as the Clinton administration supported a UN Security Council resolution designed to help rebuild Somalia's system of civil government and disarm its various warring factions. The new dimension to the UN mission amounted to 'nation-building', a term Americans had become familiar with in Vietnam. The US had initially deployed 28,000 troops to Somalia but this was now reduced to around five thousand as part of the new multinational peace enforcement operation. Despite this force-reduction, the Clinton administration's experience in Somalia moved from one that seemed to reflect the best of America's exceptional nature to one that again raised the spectre of the Vietnam War.

The major turning point came on October 3, 1993, when elite US Army Rangers launched a raid in the capital, Mogadishu, to arrest members of the Somali faction, led by Mohammed Farah Aideed, suspected of having killed 24 Pakistani peacekeepers in June. A bloody street battle ensued as 18 Rangers died and 77 were wounded defending a downed US helicopter. Some 300 Somalis were killed and over 700 wounded, 30 per cent of them women and children. One of the dead American soldiers was dragged through the streets by a crowd of jubilant Somalis in front of American television cameras. The US Congress reacted with immediate outrage and called for American troops to be withdrawn. Comparisons were made with the bungled mission in Lebanon during the Reagan administration and, inevitably, with Vietnam itself.[43]

Clinton responded by reinforcing the existing troop deployment in Somalia but pledged that all US forces would be withdrawn and replaced with other UN forces by March 31, 1994. He declared that what Somalia needed was an 'African solution for an African problem'.[44] The initial humanitarian objective of the Somalia mission had nevertheless been achieved. The famine was ended with what Clinton claimed were a million lives saved. The further objectives added under Clinton's 'mission creep' were not accomplished, however. There was no successful 'political reconstruction, disarming of the factions, or a resolution of the conflict' in Somalia.[45] Clinton admitted, 'our ability to stop people within national boundaries from killing each other is somewhat limited, and will be for the foreseeable future.'[46]

There were clearly limits to what the indispensable nation could achieve. Indeed, the transition in Somalia from the US-led operation to distribute food to the UN-led nation-building operation demonstrated that the Vietnam syndrome had become further institutionalized in US military planning. As Karin von Hippel observes, the policy was 'derived from the lessons learned in the Vietnam War and the subsequent desire to avoid "mission creep". Based on the "Powell doctrine", the emphasis is on initial, overwhelming force, with the baton passed to a multi-national operation within a short time period'.[47] The problem in Somalia, however, was that the transition did not go smoothly and mission creep did occur.

The nation-building effort was greatly hindered by the legacy of long-term state collapse in Somalia. There was also friction between the US and UN over the control of the operation.[48] Significantly, though, the biggest problem – admitted in a UN report on the lessons learned from Somalia – was that the 'operation's mandate was vague, changed frequently during the process and was open to myriad interpretations'.[49] The first requirement of the Vietnam syndrome, that objectives should be clear and attainable, was broken by the Somalia intervention and precipitated the American withdrawal, especially once it became obvious that those objectives would not be achieved quickly and decisively with a minimum number of casualties. Somalia was looking more and more like a Vietnam-style quagmire. In the US Congress, opposition to the mission had been growing throughout the summer.[50] Following the deaths of the Army Rangers, Representative Sherrod Brown of Ohio called for an American withdrawal, because 'our mission [has] become clouded in Somalia and our role [is] undefined'.[51] Representative Jim Ramstad of Minnesota was even more forthright: 'the President had better get his foreign policy act together before Somalia becomes another Vietnam.' The US was 'getting bogged down in a prolonged and deadly operation' that he described as 'the height of foreign policy folly'.[52]

Von Hippel asks why the 'fear of body bags' could be overcome in the 1989 Panama invasion where 23 US soldiers died but not in Somalia when 18 were killed? The answer is that the Vietnam syndrome is not simply about casualties. The American public has shown that it will maintain support for military interventions even if casualty figures rise, provided that the other requirements of the Vietnam syndrome are being met. In Panama, the objectives appeared clear and were achieved rapidly despite the loss of American life. In Somalia, the fear was that further sacrifices would be a waste of lives since it seemed highly unlikely that the stated objectives of the operation would be achieved sufficiently in the foreseeable future. Thus the Vietnam analogy rose to the forefront of debate and an apparent consensus to 'Get Out' of Somalia was forged rapidly. As Linda Miller argues: 'The televised pictures of a US raid gone wrong, with 18 men killed, hardened public opinion against using American forces in the internecine quarrels of a homogeneous people in a far-away place.'[53] Some polls showed support for the Somalia mission falling to a low of 33 per cent in the aftermath of the firefight. Members of Congress also claimed their offices had been inundated with constituent calls demanding the withdrawal of American troops.[54]

Other polling data and research suggest, however, that policy makers misread the public mood. Although there were clear majorities in favour of a withdrawal from Somalia, an ABC News poll found only 37 per cent of respondents wanted the troops to pull out immediately, an opinion matched by a minority of 43 per cent in a CNN/*USA Today* survey. The same polls and another by NBC also found majorities of between 55 and 61 per cent supportive of Clinton's decision to incréase the US troop commitment to Somalia in the short term followed by a gradual withdrawal. Most tellingly, ABC found 75 per cent of respondents favouring the use of a 'major military attack' if negotiations failed to secure the release of American prisoners taken in the October 3 firefight. Contrary to the conventional wisdom, as Michael McKinnon has observed, 'there was no overwhelming outcry by the public to pull out of Somalia. Rather it appears as though many members of Congress either overestimated the public's reaction, or simply presumed what it would be.'[55] The example of Somalia suggests that policy makers themselves are now more sensitive to the tenets of the Vietnam syndrome than the public at large.

Regardless of any opinion gap between public and elite views, the debacle in Somalia did reinforce the apparent lessons of Vietnam among policy makers that there should be strict limits on how and when the US employs its military might. The Bush administration had intervened in Somalia for purely humanitarian reasons. Early in Clinton's first term there had been much advocacy of the idea that American leadership in the world brought with it the responsibility to intervene in the affairs of others on humanitarian grounds. Now, however, Clinton and his advisers had lost much of their enthusiasm for 'assertive multilateralism'. This fact was clearly demonstrated by the American response to the genocidal mass killings of ethnic minority Tutsis by majority Hutus in the African state of Rwanda. In the spring of 1994, as PDD 25 was published and the Rwandan situation spun out of control, the Clinton administration opposed any increase to the small UN force in the country. This policy was followed despite the claims of the UN commander in Rwanda that with a few thousand more troops he could prevent tens of thousands of deaths. The administration even ordered its officials to avoid using the term 'genocide' to describe the slaughter so it would not have to face its obligations under the 1948 UN Genocide Convention.[56] Despite its rhetoric advocating American leadership, the benefits of global engagement, and the promotion of peace through democratic enlargement, on the African continent at least the administration's concerns for humanitarian causes seemed to be overwhelmed by the desire to avoid a difficult, long-term military commitment. The moral imperative was also not great enough, at least initially, to overcome fears of entering a potential quagmire in the Balkans.

Bosnia

During his 1992 election campaign, Clinton had heavily criticized the Bush administration's inaction over the war in Bosnia-Herzegovina. He said the US 'cannot afford to ignore what appears to be a deliberate and systematic extermination of human beings based on their ethnic origin'. Candidate Clinton's sympathies were clearly with the Bosnian Muslims. He advocated using 'air power against the Serbs to try to restore the basic conditions of humanity' and to lift the arms embargo against the Bosnian Muslims because 'they are in no way in a fair fight'.[57] Once in office, these ideas developed into the proposed policy of 'lift and strike'. Despite the diplomatic efforts of Christopher and others, however, European governments could not be convinced of the advantages of such a policy, not least because they believed it would intensify the conflict and put the mostly French and British UN troops on the ground at greater risk.[58] Clinton himself backed away from the idea after reading Robert D. Kaplan's *Balkan Ghosts*, on the origins of the region's ethnic conflict, and a *Wall Street Journal* article by Arthur Schlesinger Jr., which suggested that the Balkan conflict could scupper the president's domestic policies just as Vietnam had ruined President Johnson's.[59] During Clinton's first year in office, administration policy showed little significant change from that of his predecessor and the president came to endorse the view that, despite humanitarian concerns, the Balkans were a European problem for the Europeans to solve. The administration's inability to act decisively over Bosnia, its failure to sell its policy to the Europeans, and Clinton's apparent wavering over what course to pursue, all contributed to a growing sense among critics that the president did not sufficiently comprehend foreign affairs and that his foreign policy was a shambles. Bosnia, like Somalia, was becoming 'a symbol of Clinton's failed foreign policy'.[60]

After much hesitancy and wringing of hands, the Clinton administration finally shifted to a policy of greater engagement in Bosnia in 1994 and 1995. The major turning point was the February 6, 1994 mortar bombing of the central market in Sarajevo which killed 68 people and wounded more than 200. The moral imperative now appeared stronger to Clinton who admitted that 'more must be done' to stop the 'strangulation of Sarajevo and the continuing slaughter of innocents in Bosnia'. Clinton also now emphasized that the US had 'clear interests at stake' in the conflict. Most compelling was the prevention of a wider European conflict developing, something that had always been in the foreground of American and European concerns. Clinton also stated that NATO's credibility as a 'force for peace' was at stake and that the 'destabilizing flows of refugees' should be stemmed. He remained clear that these interests did not warrant unilateral intervention but they did 'justify the involvement of America and exercise of our leadership'.[61] For the first time, Clinton threatened the Bosnian Serbs with NATO air strikes unless they withdrew their heavy weapons from around Sarajevo.

Martin Walker argues that the 'crucial new factor in the White House was Clinton's political will, and his readiness to deploy US military power'.[62] Yet the ghosts of Vietnam and the more recent experience in Somalia remained very much present. The threat of force against the Bosnian Serbs was still confined within strict limits. Clinton made clear that NATO would not 'commit itself to any objectives it cannot achieve'. He was adamant that the use of air power would not lead to an escalating intervention: 'I have not sent American ground units into Bosnia. And I will not send American ground forces to impose a settlement that the parties to that conflict do not accept.' US intervention would be limited to the use of aircraft in NATO operations designed to force the Bosnian Serbs to accept a negotiated settlement, but US ground forces would not be put in harm's way in Bosnia. Clinton admitted that the use of air power was not without risk and that the US might suffer losses, but he assured the public that all precautions would be taken to minimize the likelihood of American casualties.[63]

On this occasion, the threat worked and the air strikes were called off after the Bosnian Serb leader, Radovan Karadzic, agreed to withdraw heavy weapons from around Sarajevo. In the following months, however, NATO did use limited air strikes to punish various Serb actions. Far from deterring the Serbs in Bosnia, however, these 'slaps on the wrist'[64] emboldened them to seize UN peacekeepers as hostages and use them as human shields against further air strikes from late 1994. On July 9, 1995, the full ineffectiveness of

UN forces on the ground and NATO air cover was revealed dramatically and tragically. Despite the presence of Dutch UN peacekeepers, the 'safe haven' of Srebrenica was overrun by Serb forces who massacred several thousand Bosnian Muslims. Two weeks later the same fate befell another safe area, Zepa. The situation in Bosnia appeared to be worsening daily rousing a debate over whether UN and NATO operations should be enhanced or whether they should extricate themselves from the conflict.[65] The decision was taken to remain and, in Clinton's words, to threaten a 'sustained and decisive use of air power' to 'raise the price of Serb aggression'.[66] He promised that future NATO responses would be 'broad, swift, and severe, going far beyond the narrow attacks of the past'.[67]

At every stage in this gradual escalation of the threat level against the Serbs there appeared a consistent reluctance to engage further. The administration seemed determined to avoid 'mission creep', although effectively this is exactly what was occurring. Throughout this period, however, Clinton never wavered in his conviction that deploying US ground troops to force an end to the conflict was not an answer to Bosnia's problems, or at least was not an acceptable policy option. On May 23, 1995, as the Serbs resumed their shelling of Sarajevo, Clinton insisted that the US was 'doing, at the moment, all we can do. ... I do not believe the United States has any business sending ground troops there'.[68] On June 3, with over 300 UN troops held hostage, he reiterated: 'we certainly should not have ground forces there, not as a part of the military conflict nor as a part of the United Nations peacekeeping mission.' Clinton offered continued support to America's allies, should they decide to remain in Bosnia, but only within 'very careful limits': 'I want to make clear again what I have said about our ground forces. We will use them only if, first, there is a genuine peace with no shooting and no fighting and the United States is part of policing that peace.' He did add, however, that he would countenance a strictly limited, temporary use of ground troops to help with the withdrawal of UN forces should this occur, or to help extricate any UN unit that should become stranded or pinned down. On the whole, he argued, America's allies in the conflict 'do not want us, they do not expect us to put American ground troops into Bosnia. But we do have an interest in doing what we can short of that to contain the conflict and minimize and eventually end the human suffering'. Frustrating as this might be at times, Clinton concluded, this was the 'appropriate, acceptable, proper policy for the United States'. In the end, he argued, 'the conflict will only be resolved by diplomacy'.[69]

The endgame to the Bosnian conflict, however, was finally approaching. In August 1995, the Croatians and their Bosnian Muslim allies launched a major offensive against the Serbs, reclaiming territory that had been seized within Croatia and making large gains within Serb-controlled areas of western Bosnia. In the same month, Clinton vetoed congressional legislation that would have unilaterally lifted the arms embargo on the Bosnian

Muslims.[70] On August 28, the Serb forces around Sarajevo finally pushed NATO's patience too far by launching another mortar attack against a crowded marketplace, killing 37 people and wounding 85. Two days later, after a final ultimatum to the Serbs was ignored, NATO began a sustained, US-led bombing campaign against Serb targets.

The combination of NATO bombing and the western offensive had a marked effect on the Serbian willingness to negotiate. Talks led by US Assistant Secretary of State for European and Canadian Affairs Richard Holbrooke intensified throughout the autumn, leading ultimately to the Dayton Agreement which ended the war on November 21, 1995. The agreement was not unlike the plan UN envoys Cyrus Vance and Lord Owen had been negotiating three years earlier, which the Clinton administration had initially rejected. Bosnia would survive as a single, multi-ethnic nation, but the Federation of Bosnian Muslims and Croats would control 51 per cent of its territory, while the Bosnian Serbs would hold the remaining 49 per cent as Republika Srpska.[71]

The Dayton Agreement called for an international force of 60,000 troops to enter Bosnia to implement the peace. NATO would command the forces with the US providing some 20,000 troops. As the negotiations in Ohio were about to get under way, Clinton again assured Americans that although US participation in any implementation process was essential for its success he would not be sending any ground troops into Bosnia 'until the parties reach a peace agreement'. Even then he would ensure they only participated if they had 'clear rules of engagement and a clearly defined mission'.[72] Once the agreement was signed, Clinton assured the nation that 'America's role will not be about fighting a war; it will be about helping the people of Bosnia to secure their own peace agreement'.[73] He was 'satisfied that the NATO implementation plan is clear, limited, and achievable and that the risks to our troops are minimized'.[74]

The use of American ground troops to implement the Dayton Agreement would meet the conditions of the Vietnam syndrome. Clinton argued the cause was just since: 'Without us, the hard-won peace would be lost, the war would resume, the slaughter of innocents would begin again – and the conflict that already has claimed so many people could spread like poison throughout the entire region.'[75] The credibility of the US and NATO was also at stake, as 'America's commitment to leadership will be questioned if we refuse to participate in implementing a peace agreement that we brokered.' The objectives were also clear and attainable: 'the mission will be precisely defined with clear, realistic goals that can be achieved in a definite period of time.' The Implementation Force (IFOR) would oversee the disengagement of forces and police the ceasefire to create a secure environment for the rebuilding of a peaceful Bosnia. With memories of Somalia still fresh, Clinton also stressed that 'a separate program of humanitarian relief and reconstruction' would be undertaken by international 'civilian agencies'.[76]

He was adamant that: 'There will be no "mission creep".'[77] Clinton insisted that sufficient force was being deployed to effectively and efficiently achieve the mission's objectives while minimizing the likelihood of American casualties. US troops would be 'heavily armed and thoroughly trained. By making an overwhelming show of force, they will lessen the need to use force'. Unlike UN forces deployed during the Bosnian war, IFOR troops would have 'the authority to respond immediately and the training and equipment to respond with overwhelming force to any threat to their own safety or any violations of the military provisions of the peace agreement'. He admitted that 'no deployment of American troops is risk-free, and this one may well involve casualties' but he promised to 'take every measure possible to minimize these risks'. He warned that: 'Anyone – anyone – who takes on our troops will suffer the consequences. We will fight fire with fire – and then some.'[78]

Holbrooke admits in his memoirs that the US had intervened 'belatedly and reluctantly' in Bosnia, but he argues that without that intervention 'the war would have continued for years and ended disastrously'.[79] Clinton and others in his administration emphasized that it was American leadership that had finally brought an end to the Bosnian War. They argued, however, that it was not only American military power that explained that leadership role, but also the exceptional nature of the US as a nation among nations. Strobe Talbott argued that:

> One of the greatest strengths of our country's foreign policy is that when it is at its best, it is rooted as solidly in American idealism as it is in American pragmatism. The world continues to look to us for leadership not just because of our economic and military might but also because, despite our initial reluctance to undertake what George Washington described as 'foreign entanglements,' we as a people have at crucial moments been willing to do the right thing.[80]

Clinton took up the same theme in his Address to the Nation on the Dayton Agreement on November 27, 1995: 'From our birth, America has always been more than just a place. America has embodied an idea that has become the ideal for billions of people throughout the world. Our founders said it best: America is about life, liberty, and the pursuit of happiness.' Throughout the twentieth century, Clinton argued, the US had 'done more than simply stand for these ideals. We have acted on them and sacrificed for them'. In a clear expression of the missionary strand of American exceptionalism, Clinton declared that: 'Today, because of our dedication, America's ideals – liberty, democracy, and peace – are more and more the aspirations of people everywhere in the world. It is the power of our ideas – even more than our size, our wealth and our military might – that makes America a uniquely trusted nation.'[81]

Throughout most of Clinton's first term he had been chastised for being weak and vacillating in foreign policy. According to Holbrooke, 'Dayton changed this almost overnight'. The criticisms 'ended abruptly' and 'Washington was now praised for its leadership'.[82] Indeed, the administration could boast a long list of first-term foreign policy achievements, despite all the criticisms. Walker observes that 'nothing on the planet seemed to get done without the ubiquitous Americans'.[83] Apart from the debacle in Somalia, the US had helped to broker peace in Bosnia; restored the democratic leadership of Haiti; contributed to peace negotiations in Northern Ireland; taken credit for an Israeli–Palestinian peace accord, largely due to the symbolic handshake on the White House lawn between Yitzhak Rabin and Yasir Arafat; continued to contain and occasionally punish Saddam Hussein in Iraq; prevented nuclear proliferation in North Korea; normalized relations with Vietnam; helped negotiate the removal of Russian troops from the Baltic states and nuclear weapons from Ukraine and Kazakhstan; and assisted in the stabilization of Boris Yeltsin's government in Russia. Not surprisingly, the administration felt emboldened by these successes. As Holbrooke further observes: 'After Dayton, American foreign policy seemed more assertive, more muscular. This may have been as much perception as reality, but the perception mattered.' The leadership theme that had been present from the beginning of the administration now became the main rallying cry of the Clinton foreign policy. The ideas that would lead to Albright, Clinton and others referring to the US as the world's only indispensable nation became prominent in public statements on foreign policy. Clinton claimed: 'there is no substitute for American leadership.'[84] Talbott agreed that:

> If we do not provide international leadership, then there is no other country on earth that can or will step in and lead in our place as a constructive, positive influence. America is not just another country; we are a global power with global interests. If we do not lead the way in promoting freedom, peace, and prosperity on a global scale, no one else will.

Talbott also argued that this leadership role was not only in US interests but also a reflection of the nation's deepest values and traditions: 'We believe that we face historic opportunities not just to combat threats and enemies from abroad but also to build a world that promotes our interests and reflects our ideals.'[85]

There was a strong belief within the administration following the experience in Bosnia that American diplomacy paired with the threat or actual use of US military power was a potent combination that placed the US in a position of strength in the post-Cold War world. However, it is clear that the Clinton administration remained significantly constrained by the legacy of the Vietnam War, as had all previous post-Vietnam administrations. The US would still only intervene in conflicts or crises under very specific conditions that limited the time, place and nature of America's indispensability.

Rwanda, for example, had certainly not been considered the right place or the right time.

Despite the final peace in Bosnia being won largely as a result of the American willingness to use force, criticisms of indecisiveness and weakness on the part of the administration did remain beyond Dayton. In his memoirs of the Bosnian negotiating process, for example, Lord Owen claimed that had the Clinton administration acted earlier, peace could have been forged in Bosnia in the spring of 1993, thus saving thousands of lives. Hyland argues that in 1993, Clinton was unwilling to jeopardize his domestic agenda by engaging in a 'messy foreign entanglement', whereas by 1995, with a presidential election year looming, he realized that his inaction might cost him the presidency.[86] After Dayton, Clinton admitted there were still limits to what the US could achieve globally. He reminded Americans that they 'cannot and must not be the world's policeman'. But he also insisted that the US should act when it could:

> There are times and places where our leadership can mean the difference between peace and war and where we can defend our fundamental values as a people and serve our most basic, strategic interests. My fellow Americans, in this new era there are still times when America and America alone can and should make the difference for peace.[87]

In his second term, with political scandal threatening to overshadow economic success at home, Clinton turned more and more attention to foreign affairs. He made wholesale changes to his foreign policy team with the appointments of Madeleine Albright as Secretary of State, William Cohen as Secretary of Defense, and Sandy Berger as National Security Advisor. He travelled abroad more than any previous president, particularly in his efforts to be regarded as an international peacemaker in such places as Northern Ireland and the Middle East. He also had what his aides referred to as his 'finest hour' as he dealt with another crisis in the Balkans.[88]

Kosovo

Kosovo had become an autonomous province of Serbia in 1974. This status was revoked, however, by Slobodan Milosevic's Serbian government in 1989 following protests that the Albanian majority was discriminating against the Serb minority. In the mid-1990s, the Kosovo Liberation Army (KLA) began a sporadic terrorist campaign against Serb targets that developed into a major offensive in February 1998. The KLA took control of more than 30 per cent of the province before being driven back by a Serb intervention. As winter approached, the Serbs made greater gains, there were reports of 'ethnic cleansing' and Kosovo Albanian refugees took to the hills. The threat of NATO air strikes convinced Milosevic to accept a ceasefire and withdraw

Serb forces. As the Serbs pulled out, the KLA moved back in, and Serb reprisals followed. A negotiated settlement was attempted at Rambouillet, near Paris. The KLA signed but the Serbs refused and negotiations ended on March 19, 1999. Three days later Serbia launched an offensive in Kosovo and on March 24 NATO began a three-month bombing campaign against Serbia and Serbian targets in Kosovo.[89]

Clinton told the nation that by acting with its allies against Serbia, the US was 'upholding our values, protecting our interests, and advancing the cause of peace'. He claimed: 'we have done everything we possibly could to solve this problem peacefully' but had been shunned by the Serbian government.[90] The main justification for intervention, Clinton argued, was the 'compelling humanitarian reason' of preventing thousands of people being removed from their homes or from being killed. In a television interview, he claimed: 'we are acting in defense of the defenseless. We are not carrying out an aggressive war. We are acting at a time when [Serb forces are] going through the country killing people.' According to Clinton, the 'main thing' was to resolve a 'horrible humanitarian crisis'.[91] He also contended that NATO must act to prevent a wider war and hinted that inaction would discredit the alliance. This last reason was probably more important than the 'moral imperative'. As one of Clinton's advisers told the *Washington Post*, 'there are bloodbaths all over the world and we're not intervening in them. This one's in the heart of Europe. I'd argue that the [NATO] alliance itself is at risk because if it's unable to address a major threat within Europe, it really loses its reason for being.'[92] NATO was celebrating its fiftieth anniversary in April 1999 and, as Michael MccGwire observes, the Kosovo intervention was an excellent opportunity at the time of this occasion to demonstrate 'the continuing relevance of the alliance', its right to act 'out-of-area' and 'without specific UN endorsement'.[93] Nonetheless, the administration stressed reasons for intervention that were consistent with the tradition of exceptionalism.

It is also clear that the administration advocated intervention because they believed it could meet the conditions of the Vietnam syndrome. The humanitarian imperative, as we have seen, made the intervention a just cause. Clinton also declared that the overall goal in Kosovo was clear and compelling: 'to stop the killing and achieve a durable peace that restores Kosovars to self-government.'[94] NATO air strikes, therefore, had three specific objectives, according to the president:

> Our mission is clear: to demonstrate the seriousness of NATO's purpose so that the Serbian leaders understand the imperative of reversing course; to deter an even bloodier offensive against innocent civilians in Kosovo; and, if necessary, to seriously damage the Serbian military's capacity to harm the people of Kosovo. In short, if President Milosevic will not make peace, we will limit his ability to make war.

These objectives would be achieved through an 'undiminished, unceasing, and unrelenting' bombing campaign in which NATO would 'persist until we prevail'.[95] Clinton assured the Congress and the American people that sufficient force would be used to minimize the risk to US forces and to accomplish their mission successfully.

Throughout the operation, Clinton frequently repeated the mantra that had become so commonplace during the war in Bosnia: 'I do not intend to put our troops in Kosovo to fight a war.'[96] The US would only introduce ground troops into Kosovo in order to oversee the province's demilitarization once Serbia had accepted the peace agreement. The Vietnam syndrome clearly influenced Clinton's decision to restrict the use of force to an air war. As he told Dan Rather of CBS News on March 31:

> [T]he thing that bothers me about introducing ground troops into a hostile situation – into Kosovo and into the Balkans – is the prospect of never being able to get them out. If you have a peace agreement, even if it's difficult and even if you have to stay a little longer than you thought you would, like in Bosnia, at least there is an exit strategy, and it's a manageable situation. If you go into a hostile environment... you could be put in a position of, for example, creating a Kosovar enclave that would keep you there forever.[97]

NATO military analysts had produced a study in October 1998 that suggested up to 200,000 troops would be needed to effectively secure and protect Kosovo. Even a lower estimate of 75,000 troops fighting their way into Kosovo after a major air assault was deemed unacceptably high by the White House, where one senior official claimed, 'The idea of troops never had any traction that I remember.' The decision not to invade with ground forces was apparently taken 'easily and with little internal dissent'.[98] It appeared that the use of air power rather than ground troops to resolve conflicts was becoming an established strategy and clearly one designed with the Vietnam syndrome in mind. The *Washington Post* characterized the Clinton presidency as one 'full of tempered violence abroad, delivered nearly always by air and most often by pilotless "standoff munitions"' such as cruise missiles.[99] This method had proved successful in Bosnia, in ongoing punitive strikes against Iraq, and in response to terrorist acts perpetrated by the al-Qaeda network led by Osama Bin Laden. Arnold Kanter, a former member of the Bush administration, referred somewhat mockingly to this approach as 'a doctrine of immaculate coercion'.[100]

Although there were no NATO casualties and the Milosevic government finally submitted to NATO demands on June 10, the operation went far from smoothly. In the early days of the bombing campaign, bad weather diminished the effectiveness of NATO's attacks and Serb forces systematically escalated their campaign to 'ethnically cleanse' Kosovo Albanians from the province. During NATO's war against Yugoslavia some 800,000 Albanians fled Kosovo and tens of thousands more sought refuge in the hills. The administration was criticized for having exacerbated a situation it claimed to have intervened to stop. As MccGwire argues, 'while Serb forces were clearly the instrument of the unfolding "humanitarian disaster", NATO's long-trailered urge to war was undoubtedly a primary cause'.[101] If this fact raised questions about the morality of the intervention, greater criticism still could be levelled against the way NATO, led by the US, had conducted the war. Although it succeeded in its objective of deploying a NATO force into Kosovo to demilitarize the province and protect its population, the alliance 'took unto itself the role of judge, jury and executioner'. While claiming to act on behalf of the international community, NATO was prepared to 'slight the UN and skirt international law in order to enforce its collective judgement'.[102]

The legitimacy of many of NATO's targets was also open to question. Between March 24 and June 10, NATO flew over 27,000 sorties and delivered more than 23,000 bombs and missiles in the first attack on a sovereign nation in its 50-year history. There was considerable disquiet throughout the bombing campaign and at its conclusion about the apparent preponderance of civilian targets being hit, whether deliberately or by mistake. In late March, Clinton had insisted, 'We have worked very hard to minimize the risks of collateral damage.' He admitted though that civilians were at risk: 'I don't want a lot of innocent Serbian civilians to die because they have a man running their country that's doing something atrocious. But some of them are at risk because of that and must be, because we have targets that we need to go after.'[103]

Around 1500 Serb civilians were killed in the NATO onslaught, not least because as the bombing campaign continued the list of legitimate targets was extended to include those of 'dual' civilian and military use such as bridges, factories, television and radio stations, water and electrical supply stations, and heating plants. Although the Pentagon emphasized the use of 'precision-guided weapons' and 'surgical hits' there were several embarrassing mistakes such as bombing a railway bridge in Serbia as a civilian train passed onto it, strafing a convoy of refugees in Kosovo, and the diplomatically disastrous destruction of a wing of the Chinese Embassy in Belgrade. The many attacks on targets in heavily populated areas of Belgrade and other cities seemed in contravention of the 1977 protocol of the Geneva Convention that prohibited 'attacks on undefended or demilitarised areas' or those that would lead to 'an excessive loss of life or injury to civilians'. Unease about the level of civilian casualties was reflected in opinion polls. In late May, Gallup found that while 48 per cent of Americans believed the Clinton administration was 'doing everything possible' to minimize civilian casualties, almost as many (46 per cent) believed it 'could do more'.[104] The tactic that received the greatest criticism was the use of cluster bombs, since many of those dropped over Kosovo and Serbia went astray, killing and maiming civilians, and over 11,000 bomblets were thought to remain unexploded across Yugoslavia. *Washington Post* reporter Michael Dobbs concluded that:

> As a democracy committed to upholding international law, we have an obligation to hold our own side to even higher moral standards than those we impose on others. ... Unlike the Serbian paramilitary troops, American pilots did not set out intentionally to murder women and children, and could not see the faces of the people they killed. But from the point of view of the victims, the end result was much the same.[105]

The US had fought what it considered to be a just war in Kosovo, based on humanitarian concerns that were in the finest tradition of American values and principles to defend. Yet the methods used raised serious questions about whether the US was acting in ways consistent with its supposedly exceptional role in world affairs.

It has been suggested that Kosovo, together with Bill Clinton's various other diplomatic successes, may provide the best opportunity for him to have a lasting foreign policy legacy.[106] However, the American public were far from convinced that the victory in Kosovo was a major success for Clinton or that it demonstrated his resolve to effectively use force in the pursuit of an apparently just cause and thus re-establish the credibility of the US internationally. Only 46 per cent of Americans in the immediate aftermath of the conflict saw it as 'a significant US foreign policy achievement' and 48 per cent believed it was not. The public was also evenly divided over whether the situation in Kosovo had been worth going to war for in the first place. Clinton himself was given 'minimal credit' for achieving a solution to the crisis and, unlike other presidents who had led successful military operations, did not find his approval rating boosted by victory. Two-thirds of Americans also did not believe the war in Kosovo would help deter 'other governments around the world from committing human rights atrocities such as mass killings or ethnic cleansing'. Yet despite these relatively negative views of the Kosovo intervention, Gallup also found that Americans remained 'decidedly internationalist'. A sizeable majority (61 per cent) continued to believe that it was better for the US to 'take an active part in world affairs' rather than to stay out of them. Three-quarters of Americans approved of US troops participating in peacekeeping operations under UN command. Most significantly perhaps, two-thirds of those polled believed that the US should 'continue to respond to international human rights atrocities with military force'.[107] As with earlier evidence concerning the public reaction to the Somalia debacle, it would appear that Americans have a greater tolerance for their government exercising its military might than their public officials are usually willing to give them credit for. Yet the relatively muted popular response to the conflict over Kosovo suggests that attitudes towards the use of force remain somewhat ambiguous and that the debate over when, where and how to intervene in the post-Vietnam era, even in support of causes perceived as humanitarian in nature, is far from being resolved.

Conclusions

Bill Clinton did leave office with a higher approval rating than any previous president since polling began in the 1930s. In December 2000, 66 per cent of Americans approved of the way Clinton was running the country, three points higher than Ronald Reagan at the end of his presidency. Throughout his final year in office, Clinton maintained an unusually high 59 per cent average approval rating. His continued popularity, however, seemed to owe more to the extraordinary economic boom he presided over than to his foreign policy achievements.[108] Indeed, throughout 2000, only 4–5 per cent of Americans considered foreign affairs to be the most pressing issue facing the country. In an election year it was education, social security and the maintenance of the economy that occupied the public's minds.[109] Given that Clinton's stated objective on becoming president was to revive the US economy, his presidency could be considered a resounding success.

Foreign affairs did, however, occupy a considerable amount of Clinton's time, increasingly so during his second term. From the beginning of his presidency he had attempted to pursue a foreign policy that was 'highly moralistic and seemingly based on ideals'. Clinton clearly shared with his predecessors 'a motivating sense of American exceptionalism'.[110] In his public pronouncements he frequently asserted that the US had an important leadership role to play in world affairs and went so far as to proclaim that it was the world's only indispensable nation. The policy of enlargement was rooted in ideas of the universal applicability of American values and principles. The administration claimed that an overarching concern for humanitarianism deeply influenced its policies towards Somalia, Bosnia, Kosovo, Haiti and elsewhere. Clinton and his advisers were also keen, particularly in the early months of the administration, to advocate the multilateral resolution of international problems, although usually under the leadership of the US, in order to lend greater legitimacy to its actions.

As his presidency progressed, however, the realities of international relations and the administration's ability to do something about them, together with domestic challenges such as the Republican takeover of the Congress in the 1994 mid-term elections, meant Clinton's 'heavy foreign policy idealism' was increasingly tempered by 'a greater sense of political realism'.[111] Most of all, it became apparent that the 'indispensable nation' could not solve all the world's problems and that there remained strict limits to what the US could achieve internationally. The enlargement policy is an instructive example. From its beginnings, critics such as Henry Kissinger condemned the strategy for lacking 'operational terms', and so it proved in many ways. The policy was a 'less-than-adequate foreign policy guide for addressing specific problems in Somalia, Bosnia, Rwanda, Russia, and Central Europe'.[112] In each of these cases, more political and strategic concerns about the national interest came to govern policy and made the US slow to act, if it did at all, even when pressing humanitarian issues were present.

In 1998 and early 1999, the Monica Lewinsky affair and the subsequent impeachment and trial of President Clinton dominated the American political agenda. During this time, the president seemed to become increasingly interested in foreign affairs and began to travel abroad more. McCormick suggests that Clinton did so 'to illustrate that he was continuing to conduct the matters of state, to present a sense of normalcy, and to downplay [the Lewinsky] issue'.[113] Critics suggested, however, the president was deliberately turning more and more to foreign policy in order to deflect attention away from his domestic troubles. The timing of certain foreign policy actions seemed particularly suspicious. On August 20, 1998, immediately after his grand jury testimony in the Lewinsky affair, Clinton ordered airstrikes against targets in Sudan and Afghanistan in response to terrorist acts perpetrated by the al-Qaeda network. On December 17, on the eve of the vote on articles of impeachment in the House of Representatives, Clinton again ordered airstrikes, this time against Iraq due to its resistance to UN weapons inspections. The Republican Senate Majority Leader Trent Lott led congressional criticisms saying he could not support the attack because: 'Both the timing and the policy are subject to question.' Republican House Majority Leader Richard Armey refused to accuse Clinton of manufacturing a crisis but did suggest that:

> the suspicion some people have about the president's motives in this attack is itself a powerful argument for impeachment. After months of lies, the president has given millions of people around the world reason to doubt that he has sent Americans into battle for the right reasons.[114]

Clinton, of course, denied any such charges and the public seemed to believe him, with polls showing three-quarters of Americans supporting the airstrikes and almost two-thirds rejecting claims the president had ordered the attacks to delay the House vote on impeachment or divert attention from the Lewinsky affair.[115] Nonetheless, Clinton did seem all too ready to resort to what was dubbed 'cruise missile diplomacy'.

This heavy reliance on air power to force compliance in foreign affairs was also present in Bosnia and Kosovo and is directly related to the persistence of the Vietnam syndrome during the Clinton administration. Indeed, like all his post-Vietnam predecessors, Bill Clinton adhered to the main tenets of the syndrome when deciding where, when and how to use US military force. He did so in response to all the major foreign policy crises of his presidency where the use of force was an issue: in the decision to withdraw from Somalia; during the unforced invasion of Haiti in 1994; the continued use of air power to punish Iraq for violating UN resolutions; the eventual decision to use force in Bosnia; the refusal to commit forces to halt the conflict in Rwanda; the use of airstrikes to punish Osama Bin Laden's al-Qaeda terrorist network; and the reliance on air power rather than ground troops against Serbia in the war over Kosovo. The Vietnam syndrome was also further codified in PDD 25. Although Clinton authorized the use of force on more occasions than any previous post-Vietnam president, he did so only under the strictest conditions. Air power was predominantly used in order to limit the likelihood of American casualties and to allow greater opportunities for withdrawing from conflicts without US troops becoming ensnared in long commitments in hostile environments. Clinton was adamant throughout the crises in Bosnia and Kosovo that US ground troops would not be introduced until peace agreements had been settled. For critics, such an approach raised serious questions about the ability of the US to achieve important international objectives. On January 3, 1999, for example, Andrew Bacevich gave a scathing indictment of Clinton's use of force in the *Washington Post*. He wrote of

> ...the extraordinary importance assigned to avoiding US casualties, thereby advertising America's own point of vulnerability; the hand-wringing preoccupation with collateral damage, signalling the United States has no stomach for war as such and thereby encouraging adversaries to persevere; the reliance on high technology weapons employed at long range, inviting confusion between the technical capability to hit targets and the achievement of operationally meaningful results; vaguely formulated objectives often explained in terms of 'sending messages' – allowing for facile claims of 'success' and the prompt recall of the forces engaged.[116]

It is clear that US military actions during the Clinton administration continued to be constrained by the Vietnam syndrome.

In common with other post-Vietnam presidents, Bill Clinton struggled with questions of how both values and interests, power and principle should influence US foreign policy. The belief in American exceptionalism, and in particular its missionary strand, continued to provide the framework within which this discussion took place. The Clinton administration appeared determined from the outset to base its foreign policy on traditional American principles but frequently found its ability to do so limited, often by the continuing legacy of the Vietnam War.

8
Conclusions: American Exceptionalism and the Legacy of Vietnam

The terrorist attacks in the United States on September 11, 2001 were carried out exactly eleven years to the day that George W. Bush's father first proclaimed his vision of a New World Order to the US Congress. Like his father and other presidents before him, George W. Bush responded to this crisis using words and phrases familiar to the American public. He claimed the US had been attacked because 'we're the brightest beacon for freedom and opportunity in the world'.[1] Bush was evoking the belief in American exceptionalism that, as we have seen, has persisted throughout American history. The belief has been perceived and expressed in different ways by different people at different times, but the basic premise has remained constant: the United States is a special nation with a special destiny, not only unique but superior among nations. This belief has survived and flourished despite the ample evidence available to Americans that suggests their nation is no more exceptional than any other nation.

Some Americans have believed that because the US is a special nation it should provide an example to the rest of the world but remain aloof from international disputes and conflicts. These have been identified as followers of the exemplary strand of American exceptionalism. Others have concluded that the exceptional nature of the US places certain responsibilities and duties on the nation to protect the higher values of humanity wherever they are threatened. These Americans, therefore, adhere to the missionary strand of American exceptionalism. The basic tension, or indeed conflict, between these two main strands of exceptionalism has been at the centre of debates over the appropriate course and direction of US foreign policy. Although their purposes were different, even diametrically opposed, advocates on all sides of the major debates have tended to couch their arguments in the language of American exceptionalism. They have done so even when they had perfectly good practical reasons for justifying their positions.

The anti-imperialists and the expansionists of 1898–1900, the isolationists and internationalists of the 1920s–30s, and the hawks and doves of the 1960s, all shared a common discourse based on the traditional belief that the US is a special nation, even if they did conceive of that exceptionalism in different ways.

This commonality of language persisted in the post-Vietnam period despite the different perspectives of each administration. Presidents Ford, Carter, Reagan, Bush and Clinton all had very different political agendas, presidential styles, and problems and crises to deal with. Each of them, even the so-called status quo president George Bush, spoke of taking the US in new directions. Yet each of them, in their own way, employed rhetoric steeped in the belief in American exceptionalism.

The basic assumption that the US is a special nation with a special destiny has been frequently challenged by the realities of American history. Yet the belief in exceptionalism has proved remarkably resilient. It survived, for example, the American Civil War, the Great Debate over Imperialism, and the Great Depression. This book has shown that the belief in American exceptionalism also survived the so-called trauma of the Vietnam War. As we have seen, the idea of exceptionalism does not imply that the United States is a perfect nation. Americans recognize that the US has problems the same as any other nation. Part of the belief in the exceptional nature of the United States, however, is the conviction that although problems exist, none of them is insurmountable. Americans regard themselves as being uniquely able, given time, to overcome the imperfections of their society. The US is, after all, an experiment in human society and, as with all experiments, mistakes are made that are learned from and then progress continues. Enough of this self-belief remained intact for Americans to believe they could still progress towards a more perfect union even after setbacks as apparently traumatic and divisive as Vietnam. The belief in American exceptionalism is highly resilient, largely because it can be expressed and applied in so many different ways; therefore it survived Vietnam as it had other times of trial in American history.

Post-Vietnam foreign policy and the belief in American exceptionalism

While the Vietnam War did not destroy the belief in American exceptionalism, it did have an impact upon it. Public confidence in the special nature of the US and its ability to fulfil its special destiny was shaken. Each post-Vietnam president, therefore, consistently attempted to bolster American self-confidence. In foreign policy, the Vietnam War had very specific consequences for the belief in exceptionalism. One aspect of this belief is the notion that the US is the greatest nation on earth, which, because it is superior, will always be successful and achieve its goals. The defeat in Vietnam, however, had revealed that the US was not invincible and raised serious questions about the nation's strength and resolve. Second, critics argued the US had conducted the war in Vietnam contrary to the high morals, values and principles that made the United States an exceptional nation. The task for post-Vietnam presidents, therefore, if they were to restore the belief that the United States was an exceptional nation, would be to demonstrate that: first, the US had the strength and resolve to maintain its position as the greatest nation on earth; and second, that it could conduct itself in ways consistent with its values and principles.

In each post-Vietnam administration, US foreign policy action failed to live up to the high principles and claims of presidential rhetoric. Gerald Ford sought to 'heal the nation's wounds' and made much use of the rhetoric of American exceptionalism. He attempted, through his response to the *Mayaguez* incident, to demonstrate American strength and resolve but he set a pattern for the post-Vietnam period of American presidents standing tall rhetorically while undertaking limited action abroad. The *Mayaguez* rescue operation was certainly designed to demonstrate that the US, despite Vietnam, was not unwilling to employ its military might to meet foreign policy crises, but it was a deliberately limited engagement that had little long-term effect on perceptions of American resolve. The decision making process also reveals that any moral concerns for the safety of the *Mayaguez* crew were secondary to strategic and political interests.

Jimmy Carter's self-proclaimed objective was to restore the 'moral compass' to US foreign policy making. He attempted to follow a foreign policy rooted in what he perceived as the values and principles upon which the US was founded. More than Ford, Carter was attempting to conduct a foreign policy consistent with the belief in American exceptionalism, particularly through his human rights policy. But the record of Carter's administration shows that moral principles, even in the application of the human rights policy, were usually superseded by strategic, economic and political interests. Despite repeated appeals to exceptionalist rhetoric, Carter also failed to revive American self-confidence and in fact was widely criticized for contributing to the sense that the US was in decline.

Carter's successor, Ronald Reagan, was the greatest advocate of the belief in American exceptionalism during the post-Vietnam era. Reagan imbued his public pronouncements with exceptionalist symbolism and imagery. He was a true believer in the special nature of his country. He sought to overcome the crisis of confidence in the US by largely denying that any problems existed. Reagan insisted that the United States *was* the greatest nation on earth and that so long as Americans maintained that belief they would be able to overcome any crises they faced. In foreign policy, he took a tough rhetorical stance against the Soviet Union, conducted a massive arms build-up, and demonstrated a willingness to employ force, all in an attempt to overcome the perception of weakness that had characterized Carter's presidency.

Reagan succeeded in bolstering American self-confidence but his claims that the US had renewed its strength and overcome the limits imposed by Vietnam were largely illusory. Despite standing tall rhetorically, Reagan was still reluctant to employ the full power of the US to back up his strong words. For all the posturing of his foreign policy rhetoric, the Reagan administration only employed US military force twice and then in extremely low-risk, limited operations against Grenada and Libya. The only other major deployment of armed force was as part of the ill-fated peacekeeping operation in Lebanon. Otherwise the administration was only prepared to use force by proxy in Nicaragua, El Salvador and Afghanistan. Ronald Reagan was certainly an activist foreign policy president but his interventions were more constrained than his image would suggest. Reagan did also couch all his foreign policy in terms of American exceptionalism but, as with other presidents, the major determinants of his policies were strategic, economic and political. Despite his insistence that all his actions were taken in keeping with the values and principles on which the US was founded, policies such as the covert war in Nicaragua and his exchange of arms for hostages with Iran indicated that the reality of Reagan's foreign policy did not live up to the claims of his exceptionalist rhetoric.

George Bush admitted to having a problem with what he called the 'vision thing', but he, like his predecessors, utilized the language of American exceptionalism in his foreign policy. In Panama and the Persian Gulf War, Bush authorized the two largest uses of American military force since the Vietnam War. He appeared to be demonstrating the strength and resolve of the US not only with words but also with action. Each operation, however, was carefully planned to ensure that American engagement would be limited in objectives, length and costs. Despite Bush's declarations to the contrary, American action continued to be constrained by the experience of Vietnam. Although he couched his foreign policy in exceptionalist terms, strategic, political and economic interests were the main determinants of policy during his administration.

Bill Clinton, too, couched his foreign policy in terms of American exceptionalism. He repeatedly identified the US as 'the world's only indispensable nation' and advocated American leadership in world affairs. Clinton made 'democratic enlargement' one of the cornerstones of his foreign policy. The US would actively support and promote the spread of democracy and free market economies throughout the world. This policy, like so many before it, was underpinned by the idea that unique American values, principles and practices had universal applications. Clinton also used American military power more often than any of his post-Vietnam predecessors. Despite claims of a foreign policy based on moral values and principles, however, the administration had a mixed record on intervening in conflicts to prevent humanitarian disasters, acting only belatedly in Bosnia and refusing to intervene in Rwanda. Even in more successful operations such as in Kosovo there were strict limitations placed on how US forces would be used, thus indicating that the experience of Vietnam continued to constrain US foreign policy.

Several conclusions can be drawn from this analysis of post-Vietnam US administrations. It is clear that US foreign policy is usually driven by strategic, economic, political or other practical interests and only occasionally do notions of exceptionalism provide the key stimulus for policy. Even when the belief in the exceptional nature of the US and the perception of its special duties and responsibilities do dictate the course of policy, if strategic and political concerns arise they usually will take precedence over the initial moral imperatives. This was the case in, for example, Somalia where the original decision to commit troops based on the duty to prevent a humanitarian disaster was later overturned when political and strategic interests made the continued presence of US troops unacceptable despite the humanitarian concerns remaining salient. Only very rarely have political and economic interests been overturned by moral imperatives as, for example, when Ford insisted the US had a moral duty to admit Vietnamese refugees into the country following the fall of Saigon.

The fact that all post-Vietnam presidents have, nonetheless, couched their foreign policies in the language of American exceptionalism begs the question of whether the use of exceptionalist rhetoric is simply a manipulative tool designed to win public approval for policy. Do American policy makers reach their desired policy then cloak it in terms they believe will assure the greatest possible public and congressional support? Certainly officials within each post-Vietnam administration acknowledged that couching policy in terms of exceptionalism would have positive effects on public opinion, but to suggest that this is the only reason for such language being employed would be to ignore other evidence. Nowhere in the public or archive record analysed here, including declassified accounts of NSC meetings, is it even implied that once a particular course has been chosen it will then be packaged in exceptionalist terms. In fact, exceptionalist language is not only used in public explanations of policy but is also used by policy makers themselves behind closed doors. Presidents and their foreign policy advisers frequently use arguments couched in exceptionalist language during private meetings and in personal memoranda. They do so even when perfectly good practical arguments for policy options exist and they often phrase even strategic, economic or political justifications in exceptionalist terms. The belief in American exceptionalism, therefore, provides the framework for discourse in US foreign policy making even if it is rarely the main determining factor of policy itself.

Another common thread in each post-Vietnam president's rhetoric and, indeed, that of many of their predecessors, is the invocation of some golden past when the United States did live up to its exceptional values and principles. Ford, Carter and Reagan all advocated the need for the US to *return* to their basic principles and use them to overcome contemporary problems. Yet when was this golden era of exceptionalism? At no time in American history has there been a true consensus even about what it is that makes the US so special. Moreover, Americans have struggled throughout their history with societal problems concerning race, gender, ethnicity, religion, poverty, politics, economics or some other social factor. In foreign policy too, the determination of President Carter, for example, to 'restore the moral compass' to American foreign policy assumes that at some point the US did conduct its foreign affairs in accordance with moral principles. Such an assumption, though, is problematic. Even at times when the US claimed to be conducting policy based on moral reasoning, other more practical factors were usually major determinants of American action and the actual conduct of policy was rarely beyond moral reproach. The history of US foreign relations is riddled with instances, such as the Spanish–American War and the subsequent Philippine–American War, where moral imperatives were superseded by strategic and economic interests. Nevertheless, part of the belief in exceptionalism is for Americans to redefine, or even ignore, the problems of the past if they do not seem to fit with the conviction that the US has nothing but benign intentions towards the rest of the world.

American self-confidence has largely recovered from the doubts and concerns raised by the Vietnam period. The Reagan presidency in particular was successful in revitalizing American self-belief, mostly through a determined application of exceptionalist rhetoric. American self-belief remains vulnerable, however, not least because positive rhetoric and a strong foreign policy are often not enough to guarantee a general mood of confidence in the country. As Presidents Ford, Carter and Bush found to their detriment, the health of the American economy has often outweighed all other concerns during the post-Vietnam period. The failure of each of those presidents to secure a second period in office was due largely to their inability to overcome problems in the economy. Conversely, President Clinton's high approval rating, even when he was facing impeachment, can be attributed on the whole to his presiding over a booming American economy. While the use of exceptionalist rhetoric and the pursuit of a strong foreign policy will continue to buoy American self-confidence, the impact of the domestic agenda must not be forgotten.

American exceptionalism and the legacy of Vietnam

While American exceptionalism has continued to provide the framework for foreign policy discourse in the post-Vietnam era, the Vietnam syndrome has emerged as a major influence upon policy making concerning the use of force. Although there is no nationwide consensus on the lessons of the Vietnam War, a pattern has developed in policy making that has remained relatively consistent across post-Vietnam administrations. When an administration is confronted with a foreign policy crisis it will only authorize the use of force if just cause can be demonstrated, the objectives are clear and compelling, and victory can be achieved swiftly and with minimal casualties. These conditions for the use of force form the content of the Vietnam syndrome and have become increasingly institutionalized with each successive administration. They have been codified in the Weinberger Doctrine and the Powell Doctrine. Even though, as Colin Powell himself has argued, administration officials do not formally go down a list checking off the specific conditions of the Vietnam syndrome, it is clear from public and archival accounts of the decision making process that deliberate steps are taken to ensure these conditions are met before force is authorized. The planning and conduct of all major uses of force since the Vietnam War – the *Mayaguez* operation; the aborted Iranian hostage rescue; Lebanon; Grenada; Libya; Panama; the Gulf War; Somalia; Bosnia; Kosovo – have been directly influenced by the Vietnam syndrome. In conjunction with various economic, strategic, political and sometimes moral interests, the Vietnam syndrome has been a central factor determining how, when and where US administrations have threatened or used force since the end of the Vietnam War.

The Vietnam syndrome and the belief in American exceptionalism are not unconnected. The syndrome actually has the effect of reinforcing and perpetuating crucial elements of the belief in American exceptionalism. The Vietnam syndrome is designed specifically to ensure that the US does not commit itself to another conflict like the Vietnam War. A central purpose of the syndrome is to avoid situations in which the US could suffer another military defeat. By following policy based on the Vietnam syndrome, US policy makers can be reasonably assured of achieving victory and thus reinforcing the belief that the United States is an exceptional nation that always succeeds in its objectives. The Vietnam syndrome also prevents the US from undertaking military commitments involving long-term occupations of hostile foreign territory. This requirement perpetuates the exceptionalist notion that the US does not seek the conquest and subjugation of foreign nations. Finally, and most significantly, if it follows the Vietnam syndrome, the US will only use force in situations where Americans can perceive a just cause. As noted throughout this book, whenever a just cause is conceived by American policy makers, no matter whether its roots are economic, strategic, political, or otherwise, it will be couched in terms of American exceptionalism. By following what is perceived as a just cause, any administration will perpetuate the belief that the US only pursues policy which is consistent with its exceptional values and principles. In this sense, the belief in exceptionalism is self-perpetuating and the Vietnam syndrome does nothing to change that situation; in fact it reinforces it. The Vietnam syndrome developed in direct response to the perceived military, political and strategic costs of the Vietnam War. However, because the belief in American exceptionalism provides the framework for foreign policy discourse, the tenets of the Vietnam syndrome are couched in terms that embody certain notions of exceptionalism.

The Vietnam syndrome acts as a constraint on American action in world affairs. It places limits on the strength, resolve and capabilities of a nation which Americans regard as all-powerful and superior to other nations. In this sense the power of the Vietnam syndrome in American foreign policy making suggests that the US is no longer an exceptional nation but is just as limited in its action as any other country. Yet, paradoxically, the Vietnam syndrome actually acts as a guarantor of the continued acceptance of the belief in American exceptionalism. If the Vietnam syndrome is followed then the US can continue to be at least perceived as an exceptional nation because it will always win its wars, it will remain committed to its tradition of not conquering foreign land for territorial expansion, and it will only resort to force in the pursuit of just causes.

The nature of the Vietnam syndrome is a clear example, then, of how the belief in American exceptionalism frames the discourse of US foreign policy. This discourse affects policy in an almost unseen, unthinking manner. It appears automatic for American public officials to conceive their policies in terms that represent some notion of the exceptional nature of the US. They do so not simply because it will be politically advantageous but because those terms form a natural part of the language they use to understand the world around them.

This book has shown that in the post-Vietnam period, Americans have continued to conceive their foreign policy, debate its course, and criticize its faults in terms that consistently reflect some notion of the exceptional nature of the United States. Although practical considerations will remain central to US foreign policy making, the belief in American exceptionalism will persist as an essential element of the cultural and intellectual framework within which policy is made. As National Security Advisor Condoleeza Rice has argued: 'I am a realist. Power matters. But there can be no absence of moral content in American foreign policy and, furthermore, the American people wouldn't accept such an absence.'[2] This view is further reflected in the recent US National Security Strategy. According to the published strategy, it is 'based on a distinctly American internationalism that reflects the union of our values and our national interests'. The document sits firmly within the tradition of the missionary strand of the belief in American exceptionalism. It advocates American leadership in world affairs and argues that the 'aim of this strategy is to help make the world not just safer but better'.[3]

The Vietnam syndrome will also maintain its prevalence in foreign policy decision making for the foreseeable future, meaning that US military force will only be employed under relatively strict conditions. American presidents have become more willing to use force in order to achieve foreign policy objectives as the memory of Vietnam has become an ever more distant memory. However, the legacy of the war continues to shape where, when and how force will be applied. The main long-term consequences have been a general reluctance to commit ground forces to potentially difficult combat situations and an increasingly heavy reliance on massive air power to fight America's wars. There is a certain irony to this latter consequence since the massive air bombardments of Vietnam, Laos and Cambodia failed to prevent American objectives being defeated thirty years ago. It would be perfectly reasonable to conclude that one lesson of the Vietnam War is that large scale strategic bombing is ineffective. Yet this tactic has been employed more and more in the post-Vietnam era, as the analysis of US interventions in this book has shown. Meanwhile, the assumption that the Vietnam syndrome is sustained by public sensitivity towards American casualties appears increasingly misplaced. Recent evidence from the Clinton presidency suggests that elite perceptions of public sensitivity are overstated and that the Vietnam syndrome holds greater sway over policy makers than it does the public at large. Nonetheless, if a US military intervention should become long, bloody and, most importantly, inconclusive, then opponents will invoke the memory of Vietnam and call for the withdrawal of American forces as they did in Somalia.

George W. Bush and the war on terrorism

The discourse of American exceptionalism and the dynamics of the Vietnam syndrome have been conspicuously present in George W. Bush's campaign against international terrorism since September 11, 2001. As we have seen, Bush believes that the al-Qaeda network, led by Osama Bin Laden, launched its attacks against targets in the United States for the very fact that the US is an exceptional nation. Bush called the attacks 'acts of war' and declared his administration's determination to root out international terrorists and those who harbour them. Bush claimed that 'Freedom and democracy are under attack' and described the ensuing conflict in stark Manichean terms: 'This will be a monumental struggle of good versus evil. But good will prevail.'[4]

Bush made clear that although the attacks had taken the lives of civilians of many nationalities, and although the war on terrorism would be pursued by a multilateral coalition, the US was very much its leader. He told the Congress: 'We will rally the world to this cause.' He claimed that the world relied on American leadership: 'The advance of human freedom... now depends on us.' In words reminiscent of so many of his predecessors, Bush declared, 'this country will define our times, not be defined by them. As long as the United States of America is determined and strong, this will not be an age of terror; this will be an age of liberty, here and across the world.' It was not only American national interests, security and credibility that were at stake. According to Bush: 'We are in a fight for our principles.'[5]

On September 19, 2001, Bush claimed in a news conference that the 'mindset of war must change' in the campaign against terrorism. He argued that: 'It is a different type of battle. It's a different type of battlefield. It's a different type of war.'[6] Yet US military tactics in the first campaign of the war on terrorism bore a remarkable resemblance to those used in other recent conflicts such as Kosovo and the Gulf War. The war on terrorism began with operations to destroy al-Qaeda's bases in Afghanistan and to punish the country's leadership, the Taliban, for harbouring Bin Laden and his organization. The focus was on the use of massive air bombardments of Taliban and al-Qaeda targets. The use of ground troops was largely limited to sporadic and swift special forces operations and the deployment of US advisers and operatives with the Northern Alliance forces who had been fighting a long-term war against the Taliban. A *New York Times*/CBS News poll found that a majority of Americans were 'prepared to accept the deaths of several thousand American troops' in the war against terrorism. The attacks on New York and Washington would, the *New York Times* suggested, 'give any United States decision to dispatch ground forces a kind of moral imperative that American involvement in Vietnam lacked'.[7] Nonetheless, the Bush administration was hesitant to commit large numbers of US ground troops, preferring to leave the majority of the ground fighting to Northern Alliance forces. As the war progressed, the hunt for Bin Laden and other al-Qaeda leaders moved into the caves of the mountainous Tora Bora region. Even then, incentives such as weapons, clothing and money were given to Northern Alliance commanders to encourage them to search the cave networks rather than committing large numbers of US ground troops to fulfil this potentially dangerous mission.[8] Conservative columnist William Kristol criticized the Bush administration for trying to fight the war 'with half-measures' and Senator John McCain, a Vietnam veteran, also accused the president of making the Pentagon wage war 'with one hand tied behind its back'. Not all lawmakers seemed to agree, however, since they were still 'haunted by the ghosts of Vietnam' which *New York Times* reporters claimed had risen like 'an unwelcome specter from an unhappy past'. It seemed clear that while Secretary of Defense Donald Rumsfeld and other Pentagon spokespeople were 'careful not to exclude a substantial ground force' they were 'clearly holding out the hope that it will not be needed'.[9] It was clear that the fear of the war in Afghanistan turning into another quagmire like Vietnam had an important influence on the way American military force was employed.

When Bush claimed the war on terrorism was 'a fight for our principles' he also claimed that 'our first responsibility is to live by them'.[10] Yet the administration was often criticized for undermining those principles in the conduct of the war. The treatment of prisoners-of-war came under particular scrutiny. In November 2001, an estimated 230 al-Qaeda and Taliban prisoners were killed in bombing raids on the Qala-i-Jhangi fort during a siege following an attempted prisoner break-out. Amnesty International was among the organizations that questioned the 'proportionality of the response'.[11] In January 2002, the Bush administration began flying captured al-Qaeda and Taliban prisoners from Afghanistan to the US military base in Guantanamo Bay, Cuba, where they were held under conditions which drew scrutiny from the world's media and the International Red Cross. Prisoners were shackled, hooded, forced to shave their beards and heads, and kept in small cages exposed to the elements. The greatest criticisms were levelled at the administration's refusal to accord the captives rights as prisoners-of-war under the Geneva Conventions. They were instead characterized as 'unlawful combatants', a term not recognized in international law. It was argued by critics that through this denial of the basic human rights of prisoners the US would 'squander' the moral high ground it had occupied since September 11.[12]

From the outset, President Bush warned the American people that the war on terrorism might be long and arduous: 'You will be asked for your patience; for, the conflict will not be short. You will be asked for resolve; for, the conflict will not be easy. You will be asked for your strength, because the course to victory may be long.'[13] The unprecedented popularity of the president and his handling of the war seemed to indicate that the US was finally willing again to conduct military interventions other than those that are short, low-risk, and easily achieved. Nonetheless, as argued here, steps have been taken to meet the ongoing requirements of the Vietnam syndrome in this conflict. It is also possible, if not likely, that the war's popularity will begin to fade as it becomes more prolonged and success and progress less easy to measure. At the time of writing, Osama Bin Laden is still at large and al-Qaeda continues to perpetrate acts of terrorism throughout the world. With the Bush administration poised to take the fight to Iraq next, the potential quagmire that George W. Bush's father deliberately avoided may be entered into soon.

The war on terrorism shows that the formation and presentation of US foreign policy continues to be couched in exceptionalist terms. The belief in American exceptionalism still provides the framework for the discourse of US foreign policy making and conduct. The legacy of the Vietnam War, however, also still influences the way in which policy is conducted, particularly in the application of the use of force. While the US will attempt to 'fight freedom's fight' in order to 'lead the world toward the values that will bring lasting peace',[14] it will do so in ways that minimize the possibility that the country will become ensnared in another Vietnam that could further challenge the belief in American exceptionalism.

Notes

1   American Exceptionalism: An Introduction

1. George W. Bush, 'Statement by the President in His Address to the Nation, September 11, 2001', White House Office of the Press Secretary.
2. Bush's response to the attacks was particularly well received in the immediate aftermath of the events. A Gallup poll conducted on September 14–15, 2001 saw the president's approval rating jump 35 points to 86 per cent (the previous poll was conducted from September 7–10). This was the highest rallying effect on presidential approval in Gallup's polling history and the fourth highest approval rating ever measured for a president. One week after the attacks, following a nationwide address announcing a war on terrorism, Bush scored the highest ever rating for a president when his approval reached 90 per cent. See 'Attack on America: Review of Public Opinion', *Gallup News Service*, September 17, 2001; David W. Moore, 'Bush Job Approval Reflects Record "Rally" Effect', *Gallup News Service*, September 18, 2001; and Moore, 'Bush Job Approval Highest in Gallup History', *Gallup News Service*, September 24, 2001.
3. Alexis de Tocqueville, *Democracy in America*, trans. George Lawrence, ed. J. P. Mayer (New York: Harper Perennial, 1988); Jack P. Greene, *The Intellectual Construction of America: Exceptionalism and Identity from 1492 to 1800* (Chapel Hill, NC: University of North Carolina Press, 1993).
4. Benedict Anderson, *Imagined Communities: Reflections on the Origin and Spread of Nationalism*, revised edn (London: Verso, 1991).
5. Michael H. Hunt, *Ideology and US Foreign Policy* (New Haven, CT: Yale University Press, 1987) 14–15.
6. Daniel Bell, 'The End of American Exceptionalism', *The Public Interest* (Fall 1975), reprinted in Bell, *The Winding Passage: Essays and Sociological Journeys 1960–1980* (New York: Basic Books, 1980) 249, 270–1.
7. Bell, ' "American Exceptionalism" Revisited: The Role of Civil Society', *The Public Interest*, no. 95 (Spring 1989) 38–56.
8. Byron E. Shafer, ed., *Is America Different? A New Look at American Exceptionalism* (Oxford: Clarendon Press, 1991); emphasis in the original.
9. See, for example, Byron E. Shafer, ' "Exceptionalism" in American Politics?' *PS: Political Science & Politics*, vol. 22, no. 5 (September 1989) 588–94; Kim Voss, *The Making of American Exceptionalism: The Knights of Labor and Class Formation in the Nineteenth Century* (Ithaca, NY: Cornell University Press, 1993); Rick Halpern and Jonathan Morris, eds, *American Exceptionalism? US Working-Class Formation in an International Context* (Basingstoke: Macmillan – now Palgrave Macmillan, 1997); Richard Rose, 'How Exceptional is the American Political Economy?' *Political Science Quarterly*, vol. 104, no. 1 (Spring 1989) 91–115; Edward A. Tiryakian, 'American Religious Exceptionalism: A Reconsideration', *Annals of the American Academy of Political and Social Science*, vol. 527 (May 1993) 40–54; Sven H. Steinmo, 'American Exceptionalism Reconsidered: Culture or Institutions?' in Lawrence C. Dodd and Calvin Jillson, eds, *The Dynamics of American Politics: Approaches and Interpretations* (Boulder CO: Westview Press, 1994) 106–31; Andrei S. Markovits and Steven L.

Hellerman, *Offside: Soccer and American Exceptionalism* (Princeton, NJ: Princeton University Press, 2001).

10. Seymour Martin Lipset, *American Exceptionalism: A Double-Edged Sword* (New York: W. W. Norton, 1996).

11. Bell, ' "American Exceptionalism" Revisited', 41; emphasis in the original.

12. Joseph Lepgold and Timothy McKeown, 'Is American Foreign Policy Exceptional? An Empirical Analysis', *Political Science Quarterly*, vol. 110, no. 3 (Fall 1995).

13. Lepgold and McKeown, 'Is American Foreign Policy Exceptional?' 380–4.

14. Michael Kammen, 'The Problem of American Exceptionalism: A Reconsideration', *American Quarterly*, vol. 45, no. 1 (March 1993) 11.

15. Hunt, *Ideology*, ch. 1–2.

16. Roger S. Whitcomb, *The American Approach to Foreign Affairs: An Uncertain Tradition* (Westport, CT and London: Praeger, 1998) esp. ch. 1–2.

17. Ibid., 18–24.

18. H. W. Brands, *What America Owes the World: The Struggle for the Soul of Foreign Policy* (Cambridge: Cambridge University Press, 1998); see Preface for quotations.

19. John Fousek, *To Lead the Free World: American Nationalism and the Cultural Roots of the Cold War* (Chapel Hill, NC: University of North Carolina Press, 2000) 2–7.

20. Siobhán McEvoy-Levy, *American Exceptionalism and US Foreign Policy: Public Diplomacy at the End of the Cold War* (Basingstoke: Palgrave – now Palgrave Macmillan, 2001) 64–5, 143.

21. Hunt, *Ideology*, p. 16.

22. Anders Stephanson, *Manifest Destiny: American Expansion and the Empire of Right* (New York: Hill & Wang, 1995) xiv.

23. Hunt, *Ideology*; McEvoy-Levy, *American Exceptionalism*; John Dumbrell, *The Making of US Foreign Policy* (Manchester: Manchester University Press, 1990).

24. David Ryan, *US Foreign Policy in World History* (London: Routledge, 2000) 15.

25. Hans Kohn, *American Nationalism: An Interpretive Essay* (New York: Macmillan, 1957) 8–9.

26. Samuel P. Huntington, *American Politics: The Promise of Disharmony* (Cambridge, MA: Belknap Press, 1981) 13–30.

27. Abraham Lincoln, 'Speech at Chicago, Illinois. July 10, 1858', *The Collected Works of Abraham Lincoln, Volume II, 1848–1858*, ed. Roy P. Basler (New Brunswick, NJ: Rutgers University Press, 1953) 499–500.

28. Huntington, *American Politics*; Seymour Martin Lipset, 'American Exceptionalism Reaffirmed' in Shafer, ed., *Is America Different?* 7.

29. Eric Hobsbawm and Terence Ranger, eds, *The Invention of Tradition* (Cambridge: Cambridge University Press, 1983) 10–11.

30. Robert N. Bellah, 'Civil Religion in America', *Daedalus*, vol. 96, no. 1 (Winter 1967) 1–21.

31. Hobsbawm and Ranger, *Invention of Tradition*, 9.

32. Joyce Appleby, Lynn V. Hunt and Margaret C. Jacob, *Telling the Truth About History* (New York: W. W. Norton, 1994) 92.

33. Anthony D. Smith, *Myths and Memories of the Nation* (Oxford: Oxford University Press, 1999) 13.

34. Ryan, *US Foreign Policy*, 10.

35. Whitcomb, *American Approach*, 52.

36. Fousek, *Lead the Free World*, 5.

37. As noted above, H. W. Brands uses the terms 'exemplarist' and 'vindicationist' to describe the two main strands of exceptionalist belief; see Brands, *What America*

Owes the World. Similarly, Michael Hunt identifies two persistent 'visions' of American national greatness: 'the dominant vision equating the cause of liberty with the active pursuit of national greatness in world affairs and the dissenting one favoring a foreign policy of restraint as essential to perfecting liberty at home.' See Hunt, *Ideology*, 43. See also Trevor B. McCrisken, 'Exceptionalism' in Alexander DeConde, Richard Dean Burns, and Fredrik Logevall, eds, *Encyclopedia of American Foreign Policy*, 2nd edn (New York: Charles Scribner's Sons, 2001) vol. 2, 63–80.

38. See Stephanson, *Manifest Destiny*, 6–10.
39. John Winthrop, 'A Modell of Christian Charity', *Winthrop Papers*, vol. II, 1623–1630 (Massachusetts Historical Society, 1931) 294–5.
40. George Washington, 'First Inaugural Address in the City of New York, April 30, 1789', *Inaugural Addresses of the Presidents of the United States from George Washington 1789 to George Bush 1989* (Washington, DC: United States Government Printing Office, 1989) 2.
41. See Robert Booth Fowler and Allen D. Hertzke, *Religion and Politics in America: Faith, Culture, and Strategic Choices* (Boulder, CO: Westview Press, 1995) esp. ch. 1, 2 and 12.
42. Stephanson, *Manifest Destiny*, 7–8.
43. Thomas Paine, *Common Sense*, ed. Isaac Kramnick (Harmondsworth: Penguin, 1987) 91.
44. J. Hector St. John de Crèvecoeur, *Letters from an American Farmer and Sketches of Eighteenth-Century America*, ed. Albert E. Stone (Harmondsworth: Penguin, 1986) 70.
45. See Richard Hofstadter, *The American Political Tradition and the Men Who Made It* (New York: Alfred A. Knopf, 1948) ch. 1.
46. George Washington, 'Farewell Address, United States, September 17, 1796', *A Compilation of the Messages and Papers of the Presidents, 1789–1902*, ed., James D. Richardson (Washington, DC: Bureau of National Literature and Art, 1907) vol. I, 222.
47. Thomas Jefferson, 'First Inaugural Address at Washington, D.C., March 4, 1801', *Inaugural Addresses*, 15.
48. John Quincy Adams, 'Mr. Adams' Oration', *Niles' Weekly Register* (Baltimore) New series no. 21, vol. VIII: whole no. 515 (July 21, 1821) 331–2.
49. See Serge Ricard, 'The Exceptionalist Syndrome in US Continental and Overseas Expansionism', in David K. Adams and Cornelis A. van Minnen, eds, *Reflections on American Exceptionalism* (Keele: Keele University Press, 1994) 73.
50. Washington, 'Farewell Address', 222–3.
51. Jefferson, 'First Inaugural', 15.
52. Arthur M. Schlesinger, Jr., *The Cycles of American History* (Boston MA: Houghton Mifflin, 1986) 16.
53. Albert K. Weinberg, *Manifest Destiny: A Study of Nationalist Expansionism in American History* (Baltimore, MD: Johns Hopkins University Press, 1935; Chicago: Quadrangle, 1963) 8, 62.
54. Richard Hofstadter, 'Manifest Destiny and the Philippines', in *America in Crisis: Fourteen Crucial Episodes in American History*, ed. Daniel Aaron (New York, Alfred A. Knopf, 1952) 173–200.
55. Quoted in Robert L. Beisner, *Twelve Against Empire: The Anti-Imperialists, 1898–1900* (Chicago: University of Chicago Press, 1985) 81.
56. Woodrow Wilson, 'A Commencement Address, June 5, 1914', *The Papers of Woodrow Wilson*, ed. Arthur S. Link (Princeton, NJ: Princeton University Press, 1989) vol. 30, 146–8.

57. Quoted in Walter LaFeber, *The American Age: US Foreign Policy at Home and Abroad, 1750 to the Present*, 2nd edn (New York: W. W. Norton, 1994) 281.
58. Franklin D. Roosevelt, 'Address to the Congress on the State of the Union, January 6, 1942', *The Public Papers and Addresses of Franklin D. Roosevelt, 1942 Volume: Humanity on the Defensive* (New York: Harper, 1950) 35.
59. See Fousek, *To Lead the Free World*, 41–4.
60. For a fuller account of how the two main strands of exceptionalism developed throughout US history see McCrisken, 'Exceptionalism', 67–72.
61. See David W. Moore, 'Public Trust in Federal Government Remains High', *Gallup News Service*, January 8, 1999.
62. See Frank Newport, 'President-Elect Bush Faces Politically Divided Nation, But Relatively Few Americans Are Angry or Bitter Over Election Outcome', *Gallup News Service*, December 18, 2000.
63. See Michael Omi and Howard Winant, *Racial Formation in the United States: From the 1960s to the 1990s*, 2nd edn (New York & London: Routledge, 1994); Arthur M. Schlesinger, Jr., *The Disuniting of America: Reflections on a Multicultural Society*, revised and enlarged edition (New York: W. W. Norton, 1998); Adalberto Aguirre, Jr. and Jonathan H. Turner, *American Ethnicity: The Dynamics and Consequences of Discrimination*, 2nd edn (Boston: McGraw-Hill, 1998).
64. Winthrop, 'Modell of Christian Charity', 294–5.
65. Tocqueville, *Democracy in America*, 237, 256, 374, 569.
66. Ryan, *US Foreign Policy*, 9. Ryan also points out that 'Some experiences (slavery and slaughter) that were incompatible with the righteous image of the nation were basically written out of the sites of collective memory' (10–11).
67. Mort Rosenblaum, *Mission to Civilize: The French Way* (San Diego, CA: Harcourt Brace Jovanovich, 1986).
68. Kathryn Tidrick, *Empire and the English Character* (London: IB Tauris, 1990).
69. Alan Bullock, *Hitler: A Study in Tyranny*, revised edn (London: Odhams Books, 1964).
70. Quoted in Richard J. Ellis, ed., *Speaking to the People: The Rhetorical Presidency in Historical Perspective* (Amherst, MA: University of Massachusetts Press, 1998) 1.
71. Ryan, *US Foreign Policy*, 7.
72. Hunt, *Ideology*, 15.

2   The End of American Exceptionalism? The Cold War and Vietnam

1. Henry R. Luce, 'The American Century', Life, vol. 10, no. 7 (February 17, 1941) 61–5.
2. George H. Gallup, 'Foreign Affairs, October 21, 1945', *The Gallup Poll: Public Opinion 1935–1971, Volume One, 1935–1948* (New York: Random House, 1972) 534.
3. Dwight D. Eisenhower, 'First Inaugural Address, January 20, 1953', *Inaugural Addresses*, 260.
4. Fousek, *Lead the Free World*.
5. Stephanson, *Manifest Destiny*, 124.
6. Fousek, *Lead the Free World*, 45–6.
7. Harry S Truman, 'Address of the President of the United States – Greece, Turkey, and the Middle East (H. Doc. No. 171)', *Congressional Record*, 80th Cong., 1st Sess. (March 12, 1947) vol. 93, part 2, 1981.

8. X [George Kennan], 'The Sources of Soviet Conduct', *Foreign Affairs*, vol. 25, no. 4 (July 1947) 582.
9. Hunt, *Ideology*, 158.
10. 'NSC 68, April 7, 1950,' *Foreign Relations of the United States, 1950*, vol. 1 (Washington, DC: USGPO, 1977) 235–92.
11. Fousek, *Lead the Free World*, 130.
12. See Mary L. Dudziak, *Cold War Civil Rights* (Princeton, NJ: Princeton University Press, 2000).
13. Fousek, *Lead the Free World*, 148.
14. Michael E. Latham, *Modernization as Ideology: American Social Science and 'Nation-Building' in the Kennedy Era* (Chapel Hill, NC: University of North Carolina Press, 2000) 67, 101.
15. See Bruce Cumings, *The Origins of the Korean War, Volume II: The Roaring of the Cataract, 1947–1950* (Princeton, NJ: Princeton University Press, 1990).
16. Harry S Truman, 'Special Message to the Congress Reporting on the Situation in Korea, July 19, 1950', *Public Papers of the Presidents of the United States: Harry S. Truman, 1950* (Washington, DC: USGPO, 1965) 531–6. Hereafter, *Public Papers* with date.
17. Kennedy, 'Inaugural Address,' 1–3.
18. John F. Kennedy, 'Radio and Television Report to the American People on the Soviet Arms Build-up in Cuba, October 22, 1962', *Public Papers, 1962*, 809.
19. Lyndon B. Johnson, 'Address at Johns Hopkins University: "Peace Without Conquest." April 7, 1965', *Public Papers, 1965*, book 1, 394–8.
20. William S. Turley, *The Second Indochina War: A Short Political and Military History, 1954–1975* (New York: Mentor, 1987) 89, 201–3.
21. See, for example, Paul M. Kattenburg, *The Vietnam Trauma in American Foreign Policy, 1945–75* (New Brunswick, NJ: Transaction Books, 1982).
22. Alexander Kendrick, *The Wound Within: America in the Vietnam Years, 1945–1974* (Boston: Little, Brown, 1974) 4.
23. Stanley Karnow, *Vietnam: A History* (New York: Viking Press, 1983) 9.
24. Bell, 'End of American Exceptionalism'.
25. Quoted in Fred Halstead, *Out Now! A Participant's Account of the American Movement Against the Vietnam War* (New York: Monad Press, 1978) 41–2.
26. David W. Levy, *The Debate Over Vietnam*, 2nd edn (Baltimore, MD: Johns Hopkins University Press, 1995) 46.
27. For a full debate over the legal aspects of US intervention in Vietnam see Richard A. Falk, ed., *The Vietnam War and International Law*, 4 vols (Princeton, NJ: Princeton University Press, 1968–76).
28. US Congress, Senate, S. J. Res. 189, *Congressional Record*, 88th Cong., 2nd Sess. (August 5, 1964) vol. 110, part 14, 18133.
29. Loren Baritz, *Backfire: A History of How American Culture Led Us into Vietnam and Made Us Fight the Way We Did* (New York: Ballantine, 1985) 128–9; George C. Herring, *America's Longest War: The United States and Vietnam, 1950–1975*, 2nd edn (New York: Alfred A. Knopf, 1986) 119–23; and Neil Sheehan, *A Bright Shining Lie: John Paul Vann and America in Vietnam* (New York: Vintage Books, 1988) 379.
30. Quoted in LaFeber, *American Age*, 406.
31. The National Liberation Front was the communist-led political and military organization formed in 1959 to lead the insurgency in South Vietnam against the Saigon government.
32. Anthony A. D'Amato, Harvey L. Gould and Larry D. Woods, 'Bombardment of Non-Military Targets', in 'War Crimes and Vietnam: The "Nuremburg Defense"

and the Military Service Resister', *California Law Review*, vol. 57 (November 1969) reprinted in Falk, *The Vietnam War and International Law*, vol. 3, 433–43.

33. Todd Gitlin, *The Sixties: Years of Hope, Days of Rage* (New York: Bantam, 1989) 265.

34. Bill Moyers, 'What is Left of Conscience?' *Saturday Review*, February 13, 1971, reprinted in Steven Cohen, *Vietnam: Anthology and Guide to a Television History* (New York: Alfred A. Knopf, 1983) 379.

35. See Telford Taylor, *Nuremberg and Vietnam: An American Tragedy* (Chicago: Quadrangle, 1970).

36. Quoted in J. Justin Gustainis, *American Rhetoric and the Vietnam War* (Westport, CT: Praeger, 1993) 44.

37. Frances FitzGerald, *Fire in the Lake: The Vietnamese and the Americans in Vietnam* (New York: Atlantic-Little, 1972; Vintage Books, 1989) 455.

38. Quoted in Herring, *America's Longest War*, 187.

39. John E. Mueller, *War, Presidents, and Public Opinion* (New York: John Wiley, 1973) 54–7.

40. Karnow, *Vietnam*, 546–7.

41. Johnson, 'The President's Address to the Nation Announcing Steps to Limit the War in Vietnam and Reporting His Decision Not to Seek Reelection, March 31, 1968', *Public Papers, 1968*, book I, 476.

42. Karnow, *Vietnam*, 559; Herring, *America's Longest War*, 201–2.

43. Richard M. Nixon, 'Address to the Nation on the War in Vietnam, November 3, 1969', *Public Papers, 1969*, 902.

44. Quoted in Herring, *America's Longest War*, 223.

45. Nixon, 'Address to the Nation, November 3, 1969', 903.

46. Leslie H. Gelb and Richard K. Betts, *The Irony of Vietnam: The System Worked* (Washington, DC: Brookings Institution, 1979) 349–50.

47. Quoted in Sheehan, *Bright Shining Lie*, 739.

48. Herring, *America's Longest War*, 225–55; Karnow, *Vietnam*, 604–69.

49. Herring, *America's Longest War*, 255–6.

50. Ibid., 256.

51. Ibid.; Turley, *Second Indochina War*, 89.

52. Frank Snepp, *Decent Interval: The American Debacle in Vietnam and the Fall of Saigon* (New York: Random House, 1977).

53. Nixon, 'Address to the Nation, November 3, 1969', 909.

54. Ibid.

55. J. William Fulbright, *The Arrogance of Power* (New York: Vintage, 1966) 4–5, 20–1, 245–7, 254–6.

56. Robert E. Lane and Michael Lerner, 'Why Hard Hats Hate Hairs', *Psychology Today* (November 1970) 45, quoted in Gustainis, *American Rhetoric*, 110.

57. Gitlin, *The Sixties*, 107.

58. Quoted in Kenneth J. Heineman, *Campus Wars: The Peace Movement at American State Universities in the Vietnam Era* (New York: New York University Press, 1993) 89.

59. Ibid., 207.

60. Quoted in 'M-Day's Message to Nixon', *Time*, vol. 94, no. 17 (October 24, 1969) 17.

61. Daniel Yankelovich, 'A Crisis of Moral Legitimacy?' *Dissent* (Fall 1974) 526–7, 530–2.

62. 'The Tarnished Age', *New Republic*, vol. 171, no. 17 (October 26, 1974) 3.

63. Quoted in Halstead, *Out Now!* 360.

64. See Louis Fisher, *Presidential War Power* (Lawrence, KS: University Press of Kansas, 1995) ch. 6–9.

65. See, for example, Ole R. Holsti and James N. Rosenau, *American Leadership in World Affairs: Vietnam and the Breakdown of Consensus* (Boston: Allen & Unwin, 1984); Richard A. Melanson, *American Foreign Policy Since the Vietnam War: The Search for Consensus from Nixon to Clinton*, 2nd edn (Armonk, NY: M. E. Sharpe, 1996) ch. 1.
66. See, for example, Richard Nixon, *No More Vietnams* (London: W. H. Allen, 1986).

3   Gerald Ford and the Time for Healing

1. Gerald R. Ford, 'Remarks on Taking the Oath of Office. August 9, 1974', *Public Papers of the Presidents of the United States: Gerald R. Ford 1974*, 1. Hereafter *Public Papers* followed by the year.
2. Gerald R. Ford, *A Time to Heal: The Autobiography of Gerald R. Ford* (New York: Harper & Row, 1979) 124, 144.
3. Robert T. Hartmann, *Palace Politics: An Inside Account of the Ford Years* (New York: McGraw-Hill, 1980) 165.
4. Ford's approval rating was 71 per cent with 26 per cent of those polled holding 'no opinion'. See George H. Gallup, *The Gallup Poll: Public Opinion 1972–1977, Vol. One, 1972–75* (Wilmington, DE: Scholarly Resources Inc, 1978) 347.
5. Gallup, *Gallup Poll, 1972–75*, 347, 364.
6. Ford, 'Address Before a Joint Session of the Congress Reporting on the State of the Union, January 15, 1975', *Public Papers, 1975*, 44.
7. Ford, 'Address to a Joint Session of the Congress. August 12, 1974', *Public Papers, 1974*, 12.
8. Draft Presidential Address (NSC Portion), August 12, 1974, folder 8/12/74 Joint Session of Congress (1), box 171, Robert T. Hartmann Papers, Gerald R. Ford Library (hereafter GRFL).
9. Ford, 'Address at the Continental Congress of the Daughters of the American Revolution, April 15, 1975', *Public Papers, 1975*, 482.
10. Ford, 'State of the Union, 1975', 45–6.
11. Minutes, National Security Council Meeting, April 9, 1975 [declassified], box A6, folder NSC Meeting April 9, 1975 Minutes, Henry Kissinger & Brent Scowcroft Files 1974–77 Temporary Parallel File, GRFL; Ford, 'Special Message to the Congress Requesting Supplemental Assistance for the Republic of Vietnam and Cambodia, January 28, 1975', *Public Papers, 1975*, 119–23; Ford, 'Letter to the Speaker of the House Urging Action on Supplemental Military and Economic Assistance for Cambodia, February 25, 1975', *Public Papers, 1975*, 279–80; Ford, 'Address Before a Joint Session of the Congress Reporting on United States Foreign Policy, April 10, 1975', *Public Papers, 1975*, 459–73.
12. Greene, *Gerald R. Ford*, 117–19.
13. Ibid., 134–8; Memo, Bob Wolthuis to Jack Marsh, 'Congressional Reaction to Viet Nam and Cambodia', April 9, 1975, folder National Security: Wars – Cambodia (1), box 33, Presidential Handwriting File, GRFL.
14. Ford, 'Address at a Tulane University Convocation, April 23, 1975', *Public Papers, 1975*, 568–73.
15. Message, Ambassador Graham Martin to Dr. Henry A. Kissinger, April 19, 1975 [declassified], folder Backchannel Series, box A1, Henry Kissinger & Brent Scowcroft Files 1974–1977 Temporary Parallel File, GRFL.
16. Quoted in 'After the Fall: Reactions and Rationales,' *Time*, May 12, 1975, 23.
17. Roy Rowan and William Stewart, 'The Last Grim Goodbye', *Time*, May 12, 1975, 6–7.

18. Summary, 'Worldwide Treatment of Current Issues: Indochina and US Policy Reassessment,' no. 28, April 7, 1975, box 33, folder National Security Wars – Vietnam (1), Presidential Handwriting File, GRFL.

19. Memo, Ron Nessen to the President, 'UPI Story on Public Opposition to Vietnamese Refugees', May 3, 1975, folder National Security: Refugees – Vietnam, box 32, Presidential Handwriting File, GRFL.

20. 'A Cool and Wary Reception', *Time*, May 12, 1975, 24.

21. Ford, *Time to Heal*, 257.

22. Ford, 'Statement on House Action Rejecting Vietnam Humanitarian Assistance and Evacuation Legislation, May 1, 1975', *Public Papers, 1975*, 619.

23. Memo, Roland L. Elliott to the President, 'Support from Organizations on Refugee Resettlement', May 12, 1975, folder National Security: Refugees – Vietnam, box 32, GRFL.

24. Talking Points, Meeting with Republican Congressional Leaders, May 6, 1975, folder Republican Congressional Leaders 5/6/75, box 44, James M. Cannon Files, GRFL.

25. 'A Warmer Welcome for the Homeless', *Time*, May 19, 1975, 10.

26. Folder National Security: Refugees – Vietnam, box 32, Presidential Handwriting File, GRFL.

27. Memo, Jack Marsh to Donald Rumsfeld, 'Statement of Senator Mike Mansfield', April 7, 1975, folder 4/10/75 Foreign Policy Address (4), box 174, Robert T. Hartmann Papers, GRFL.

28. Ford, 'The President's News Conference of May 6, 1975', *Public Papers, 1975*, 641.

29. Ford, 'The President's News Conference of June 9, 1975', *Public Papers, 1975*, 791.

30. Chronology of Events of the Mayaguez Incident, folder Mayaguez Situation – GAO Report, box 25, Philip Buchen Files, GRFL; Greene, *Gerald R. Ford*, 143–9.

31. Memo, Jerry Jones to Dick Cheney, May 27, 1975, folder National Security: Wars – Cambodia (2), box 33, Presidential Handwriting File, GRFL.

32. Newspaper clipping, *Detroit Free Press*, May 15, 1975, folder National Security: Wars – Cambodia (2), box 33, Presidential Handwriting File, GRFL.

33. Memo, 'Latest Reaction to *Mayaguez* Incident', May 16, 1975, folder 'Mayaguez' S.S., box 2056, White House Central Files – Name File, GRFL; Memo, Roland L. Elliott to The President, May 16, 1975, folder National Security: Wars – Cambodia (1), box 33, Presidential Handwriting File, GRFL.

34. Telegram, Mr & Mrs L. Baltz, Naugatuck, Conn. and Mr & Mrs J. Howe, Granby, Conn. to President Gerald Ford, May 15, 1975, folder National Security: Wars – Cambodia (1), box 33, Presidential Handwriting File, GRFL.

35. Memo, Max Friedersdorf to The President, May 16, 1975, folder 'Mayaguez' Situation – General (2), box 25, Philip Buchen Files, GRFL.

36. Memo, US Congressman Carroll Hubbard to News Media, May 15, 1975, folder 'Mayaguez' – General, box 14, Ron Nessen Papers, GRFL.

37. Gallup, *Gallup Poll*, 1972–75, 519.

38. Gerald R. Ford, 'Letter to the Speaker of the House and the President Pro Tempore of the Senate Reporting on United States Actions in the Recovery of the SS *Mayaguez*, May 15, 1975', *Public Papers, 1975*, 669–70.

39. Minutes, National Security Council Meeting, Monday May 12, 1975, 12:05 pm to 12:50 pm [declassified], folder NSC Meeting May 12, 1975 Minutes, box A6, Henry Kissinger & Brent Scowcroft Files 1974–77 Temporary Parallel File, GRFL.

40. Ibid.

41. Minutes, National Security Council Meeting, Tuesday May 13, 1975, 10:40 pm to 12:25 am [declassified], folder NSC Meeting May 13, 1975 Minutes, box A6, Henry Kissinger & Brent Scowcroft Files 1974–77 Temporary Parallel File, GRFL.

42. Handwritten Notes, Untitled, Not Dated, folder Mayaguez Situation – General (1), box 25, Philip Buchen Files, GRFL; emphasis in the original.
43. Minutes, National Security Council Meeting, Tuesday May 13, 1975, 10:22 am to 11:17 am, [declassified], folder NSC Meeting May 13, 1975 Minutes, box A6, Henry Kissinger & Brent Scowcroft Files 1974–77 Temporary Parallel File, GRFL.
44. NSC Meeting, May 13, 1975, 10:40 pm to 12:25 am.
45. Transcript, News Conference at the White House with Ron Nessen, May 19, 1975, folder May 19, 1975 (No. 223), box 9, Ron Nessen Files, GRFL.
46. Memo, Friedersdorf to The President, May 16, 1975.
47. Minutes, NSC, May 12, 1975.
48. Minutes, NSC, May 14, 1975.
49. Ford, *Time to Heal*, 284.
50. *New York Times*, May 19, 1975, 29, quoted in Fisher, *Presidential War Power*, 138.
51. Gallup, *Gallup Poll*, 1972–75, 488.
52. Ford, 'Interview with European Journalists, May 23, 1975', *Public Papers, 1975*, 706.
53. Ford, *Time to Heal*, 284.
54. See, for example, Richard A. Melanson, *American Foreign Policy Since the Vietnam War: The Search for Consensus from Nixon to Clinton*, 2nd edn (Armonk, NY: M. E. Sharpe, 1996) which treats Ford's foreign policy perfunctorily in a chapter on the Nixon administration.
55. Hugh Sidey, 'Closing Out an Interim Chapter', *Time*, November 15, 1976, 28.
56. The speeches were published in a small volume entitled *The American Adventure: The Bicentennial Messages of Gerald R. Ford, July 1976*.
57. *Newsweek*, July 12, 1976, 3.
58. 'The Big 200th Bash', *Time*, 5 July 1976, 8.
59. Ford, *Time to Heal*, 393.
60. Greene, *Gerald R. Ford*, on Sinai Accords: 127–9, 153–5; on Soviet policy: 120–6
61. Ibid., ch. 7.

4 Jimmy Carter – Morality and the Crisis of Confidence

1. Jimmy Carter, 'Inaugural Address of President Jimmy Carter, January 20, 1977' *Public Papers of the Presidents of the United States: Jimmy Carter, 1977*, 1. Hereafter *Public Papers* followed by year.
2. Carter, 'Nomination Acceptance Speech at the 1976 Democratic National Convention', *Why Not The Best?* Presidential edition (Eastbourne: Kingsway, 1977) 185.
3. Carter, *Why Not The Best?* 11.
4. Zbigniew Brzezinski, *Power and Principle: Memoirs of the National Security Adviser, 1977–1981* (London: Weidenfeld & Nicolson, 1983) 81.
5. Carter, 'University of Notre Dame: Address at Commencement Exercises at the University, May 22, 1977', *Public Papers, 1977*, 957.
6. Carter, 'Charleston, South Carolina: Remarks at the 31st Annual Meeting of the Southern Legislative Conference, July 21, 1977', *Public Papers, 1977*, 1312.
7. Carter, 'Inaugural Address', 1–4.
8. Gaddis Smith, *Morality, Reason, and Power: American Diplomacy in the Carter Years* (New York: Hill & Wang, 1986) 35–40; Brzezinski, *Power and Principle*, 3–15, 36.
9. Smith, *Morality, Reason, and Power*, 40–1; Cyrus Vance, *Hard Choices: Critical Years in America's Foreign Policy* (New York: Simon & Schuster, 1983) 26–9.

10. Brzezinski, *Power and Principle*, 42–3.
11. Memo, Zbigniew Brzezinski to President Carter, April 18, 1977, folder Four Year Goals (4/77), box 23, Zbigniew Brzezinski Collection, Jimmy Carter Library (hereafter JCL).
12. Carter, 'Notre Dame Address', 955.
13. Ibid., 956.
14. Memo, Jerry Doolittle to Jim Fallows, forwarded to President Carter, May 20, 1977, folder 5/22/77 Notre Dame Speech (4), box 6, Staff Offices Speechwriters – Chron File, JCL.
15. Brzezinski, *Power and Principle*, 124.
16. Vance, *Hard Choices*, 29.
17. Carter, 'Notre Dame Address', 961.
18. Brzezinski, *Power and Principle*, 53; Carter, 'Notre Dame Address', 957.
19. Carter, 'Notre Dame Address', 962.
20. Carter, 'United States Foreign Policy: Remarks to the People of Other Nations on Assuming Office, January 20, 1977', *Public Papers, 1977*, 4.
21. Carter, 'Inaugural Address', 2.
22. Carter, 'SLC Remarks', 1311.
23. Presidential Directive/NSC-18: US National Strategy, August 24, 1977 [partially declassified], folder Presidential Directives, Vertical File, JCL.
24. Vance, *Hard Choices*, 23–7.
25. Carter, 'Notre Dame Address', 957.
26. Carter, 'Inaugural Address', 3.
27. Carter, 'Notre Dame Address', 957.
28. Presidential Directive/NSC-30: Human Rights, February 17, 1978 [declassified], folder Presidential Directives, box Vertical File, JCL. Hereafter PD-30.
29. Carter, 'European Newspaper Journalists Question-and-Answer Session, April 25, 1977', *Public Papers, 1977*, 782.
30. Carter, 'Yazoo City, Mississippi: Remarks and a Question-and-Answer Session at a Public Meeting, July 21, 1977', *Public Papers, 1977*, 1328.
31. Ibid., 1324.
32. Carter, 'Interview with the President: Remarks and a Question-and-Answer Session with a Group of Publishers, Editors, and Broadcasters, May 20, 1977', *Public Papers, 1977*, 947.
33. Presidential Review Memorandum/NSC-28: Human Rights, July 7, 1977 [declassified], folder Presidential Review Memoranda (2), Vertical File, JCL. Hereafter PRM 28.
34. Brzezinski, *Power and Principle*, 124–7.
35. PD-30.
36. Ibid.
37. Vance, *Hard Choices*, 33.
38. Carter, 'Notre Dame Address', 958.
39. PRM 28, 12–13.
40. Ibid., 4.
41. Carter, 'The President's News Conference of December 15, 1977', *Public Papers, 1977*, 2115.
42. PRM 28, 15.
43. Cited in Carter, *Keeping Faith*, 146.
44. Carter, 'United Nations: Address Before the General Assembly, March 17, 1977', *Public Papers, 1977*, 449.

45. Carter, *Keeping Faith*, 149.
46. PRM 28, 7; emphasis in original.
47. Carter, 'Notre Dame Address', 958.
48. Carter, 'Interview July 15, 1977', 1275.
49. David P. Forsythe, *Human Rights and US Foreign Policy: Congress Reconsidered* (Gainesville, FL: University of Florida Press, 1988) 61.
50. Ibid., 77.
51. Dumbrell, *Carter*, 193.
52. Jeane K. Kirkpatrick, 'Dictatorships and Double Standards', *Commentary*, no. 68 (November 1979) 34–45.
53. Joshua Muravchik, *The Uncertain Crusade: Jimmy Carter and the Dilemmas of Human Rights Policy* (Lanham, MD: Hamilton Press, 1986) 215.
54. Dumbrell, *Carter*, 186–7.
55. Memo, Hamilton Jordan to President Carter, June 1977 [declassified], folder Foreign Policy/Domestic Politics Memo, HJ Memo, 6/77, box 34, Chief of Staff Hamilton Jordan's Files, JCL.
56. Ibid.
57. Carter, *Why Not The Best?* 143–4.
58. Ibid., 135, 159.
59. Vance, *Hard Choices*, 33.
60. Interview with Hendrick Hertzberg (including Christopher Matthews, Achsah Nesmith, Gordon Stewart), Miller Center Interviews, Carter Presidency Project, vol. VIII, December 3–4, 1981, 20, JCL.
61. Brzezinski, *Power and Principle*, 49.
62. Ibid., 9, 23, 48–9.
63. Interview with Zbigniew Brzezinski, Madeleine Albright, Leslie Denend, and William Odom, Miller Center Interviews, Carter Presidency Project, vol. XV, February 18, 1982, 61, JCL.
64. Ibid.; Brzezinski, *Power and Principle*, 49.
65. Vance, *Hard Choices*, 29.
66. Carter, *Keeping Faith*, 143.
67. Privately administration officials referred to the 1903 treaty as one of the 'sins of our colonialist past' but were careful not to express this opinion publicly as it was realized that taking 'an apologetic and self-lacerating attitude' would scupper all chances for ratification. See Letter, Jim Fallows to Harlan J. Strauss, September 19, 1977, folder Panama Canal Treaty [9/16/77-11/4/77] [CF, O/A 616], box 8, Speechwriters – Fallows files, JCL.
68. Carter, *Keeping Faith*, 156.
69. Memo, Jerry Doolittle to Joe Aragon and Landon Butler, August 22, 1977, folder Panama Canal Treaty (4/14/77-8/30/77) [CF, O/A 616], box 8, Staff Offices Speechwriters – Fallows, JCL.
70. Carter, *Keeping Faith*, 152–85.
71. Quoted in Garry Wills, *Reagan's America* (New York: Penguin, 1988) 390.
72. See Memo, Hodding Carter III to Joseph Aragon, Working Paper on Panama/Public and Press Outreach Strategy, June 17, 1977, folder Panama Canal Treaty 6-7/77, box 36, Chief of Staff Hamilton Jordan files, JCL; Survey Report, An Analysis of Public Attitudes Toward the Panama Canal Treaties, Cambridge Survey Research for the Democratic National Committee, October 1977, folder Panama Canal Treaty, 10, 11, 12/77 (1), box 36, Chief of Staff Hamilton Jordan files, JCL.

73. See Summary, Poll Results on the Panama Canal Treaties, folder Panama Canal Treaties 1977 [CF, O/A 413] (3), box 50, Chief of Staff Hamilton Jordan files, JCL.
74. Carter, *Keeping Faith*, 184; Vance, *Hard Choices*, 156–7.
75. Carter, *Keeping Faith*, 184.
76. Carter, 'Panama Canal Treaties: Remarks at the Signing Ceremony at the Pan American Union Building, September 7, 1977', *Public Papers, 1977*, book II, 1543.
77. See Dumbrell, *Carter*, 150–61; Smith, *Morality, Reason, and Power*, Ch. 5; Gaddis Smith, *The Last Years of the Monroe Doctrine, 1945–1993* (New York: Hill & Wang, 1994) ch. 7.
78. See Carter, *Keeping Faith*, 186–211; Brzezinski, *Power and Principle*, 196–233; Vance, *Hard Choices*, 75–83, 113–19.
79. Quoted in Smith, *Morality, Reason, and Power*, 94.
80. Quoted ibid., 97.
81. Brzezinski, *Power and Principle*, 409–13.
82. Quoted in Elizabeth Becker, *When the War was Over: The Voices of Cambodia's Revolution and its People* (New York: Touchstone, 1987) 440. See also Christopher Brady, *United States Foreign Policy Towards Cambodia, 1977–92* (Basingstoke: Macmillan – now Palgrave Macmillan, 1999) ch. 1.
83. See Carter, *Keeping Faith*, 267–429; Brzezinski, *Power and Principle*, 83–122, 234–88; Vance, *Hard Choices*, 159–255.
84. Carter, *Keeping Faith*, 277.
85. Smith, *Morality, Reason and Power*, 9, 157–68.
86. Memo, Patrick H. Caddell to the President, Journalists Meeting, July 12, 1979, folder 7/15/79 Address to the Nation – Energy/Crisis of Confidence (2), box 50, Speechwriters Chron File, JCL. This memorandum contains a summary of Caddell's earlier report.
87. Memo, Caddell to the President, July 12, 1979.
88. Memo, Anthony Lake to James Fallows, President's Annapolis commencement speech, Attachment I to Memo, Jim Fallows to the President, Naval Academy Speech, May 23, 1978, folder 6/7/78 Naval Academy Speech (1), box 26, Speechwriters Chron File, JCL; emphasis added.
89. Memo, Jerry Doolittle and Rick Hertzberg to the President, Suggested Outline for the Annapolis Speech, June 2, 1978, folder 6/7/78 Naval Academy Speech (2), box 27, Speechwriters Chron File, JCL; Carter, 'United States Naval Academy: Address at the Commencement Exercises, June 7, 1978', *Public Papers, 1978*, 1052–7.
90. See Carter, *Keeping Faith*, 91–124.
91. Memo, Achsah Nesmith, Walter Shapiro and Gordon Stewart to Jerry Rafshoon and Rick Hertzberg, Energy Speech, June 29, 1979, folder 7/15/79 Proposed Remarks on Energy (2), box 50, Speechwriters Chron File, JCL; underline in the original.
92. Kenneth E. Morris, *Jimmy Carter: American Moralist* (Athens, GA and London: University of Georgia Press, 1996) 1.
93. Carter, 'Energy and National Goals: Address to the Nation, July 15, 1979', *Public Papers, 1979*, book II, 1236–8.
94. Memo, Jerry Rafshoon to the President, July 10, 1979, folder 7/15/79 Address, box 50, Speechwriters Files, JCL.
95. Carter, 'Energy and National Goals', 1238–41.
96. 'Carter was Speechless', *Time*, July 16, 1979, 8–11.
97. 'Carter at the Crossroads', *Time*, July 23, 1979, 29.
98. Morris, *Carter*, 6–7.

99. Quoted ibid., 261–2.
100. 'Ennui the People', *New Republic*, August 4 and 11, 1979, 5–10.
101. Ken Bode, 'It's Over for Jimmy', *New Republic*, August 4 and 11, 1979, 15–16.
102. Morris, *Carter*, 6.
103. 'Carter at the Crossroads', 24.
104. Quoted in Bode, 'It's Over for Jimmy', 15.
105. See Brzezinski, *Power and Principle*, 401 ff.
106. Carter, 'Philadelphia, Pennsylvania: Address Before the World Affairs Council of Philadelphia, May 9, 1980', *Public Papers, 1980–81*, 868.
107. Carter, 'Berlin, Federal Republic of Germany: Question-and-Answer Session at a Town Meeting, July 15, 1978', *Public Papers, 1978*, 1303.
108. Melanson, *American Foreign Policy*, 111.
109. Brzezinski, *Power and Principle*, 183–4.
110. Ibid., 44.
111. Carter, 'United States Defense Policy: Remarks to Members of the Business Council, December 12, 1979', *Public Papers, 1979*, 2233.
112. 'US Attitudes: Unity and Strength', *Time*, January 7, 1980, 18.
113. 'Flip-Flops and Zigzags', *Time*, March 17, 1980, 14–15.
114. For accounts of the decision making leading to the rescue mission and its implementation see Carter, *Keeping Faith*, 501–22; Brzezinski, *Power and Principle*, 477–500; Vance, *Hard Choices*, 408–13.
115. Brzezinski, *Power and Principle*, 480, 496.
116. Carter, *Keeping Faith*, 507.
117. Ibid., 461.
118. Carter, 'Rescue Attempt for American Hostages in Iran: Address to the Nation, April 25, 1980', *Public Papers, 1980–81*, 772–3.
119. Carter, 'Rescue Attempt for American Hostages in Iran: Letter to the Speaker of the House and the President Pro Tempore of the Senate Reporting on the Operation, April 26, 1980', *Public Papers, 1980–81*, 777–9.
120. Carter, 'Rescue Attempt Address to the Nation', 772.
121. Brzezinski, *Power and Principle*, 494–5.
122. Carter, *Keeping Faith*, 507.
123. Transcript, 'ABC News Issues and Answers, Sunday April 27, 1980', folder Hostages in US Embassy in Iran, 1980, No. 2 [CF, O/A 749] (2), box 62, Staff Offices Press Powell, JCL.
124. Memo, White House Comments Office Totals, April 25, 1980, folder Hostages in US Embassy in Iran, 1980, No. 2 [CF, O/A 749] (3), box 62, Staff Offices Press Powell, JCL.
125. George H. Gallup, *The Gallup Poll: Public Opinion 1980* (Wilmington, DE: Scholarly Resources, Inc., 1981) 102.
126. See Memo, Frank Moore to the President, April 25, 1980, folder 4/26/80, box 1833, Presidential Handwriting File, JCL.
127. 'Debacle in the Desert', *Time*, May 5, 1980, 12.
128. Gallup, *The Gallup Poll: Public Opinion 1980*, 158.
129. Minutes, Cabinet Meeting, January 7, 1980, folder Cabinet Minutes 1980, box 18, Plains File, JCL; Carter, 'Situation in Iran and Soviet Invasion of Afghanistan: Remarks at a White House Briefing for Members of Congress, January 8, 1980', *Public Papers, 1980–81*, 40.
130. Robert O. Freedman, *Moscow and the Middle East: Soviet Policy since the Invasion of Afghanistan* (Cambridge: Cambridge University Press, 1991) 71–4; M. Hassan

Kakar, *Afghanistan: The Soviet Invasion and the Afghan Response, 1979–1982* (Berkeley, CA: University of California Press, 1995) 46–50; Sarah E. Mendelson, *Changing Course: Ideas, Politics, and the Soviet Withdrawal from Afghanistan* (Princeton, NJ: Princeton University Press, 1998) 41–64.

131. Carter, 'The State of the Union: Address Delivered Before a Joint Session of the Congress, January 23, 1980', *Public Papers, 1980–81*, 197.

132. See Carter, 'Soviet Invasion of Afghanistan: Address to the Nation, January 4, 1980', *Public Papers, 1980–81*, book I, 21–4; Carter, *Keeping Faith*, 471–3, 479–83, 486–9; Brzezinski, *Power and Principle*, 426–69; Vance, *Hard Choices*, 384–97.

133. Carter, *Keeping Faith*, 568. Gary Sick has controversially argued that a secret deal was struck between the Iranians and the Reagan campaign to delay the hostages' release until after the presidential election. See Gary Sick, *October Surprise: America's Hostages in Iran and the Election of Ronald Reagan* (New York: Times Books, 1991).

134. Carter, 'Aliquippa, Pennsylvania: Remarks and a Question-and-Answer Session at a Town Meeting, September 23, 1978', *Public Papers, 1978*, 1614–15.

135. Ibid., 1615.

136. John Dumbrell, *American Foreign Policy: Carter to Clinton* (Basingstoke: Macmillan – now Palgrave Macmillan, 1997) 52.

137. Morris, *Carter*, 287.

5 Ronald Reagan – 'America is Back'

1. Lou Cannon, *President Reagan: The Role of a Lifetime* (New York: Touchstone, 1991) 793.

2. Ronald Reagan, 'Remarks at a Republican Rally, Costa Mesa, California, November 3, 1986', *Public Papers of the Presidents of the United States: Ronald Reagan, 1986*. Hereafter *Public Papers* followed by year.

3. Wills, *Reagan's America*, 127–32, 137–48.

4. Cannon, *Reagan*, 486–90; Wills, *Reagan's America*, 199–201.

5. Reagan, 'Remarks at the First Annual Commemoration of the Days of Remembrance of Victims of the Holocaust, April 30, 1981', *Public Papers, 1981*, 396–7.

6. Reagan, 'Remarks at a Ceremony Commemorating the 40th Anniversary of the Voice of America, February 24, 1982', *Public Papers, 1982*, 217.

7. See Wills, *Reagan's America*, 374–84.

8. Ibid., 383–4.

9. Quoted in Cannon, *Reagan*, 109n; Wills, *Reagan's America*, 456.

10. Wills, *Reagan's America*, 236.

11. Reagan, 'Inaugural Address, January 20, 1981', *Public Papers, 1981*, 1–4.

12. Reagan, 'Remarks at the Conservative Political Action Conference Dinner, March 20, 1981', *Public Papers, 1981*, 278.

13. Carter, 'Energy and National Goals', 1241.

14. Reagan, 'Address at Commencement Exercises at the United States Military Academy, May 27, 1981', *Public Papers, 1981*, 464.

15. Reagan, 'Address Before a Joint Session of the Congress Reporting on the State of the Union, January 26, 1982', *Public Papers, 1982*, 72–9.

16. Reagan, 'Remarks at a Mount Vernon, Virginia, Ceremony Commemorating the 250th Anniversary of the Birth of George Washington, February 22, 1982', *Public Papers, 1982*, 200.

17. Reagan, 'Address to the Nation on the Economy, February 5, 1981', *Public Papers, 1981*, 83.
18. Talking Points, Breakfast with Presidential Appointees, March 30, 1981, folder #043369, Office of the President: Presidential Briefing Papers (1981–1984) files, Ronald Reagan Library (hereafter RRL).
19. See Cannon, *Reagan*, esp. ch. 6; Wills, *Reagan's America*, esp. ch. 30 and 36.
20. Reagan, 'Remarks at the Welcoming Ceremony for the Freed American Hostages, January 27, 1981', *Public Papers, 1981*, 43.
21. Reagan, 'Address to the Nation on Strategic Arms Reduction and Nuclear Deterrence, November 22, 1982', *Public Papers, 1982*, 1510.
22. Reagan, 'Address to the Nation on the Program for Economic Recovery, September 24, 1981', *Public Papers, 1981*, 836; Reagan, 'Remarks at the Bicentennial Observance of the Battle of Yorktown in Virginia, October 19, 1981', *Public Papers, 1981*, 970.
23. Reagan, 'Remarks at a Luncheon of the World Affairs Council of Philadelphia in Philadelphia, Pennsylvania, October 15, 1981', *Public Papers, 1981*, 938.
24. Reagan, 'Remarks at the Annual Convention of the National League of Cities in Los Angeles, California, November 29, 1982', *Public Papers, 1982*, 1521.
25. Reagan, 'Inaugural Address, 1981', 3.
26. Reagan, 'Voice of America Remarks', 217.
27. Memo, Henry R. Nau to Allen Lenz, December 3, 1981, folder SP 230-82 044142 [2 of 2], box SP 230 Begin – SP 230-82 057187, White House Office of Records Management (WHORM) Subject File SP (Speeches), RRL.
28. Reagan, 'Remarks in New York City Before the United Nations General Assembly Special Session Devoted to Disarmament, June 17, 1982', *Public Papers, 1982*, 785.
29. Handwritten Letter, President Reagan to President Brezhnev, April 24, 1981 [declassified], folder Declassified Head of State (USSR), RRL.
30. Reagan, 'Remarks at the Conservative Political Action Conference Dinner, February 18, 1983', *Public Papers, 1983*, 256.
31. Reagan, 'Remarks at a Spirit of America Rally in Atlanta, Georgia, January 26, 1984', *Public Papers, 1984*, 101.
32. Reagan, 'Remarks at the Annual Washington Conference of the American Legion, February 22, 1983', *Public Papers, 1983*, 264–71.
33. Reagan, 'The President's News Conference, June 16, 1981', *Public Papers, 1981*, 520–1.
34. See Alexander M. Haig, Jr., *Caveat: Realism, Reagan, and Foreign Policy* (London: Weidenfeld & Nicolson, 1984).
35. Indeed, immediately following the assassination attempt against Reagan on March 30, 1981, a clearly flustered Haig famously misinterpreted the constitutional provisions for presidential succession. He declared to the bemused White House press corps 'I am in control here' while the President was in surgery and Vice President George Bush was returning by air from Texas. Cannon, *Reagan*, 198–9.
36. Reagan, *American Life*, 254.
37. Cannon, *Reagan*, 189–90.
38. Ibid., 404.
39. Haig, *Caveat*, 85. Although Reagan did not give a major foreign policy speech during his first year in office, his Secretaries of State and Defense did, most notably Alexander Haig, 'Address by the Secretary of State (Haig) Before the American Society of Newspaper Editors, Washington, April 24, 1981', and Caspar

Weinberger, 'Address by the Secretary of Defense (Weinberger) at the United Press International Luncheon of the American Newspaper Publishers Association Meeting, Chicago, May 5, 1981', *American Foreign Policy Current Documents 1981* (Washington, DC: Department of State, 1984) 35–42.

40. Reagan, 'Address to Members of the British Parliament, June 8, 1982', *Public Papers, 1982*, 742–8.

41. Ibid., 748.

42. Reagan, 'Address before the Bundestag in Bonn, Federal Republic of Germany, June 9, 1982', *Public Papers, 1982*, 754–9.

43. Reagan, 'Address Before a Joint Session of the Congress on the State of the Union, January 25, 1983', *Public Papers, 1983*, 108.

44. Reagan, 'American Legion', 270.

45. Reagan, 'Remarks at a Dinner Marking the 10th Anniversary of the Heritage Foundation, October 3, 1983', *Public Papers, 1983*, 1407–8.

46. Reagan, 'Remarks to Members of the National Press Club on Arms Reductions and Nuclear Weapons, November 18, 1981', *Public Papers, 1981*, 1062–7.

47. See Haig, *Caveat*, 26–7, 87; Caspar Weinberger, *Fighting for Peace: Seven Critical Years in the Pentagon* (London: Michael Joseph, 1990) 25.

48. Quoted in Cannon, *Reagan*, 162–3.

49. Frances FitzGerald, *Way Out There in the Blue: Reagan, Star Wars and the End of the Cold War* (New York: Simon & Schuster, 2000) 330–1.

50. Cannon, *Reagan*, 163.

51. Reagan, 'Remarks and a Question-and-Answer Session with Reporters on the Announcement of the United States Strategic Weapons Program, October 2, 1981', *Public Papers, 1981*, 878–80.

52. Dumbrell, *American Foreign Policy*, 64.

53. Quoted in Memo, Charles Z. Wick to President Reagan, 'Inflammatory Soviet Statements About the President and US Policy', March 21, 1984, folder Speeches SP 729 Address to National Association of Evangelicals 3/8/83 (3 of 3), box SP 729-SP 781, WHORM Subject File SP (Speeches), RRL.

54. Reagan, 'Remarks and a Question-and-Answer Session at a Working Luncheon with Out-of-Town Editors, October 16, 1981', *Public Papers, 1981*, 956–7.

55. Reagan, 'The President's News Conference, November 10, 1981', *Public Papers, 1981*, 1033.

56. Reagan, 'National Press Club', 1064–7; see also Letter, President Reagan to Leonid Brezhnev, November 17, 1981 [declassified], folder Declassified Head of State (USSR), RRL.

57. Robert Jay Lifton and Richard Falk, *Indefensible Weapons: The Political and Psychological Case Against Nuclearism* (New York: Basic Books, 1982).

58. Reagan, *American Life*, 258, 547.

59. For example: Reagan, 'Address Before a Joint Session of Congress on the State of the Union, January 25, 1984', *Public Papers, 1984*, 93.

60. Reagan, 'The President's News Conference, March 31, 1982', *Public Papers, 1982*, 398; Reagan, 'Radio Address to the Nation on Arms Control and Reduction, July 16, 1983', *Public Papers, 1983*, 1042.

61. Reagan, *American Life*, 550.

62. Mikhail Gorbachev, *Perestroika: New Thinking for Our Country and the World* (New York: Harper & Row, 1987) 243.

63. Handwritten Letter, President Reagan to Secretary General Gorbachev, November 28, 1985 [declassified], folder Declassified Head of State (USSR), RRL.

64. See Peter Schweizer, *Victory: The Reagan Administration's Secret Strategy that Hastened the Collapse of the Soviet Union* (New York: Atlantic Monthly Press, 1993).
65. Raymond L. Garthoff, *The Great Transition: American–Soviet Relations and the End of the Cold War* (Washington, DC: Brookings Institution, 1994) 764–5.
66. Richard Ned Lebow and Janice Gross Stein, *We All Lost the Cold War* (Princeton, NJ: Princeton University Press, 1994) 370.
67. Reagan, 'The President's News Conference, January 29, 1981', *Public Papers, 1981*, 57.
68. Reagan, 'Remarks at the Annual Convention of the National Association of Evangelicals in Orlando, Florida, March 8, 1983', *Public Papers, 1983*, 363–4.
69. Ibid., 364.
70. Reagan, 'Interview With Henry Brandon of the London Sunday Times and News Service on Domestic and Foreign Policy Issues, March 18, 1983', *Public Papers, 1983*, 416.
71. Reagan, 'Question-and-Answer Session with Reporters on Domestic and Foreign Policy Issues, March 29, 1983', *Public Papers, 1983*, 464.
72. Reagan, 'Radio Address to the Nation on American International Broadcasting, September 10, 1983', *Public Papers, 1983*, 1250.
73. Reagan, 'Heritage Foundation', 1407.
74. Reagan, 'Interview with Gary Clifford and Patricia Ryan of People Magazine, December 6, 1983', *Public Papers, 1983*, 1714.
75. Reagan, 'Address to the Nation and Other Countries on United States–Soviet Relations, January 16, 1984', *Public Papers, 1984*, 40–3.
76. Cannon, *Reagan*, 507–10.
77. Beth A. Fischer, *The Reagan Reversal: Foreign Policy and the End of the Cold War* (Columbia, MO: University of Missouri Press, 1997).
78. Reagan, 'Interview with Lou Cannon, David Hoffman, and Juan Williams of the Washington Post on Foreign and Domestic Issues, January 16, 1984', *Public Papers, 1984*, 63–4.
79. Memo, Tyrus W. Cobb to Robert C. McFarlane, January 18, 1984, folder SP833 (Soviet/US Relations, WH 1/16/84) 200000–204999, box SP833-SP891, WHORM Subject File SP (Speeches), RRL.
80. Reagan, 'Address at Commencement Exercises at the University of Notre Dame, May 17, 1981', *Public Papers, 1981*, 434.
81. Reagan, 'Eureka College, 1982', 582.
82. Reagan, 'Address to British Parliament', 744.
83. Reagan, 'First Inaugural Address', 4.
84. Reagan, 'Proclamation 4841 – National Day of Recognition for Veterans of the Vietnam Era, April 23, 1981', *Public Papers, 1981*, 381.
85. See for example: Reagan, 'Remarks at a Ceremony Commemorating the Initiation of the Vietnam Leadership Program, November 10, 1981', *Public Papers, 1981*, 1028.
86. Reagan, 'Remarks on Presenting the Presidential Citizens Medal to Raymond Weeks at a Veterans Day Ceremony, November 11, 1982', *Public Papers, 1982*, 1445.
87. Quoted in Arnold R. Isaacs, *Vietnam Shadows: The War, Its Ghosts, and Its Legacy* (Baltimore, MD: Johns Hopkins University Press, 1997) 49.
88. Ibid.
89. Reagan, 'First Inaugural Address', 3.
90. Reagan, 'State of the Union 1984', 92.

91. Reagan, 'Conservative Political Action Conference, 1983', 256.
92. Haig, *Caveat*, 27.
93. Haig, 'Newspaper Editors' Address, 1981', 35.
94. Haig, *Caveat*, 47.
95. Ibid., 125.
96. Colin L. Powell with Joseph E. Persico, *My American Journey* (New York: Random House, 1995) 207–8.
97. Weinberger, *Fighting for Peace*, 6, 22.
98. Shultz, *Turmoil and Triumph*, 650.
99. Ibid., 106, 294, 648–9.
100. Powell, *American Journey*, 302–3.
101. Caspar W. Weinberger, *Fighting for Peace: Seven Critical Years in the Pentagon* (New York: Warner Books, 1990) 441–2. NB: This is the US edition of Weinberger's memoirs, which includes an appendix on the Weinberger Doctrine not included in the British edition cited elsewhere in this chapter.
102. Powell, *American Journey*, 303.
103. Shultz, *Turmoil and Triumph*, 649–51.
104. Quoted ibid., 651.
105. Smith, *Monroe Doctrine*, 152–60.
106. Walter LaFeber, *Inevitable Revolutions: The United States in Central America*, 2nd edn (New York: W. W. Norton, 1993) 237–8, 282–3, 292–4, 305–7; LaFeber, *American Age*, 720–1.
107. Quoted in Robert Dallek, *Ronald Reagan: The Politics of Symbolism*, new edn (Cambridge, MA: Harvard University Press, 1999) 166.
108. Smith, *Monroe Doctrine*, 188.
109. Haig, *Caveat*, 122–3.
110. Wills, *Reagan's America*, 411.
111. Reagan, 'Address Before a Joint Session of the Congress on Central America, April 27, 1983', *Public Papers, 1983*, 601–7.
112. Reagan, 'Interview with USA Today, April 26, 1983', *Public Papers, 1983*, 587.
113. Haig, *Caveat*, 125–9.
114. Weinberger, *Fighting for Peace*, 22–3.
115. Haig, *Caveat*, 128–9.
116. Cannon, *Reagan*, 391–401.
117. Reagan, 'Remarks to Reporters Announcing the Deployment of United States Forces in Beirut, Lebanon, August 20, 1982', *Public Papers, 1982*, 1062–3; Reagan, 'Letter to the Speaker of the House and the President Pro Tempore of the Senate on the Deployment of United States Forces in Beirut, Lebanon, August 24, 1982', *Public Papers, 1982*, 1078–9.
118. Cannon, *Reagan*, 406–8.
119. Reagan, 'Address to the Nation Announcing the Formation of a New Multinational Force in Lebanon, September 20, 1982', *Public Papers, 1982*, 1187–9; Reagan, 'Letter to the Speaker of the House and the President Pro Tempore of the Senate Reporting on United States Participation in the Multinational Force in Lebanon, September 29, 1982', *Public Papers, 1982*, 1238.
120. Cannon, *Reagan*, 409–22, 436–41.
121. Reagan, 'Remarks and a Question-and-Answer Session with Regional Editors and Broadcasters on the Situation in Lebanon, October 24, 1983', *Public Papers, 1983*, 1501.
122. Cannon, *President Reagan*, 449; Reagan, 'Address to the Nation on Events in Lebanon and Grenada, October 27, 1983', *Public Papers, 1983*, 1519.

123. Cannon, *Reagan*, 444–5, 449–57.
124. Reagan, 'Radio Address to the Nation on the Budget Deficit, Central America, and Lebanon, February 4, 1984', *Public Papers, 1984*, 169.
125. Reagan, 'Statement on the Situation in Lebanon, February 6, 1984', *Public Papers, 1984*, 177.
126. Reagan, 'Statement on the Situation in Lebanon, February 7, 1984', *Public Papers, 1984*, 185.
127. Reagan, 'Remarks at a Fundraiser for Republican Women Candidates on the Occasion of Susan B. Anthony's Birthday, February 15, 1984', *Public Papers, 1984*, 216.
128. Cannon, *Reagan*, 389–457; Shultz, *Turmoil and Triumph*, 43–116; Weinberger, *Fighting for Peace*, 94–122.
129. Shultz, *Turmoil and Triumph*, 344.
130. Smith, *Monroe Doctrine*, 178–84; Hugh O'Shaughnessy, *Grenada: Revolution, Invasion and Aftermath* (London: Sphere, 1984).
131. Reagan, 'Remarks of the President and Prime Minister Eugenia Charles of Dominica Announcing the Deployment of United States Forces in Grenada, October 25, 1983', *Public Papers, 1983*, 1505–8; Reagan, 'Letter to the Speaker of the House and the President Pro Tempore of the Senate on the Deployment of United States Forces in Grenada, October 25, 1983', *Public Papers, 1983*, 1512–13; Reagan, 'Address to the Nation on Events in Lebanon and Grenada,' *Public Papers, 1983*, 1520–2; Shultz, *Turmoil and Triumph*, 328–9; Weinberger, *Fighting for Peace*, 73–4.
132. Reagan, 'Address to the Nation, Oct 27, 1983', 1521.
133. Reagan, 'Remarks in Bridgetown, Barbados, Following a Luncheon Meeting with Leaders of Eastern Caribbean Countries, April 8, 1982', *Public Papers, 1982*, 448.
134. Reagan, 'Address to the Nation on Defense and National Security, March 23, 1983', *Public Papers, 1983*, 440.
135. Letter, Rev. Herbert Daughtry to President Reagan, March 25, 1983, folder Speeches SP 735 Address to Nation on Defense and National Security 3/23/83 (7 of 8), box SP 729-781, WHORM Subject File SP (Speeches), RRL.
136. Reagan, 'Address to the Nation, October 27, 1983', 1521.
137. Reagan, 'Remarks Announcing Grenada, October 25, 1983', 1505; Reagan, 'Letter to the House & Senate, October 25, 1983', 1512–13.
138. Shultz, *Turmoil and Triumph*, 328–35.
139. Weinberger, *Fighting for Peace*, 74–82.
140. Reagan, 'Remarks Announcing Grenada, October 25, 1983', 1506.
141. Shultz, *Turmoil and Triumph*, 329.
142. Weinberger, *Fighting for Peace*, 77.
143. Ibid., 85; Reagan, 'Address to the Nation, October 27, 1983', 1521.
144. Weinberger, *Fighting for Peace*, 78.
145. Reagan, 'Remarks Announcing Grenada, October 25, 1983', 1507.
146. Reagan, 'Letter to the House & Senate, October 25, 1983', 1513.
147. Reagan, 'Remarks Announcing the Appointment of Donald Rumsfeld as the President's Personal Representative in the Middle East, November 3, 1983', *Public Papers, 1983*, 1534.
148. Reagan, 'Remarks to Military Personnel at Cherry Point, North Carolina, on the United States Casualties in Lebanon and Grenada, November 4, 1983', *Public Papers, 1983*, 1540.
149. Weinberger, *Fighting for Peace*, 84–7.

150. Ibid., 89.
151. Reagan, 'Address to the Nation, October 27, 1983', 1521.
152. Weinberger, *Fighting for Peace*, 85.
153. Reagan, 'Appointment of Donald Rumsfeld,' 1533.
154. Memo, Senator John Tower to the Senate Committee Armed Services, Subject: Grenada, November 9, 1983, folder CO 058 177165, box CO 001-075, WHORM Subject File CO (Countries), RRL.
155. William Schneider, '"Rambo" and Reality: Having It Both Ways', *Eagle Resurgent? The Reagan Era in American Foreign Policy*, ed. Kenneth A. Oye, Robert J. Lieber and Donald Rothchild (Boston, MA: Little, Brown, 1987) 59.
156. Shultz, *Turmoil and Triumph*, 339–40.
157. Margaret Thatcher, *The Downing Street Years* (New York: Harper Perennial, 1995) 328–33.
158. Quoted ibid., 340–1.
159. Quoted in Memo, Charles Z. Wick to President Reagan, 'Inflammatory Soviet Statements About the President and US Policy', March 21, 1984, folder Speeches SP 729 Address to National Association of Evangelicals 3/8/83 (3 of 3), box SP 729-SP 781, WHORM Subject File SP (Speeches), RRL.
160. Letter, President Reagan to President Brezhnev, April 24, 1981 [declassified], folder Declassified Head of State (USSR), RRL.
161. Reagan, 'Remarks to Military Personnel, November 4, 1983', 1541.
162. Shultz, *Turmoil and Triumph*, 345.
163. Weinberger, *Fighting for Peace*, 86–7.
164. Reagan, 'Remarks to Military Personnel, November 4, 1983', 1541.
165. Reagan, 'Appointment of Donald Rumsfeld,' 1534.
166. Reagan, 'Ceremony for Freed American Hostages, January 27, 1981', 42.
167. Reagan, 'Remarks and a Question-and-Answer Session with Reporters on the Pentagon Report on the Security of United States Marines in Lebanon, December 27, 1983', *Public Papers, 1983*, 1748.
168. See Shultz, *Turmoil and Triumph*, ch. 32–3.
169. Weinberger, *Fighting for Peace*, 140–1.
170. Reagan, 'Address to the Nation on the United States Air Strike Against Libya', *Public Papers, 1986*, 468–9; Larry M. Speakes, 'Statement by Principal Deputy Press Secretary Speakes on the United States Air Strike Against Libya, April 14, 1986', *Public Papers, 1986*, 468; Speakes, 'Statement by Principal Deputy Press Secretary Speakes on the United States Air Strike Against Libya, April 15, 1986', *Public Papers, 1986*, 470–1; Shultz, *Turmoil and Triumph*, 677–85; Weinberger, *Fighting for Peace*, 132–41.
171. Cannon, *Reagan*, 653–4.
172. Geir Lundestad, 'The United States and Western Europe Under Ronald Reagan', in David E. Kyvig, ed., *Reagan and the World* (Westport, CT: Greenwood Press, 1990) 54.
173. Reagan, 'Letter to the Speaker of the House of Representatives and the President Pro Tempore of the Senate on the United States Air Strike against Libya, April 16, 1986', *Public Papers, 1986*, 478.
174. Shultz, *Turmoil and Triumph*, 686.
175. Speakes, 'Statement on Libya, April 15, 1986', 470.
176. Shultz, *Turmoil and Triumph*, 687.
177. Robert I. Rotberg, 'The Reagan Era in Africa', in Kyvig, ed., *Reagan and the World*, 131.

178. '*Newsweek*/Gallup Poll on Libyan Raid, April 17–18, 1986', *Gallup Report*, no. 247 (April 1986) 3.
179. 'Gallup Poll on Reagan Popularity, May 16–19, 1986', *Gallup Report*, no. 248 (May 1986) 30–1.
180. '*Newsweek*/Gallup Poll on Libyan Raid', 8.
181. John E. Rielly, ed., *American Public Opinion and US Foreign Policy 1987* (Chicago: Chicago Council on Foreign Relations, 1987) 32–3.
182. Reagan, 'Veterans of Foreign Wars, August 15, 1983', 1174.
183. Reagan, 'Eureka College, May 9, 1982', 582–3.
184. Reagan, 'Address to the Nation About Christmas and the Situation in Poland, December 23, 1981', *Public Papers, 1981*, 1186–8.
185. Reagan, 'Statement on the Soviet Attack on a Korean Civilian Airliner, September 1, 1983', *Public Papers, 1983*, 1221.
186. Reagan, 'Remarks to Reporters on the Soviet Attack on a Korean Civilian Airliner, September 2, 1983', *Public Papers, 1983*, 1223–4; Reagan, 'Address to the Nation on the Soviet Attack on as Korean Civilian Airliner, September 5, 1983', *Public Papers, 1983*, 1227–30.
187. Reagan, 'Address to the Nation, September 5, 1983', 1228; see Draft with Handwritten Sections, Presidential Television Address: Flight 007, September 5, 1983, document 16766355, folder SP799 167662-End, box SP799-SP832-36 WHORM Subject File SP (Speeches), RRL.
188. Reagan, 'Address to the Nation, September 5, 1983', 1228.
189. Reagan, 'Radio Address to the Nation on the Soviet Attack on a Korean Civilian Airliner, September 17, 1983', *Public Papers, 1983*, book II, 1296.
190. Quoted in Cannon, *Reagan*, 742–3fn.
191. Reagan, 'Radio Address, September 17, 1983', 1296.
192. Reagan, 'Remarks at Eureka College in Eureka, Illinois, February 6, 1984', *Public Papers, 1984*, 175.
193. Reagan, 'Radio Address to the Nation on the Situation in Central America, August 13, 1983', *Public Papers, 1983*, 1157.
194. Reagan, 'Radio Address to the Nation on Central America, February 16, 1985', *Public Papers, 1985*, 173.
195. Reagan, 'Remarks at the Annual Dinner of the Conservative Political Action Conference, March 1, 1985', *Public Papers, 1985*, 229.
196. Reagan, 'Radio Address, February 16, 1985', 173.
197. Reagan, 'Address Before a Joint Session of the Congress on the State of the Union, February 6, 1985', *Public Papers, 1985*, 135.
198. Quoted in Susanne Jonas, 'Reagan Administration Policy in Central America', in Kyvig, *Reagan and the World*, 103.
199. Robert Kagan, *A Twilight Struggle: American Power and Nicaragua, 1977–1990* (New York: Free Press, 1996) 355–6.
200. Kirkpatrick, 'Dictatorships and Double Standards'.
201. Holly Sklar, *Washington's War on Nicaragua* (Boston: South End Press, 1988) 168–70, 314;
202. Ibid., 165–70; Shultz, *Turmoil and Triumph*, 306–7, 404–6, 425–6.
203. See Cannon, *Reagan*, 589–738; John Tower, Edmund Muskie and Brent Scowcroft, *The Tower Commission Report: The Full Text of the President's Special Review Board* (New York: Times Books, 1987); Lawrence E. Walsh, *Firewall: The Iran-Contra Conspiracy and Cover-up* (New York: W. W. Norton, 1997).
204. Shultz, *Turmoil and Triumph*, 688.

205. Louis Harris, *Inside America* (New York: Vintage, 1987) 310–11, 421.
206. Reagan, 'US Military Academy, May 27, 1981', 461–2.
207. Reagan, 'Interview with Representatives of West European Publications, May 21, 1982', *Public Papers, 1982*, 698.
208. Reagan, 'State of the Union, 1983', 103.
209. Reagan, 'Conservative Political Action Conference, February 18, 1983', 255.
210. Reagan, 'State of the Union, 1984', 87–8.
211. Reagan, 'Address Before a Joint Session of Congress on the State of the Union, January 25, 1988', *Public Papers, 1988–1989*, 85.
212. Reagan, 'Farewell Address, January 11, 1989', *Public Papers, 1988–1989*, 1718–23.
213. Jerry Hagstrom, *Beyond Reagan: The New Landscape of American Politics* (New York: Penguin, 1988) 13.
214. Kevin Phillips, *The Politics of Rich and Poor: Wealth and the American Electorate in the Reagan Aftermath* (New York: Random House, 1990) esp. 3–31; see also Hagstrom, *Beyond Reagan*; Lewis H. Lapham, *Money and Class in America: Notes and Observations on the Civil Religion* (London: Picador, 1989).
215. Gallup found Reagan's final approval rating to be 63 per cent while a *New York Times*-CBS poll rated him as high as 68 per cent. Cannon, *Reagan*, 894.
216. Cannon, *Reagan*, 830.
217. Reagan, 'Farewell Address'.

6 George Bush – the 'Vision Thing' and the New World Order

1. David Mervin, *George Bush and the Guardianship Presidency* (Basingstoke: Macmillan – now Palgrave Macmillan, 1996) 28–37.
2. Dilys M. Hill and Phil Williams, eds, *The Bush Presidency: Triumphs and Adversities* (Basingstoke: Macmillan – now Palgrave Macmillan, 1994) 2–3.
3. Mervin, *Bush*, 21, 33, 214.
4. Hill and Williams, *Bush Presidency*, 217.
5. Fred Barnes, 'Mr. Popularity', *New Republic*, January 8 and 15, 1990, vol. 202, nos 2 and 3, 12.
6. For example, see Charles Krauthammer, 'The Unipolar Moment' in Graham Allison and Gregory F. Treverton, eds, *Rethinking America's Security: Beyond Cold War to New World Order* (New York: W. W. Norton, 1992) 295–306.
7. See Paul Kennedy, *The Rise and Fall of the Great Powers: Economic Change and Military Conflict from 1500 to 2000* (New York: Random House, 1987) 514–35; David P. Calleo, *Beyond Hegemony: The Future of the Western Alliance* (New York: Wheatsheaf, 1987); Robert Gilpin, *The Political Economy of International Relations* (Princeton, NJ: Princeton University Press, 1987) esp. ch. 10; Samuel P. Huntington, 'The US – Decline or Renewal?' *Foreign Affairs*, vol. 67, no. 2 (Winter 1988/89) 76–96; William Pfaff, *Barbarian Sentiments: How the American Century Ends* (New York: Hill & Wang, 1989); Joseph S. Nye, Jr., *Bound To Lead: The Changing Nature of American Power* (New York: Basic Books, 1990); Henry Nau, *The Myth of America's Decline: Leading the World Economy into the 1990s* (Oxford: Oxford University Press, 1990).
8. Quoted in Mervin, *Bush*, 214.
9. George Bush, 'Inaugural Address, January 20, 1989', *Public Papers of the Presidents of the United States: George Bush, 1989* (hereafter *Public Papers* followed by year). All citations for the Bush public papers are taken from the on-line version at

<www.csdl.tamu.edu/bushlib/papers/>; see also McEvoy-Levy, *American Exceptionalism*, ch. 2.

10. Bush, 'Address on Administration Goals Before a Joint Session of Congress, February 9, 1989', *Public Papers, 1989*.
11. Ibid.
12. Bush, 'Remarks at the United States Coast Guard Academy Commencement Ceremony in New London, Connecticut, May 24, 1989', *Public Papers, 1989*.
13. Quoted in Mervin, *Bush*, 211.
14. Mervin, *Bush*, 210–13.
15. Steve Garber and Phil Williams, 'Defense Policy', in Hill and Williams, *Bush Presidency*, 187–8.
16. See Mervin, *Bush*, 160–4; Powell, *American Journey*, 329–96, 405–9; Bob Woodward, *The Commanders* (New York: Simon & Schuster, 1991) 45–67.
17. Garber and Williams, 'Defense Policy', 188.
18. Bush, 'Remarks at US Coast Guard, May 24, 1989'.
19. Bush, 'Address to Congress, February 9, 1989'.
20. Bush, 'The President's News Conference in Paris, July 16, 1989', *Public Papers, 1989*.
21. Bush, 'Remarks and a Question-and-Answer Session with Reporters on the Relaxation of East German Border Controls, November 9, 1989', *Public Papers, 1989*.
22. Russell Watson et al., 'No Time For Showboating', *Newsweek*, November 27, 1989, 30–1.
23. Bush, 'Inaugural Address'.
24. Bush, 'Remarks at the Annual Conference of the Veterans of Foreign Wars, March 6, 1989', *Public Papers, 1989*.
25. Woodward, *Commanders*, 90, 230.
26. Bush and Scowcroft, *World Transformed*, 354.
27. Ibid., 118.
28. *Newsweek*, May 22, 1989, 37.
29. Powell, *American Journey*, 420–1.
30. Ibid., 422.
31. Woodward, *Commanders*, 159.
32. Bush, 'Letter to the Speaker of the House of Representatives and the President Pro Tempore of the Senate on United States Military Action in Panama, December 21, 1989', *Public Papers, 1989*.
33. Bush, 'Address to the Nation Announcing United States Military Action in Panama, December 20, 1989', *Public Papers, 1989*.
34. Powell, *American Journey*, 426.
35. Bush, 'Address to the Nation, December 20, 1989'.
36. Bush, 'Remarks Announcing the Surrender of General Manuel Noriega in Panama, January 3, 1990', *Public Papers, 1990*.
37. Woodward, *Commanders*, 115, 139–40.
38. Bush, 'Letter to the Speaker of the House, December 21, 1989'.
39. Quoted in Fisher, *Presidential War Power*, 145–6.
40. Mervin, *Bush*, 168.
41. Woodward, *Commanders*, 194.
42. 'The Panama Invasion: A Newsweek Poll', *Newsweek*, January 1, 1990, 22.
43. Graham Hueber, 'Approval Rating Second Highest in Poll's History', *Gallup Poll Monthly*, no. 292 (January 1990) 16–17.

44. Frank Newport, 'Bush Approval Rate and What's Behind It', *Gallup Poll Monthly*, no. 293 (February 1990) 17–19.
45. Woodward, *Commanders*, 162–71.
46. Bush, 'The President's News Conference, December 21, 1989', *Public Papers, 1989*.
47. Powell, *American Journey*, 424–5; Woodward, *Commanders*, 168–9.
48. Woodward, *Commanders*, 195.
49. Powell, *American Journey*, 434.
50. Lawrence Freedman and Efraim Karsh, *The Gulf Conflict 1990–1991: Diplomacy and War in the New World Order* (London: Faber & Faber, 1993) 42–50.
51. The relevant UN Security Council Resolutions are reprinted in full in Dilip Hiro, *Desert Shield to Desert Storm: The Second Gulf War* (New York: Routledge, 1992) 526–52.
52. Bush, 'Remarks at a Fundraising Luncheon for Rep. Bill Grant, September 6, 1990', *Public Papers, 1990*.
53. Quoted in Robert W. Tucker and David C. Hendrickson, *The Imperial Temptation: The New World Order and America's Purpose* (New York: Council on Foreign Relations Press, 1992) 81.
54. Powell, *American Journey*, 463; Tucker and Hendrickson, *Imperial Temptation*, 81; Bush and Scowcroft, *World Transformed*, 322
55. Bush and Scowcroft, *World Transformed*, 316, 349.
56. Bush, 'Address to the Nation Announcing Allied Military Action in the Persian Gulf, January 16, 1991', *Public Papers, 1991*.
57. Bush, 'Address to the Nation Announcing the Deployment of United States Armed Forces to Saudi Arabia, August 8, 1990', *Public Papers, 1990*.
58. Bush and Scowcroft, *World Transformed*, 320, 328.
59. Powell, *American Journey*, 491.
60. Bush and Scowcroft, *World Transformed*, 389.
61. Ibid., 341, 358, 374–5.
62. Bush, 'Address to the Nation, January 16, 1991'.
63. Bush and Scowcroft, *World Transformed*, 375.
64. Ibid., 303–4, 313, 416.
65. 'Senate Debate on the Persian Gulf War, January 10–12, 1991', *Congressional Record*, 102nd Cong. 1st Sess. (January 10–12, 1991) vol. 137, nos. 6–8, on-line at <http://thomas.loc.gov/r102/r102.html>.
66. Quoted in John Robert Greene, *The Presidency of George Bush* (Lawrence, KS: University of Kansas Press, 2000), 124.
67. Ibid., 123.
68. Bush and Scowcroft, *World Transformed*, 428, 435, 446.
69. Ibid., 353.
70. Powell, *American Journey*, 466–7, 470; Bush, 'Remarks and an Exchange With Reporters on the Iraqi Invasion of Kuwait, August 5, 1990', *Public Papers, 1990*.
71. Bush and Scowcroft, *World Transformed*, 418.
72. Bush, 'Remarks to the American Legislative Exchange Council, March 1, 1991', *Public Papers, 1991*.
73. Bush, 'Address to the Nation on the Suspension of Allied Offensive Combat Operations in the Persian Gulf, February 27, 1991', *Public Papers, 1991*; emphasis added.
74. Bush, 'Address to the Nation, August 8, 1990'.
75. Quoted in Woodward, *Commanders*, 273.
76. Bush, 'Address to the Nation, January 16, 1991'.

77. Powell, *American Journey*, 519.
78. Quoted in Woodward, *Commanders*, 339.
79. Ibid., 306–7.
80. Powell, *American Journey*, 487.
81. Bush, 'Address to the Nation, January 16, 1991'.
82. Powell, *American Journey*, 487.
83. Bush, 'Address to the Nation, January 16, 1991'.
84. Powell, *American Journey*, 496.
85. Rick Atkinson, *Crusade: The Untold Story of the Persian Gulf War* (Boston: Houghton Mifflin, 1994); Greene, *George Bush*, 133–4.
86. Figures from US intelligence agencies, Central Command (CENTCOM) and Iraqi sources cited in Freedman and Karsh, *Gulf Conflict*, 408–9.
87. Quoted in Hiro, *Desert Shield*, 387–90.
88. Powell, *American Journey*, 519–21.
89. Bush and Scowcroft, *World Transformed*, 448.
90. Ibid., 487.
91. Ibid., 483.
92. Powell, *American Journey*, 523.
93. Freedman and Karsh, *Gulf Conflict*, 408.
94. Hiro, *Desert Shield*, 268, 310, 330, 347, 379, 481.
95. *Gallup Poll: Public Opinion 1991* (Wilmington, DE: Scholarly Resources Inc., 1992) 67–8.
96. Ibid., 57.
97. Bush, 'Radio Address to United States Armed Forces Stationed in the Persian Gulf Region, March 2, 1991', *Public Papers, 1991*.
98. Powell, *American Journey*, 532.
99. Bush, 'Remarks to the American Association for the Advancement of Science, February 15, 1991', *Public Papers, 1991*.
100. Bush and Scowcroft, *World Transformed*, 472.
101. Powell, *American Journey*, 490.
102. Bush and Scowcroft, *World Transformed*, 464.
103. Quoted in Tucker and Hendrickson, *Imperial Temptation*, 146.
104. Bush and Scowcroft, *World Transformed*, 433.
105. Quoted in Schneider, 'The Old Politics and the New World Order', in Kenneth A. Oye, Robert J. Lieber and Donald Rothchild, eds, *Eagle in a New World: American Grand Strategy in the Post-Cold War Era* (New York: HarperCollins, 1992) 66.
106. Ibid., 64, 66–7.
107. Laura Silber and Allan Little, *The Death of Yugoslavia*, rev. edn (London: Penguin, 1996) 150–2, 163–4, 201.
108. Bush, 'The President's News Conference, June 4, 1992', *Public Papers, 1992*.
109. Bush, 'The President's News Conference, August 7, 1992', *Public Papers, 1992*.
110. Bush, 'The President's News Conference in Kennebunkport, Maine, August 8, 1992', *Public Papers, 1992*.
111. 'Presidential Debate in St. Louis, October 11, 1992', *Public Papers, 1992*.
112. John L. Hirsch and Robert B. Oakley, *Somalia and Operation Restore Hope: Reflections on Peacemaking and Peacekeeping* (Washington, DC: United States Institute of Peace Press, 1995) 3–16.
113. Bush, 'Address to the Nation on the Situation in Somalia, December 4, 1992', *Public Papers, 1992*.

114. Lydia Saad, ' "Operation Restore Hope" Gets Public's Blessing', *Gallup Monthly*, no. 327 (December 1992) 18–20.
115. Bush, 'Address to the Nation, December 4, 1992'.
116. Saad, 'Operation Restore Hope', 18–20.
117. Bush and Scowcroft, *World Transformed*, 370.
118. Bush, 'Remarks at the United States Coast Guard Academy Commencement Ceremony in New London, Connecticut, May 24, 1989', *Public Papers, 1989*.
119. Bush, 'Address to the 44th Session of the United Nations General Assembly in New York, New York, September 25, 1989', *Public Papers, 1989*.
120. Bush and Scowcroft, *World Transformed*, 353–5.
121. Bush, 'The President's News Conference on the Persian Gulf Crisis, August 30, 1990', *Public Papers, 1990*.
122. Bush, 'Address Before a Joint Session of the Congress on the Persian Gulf Crisis and the Federal Budget Deficit, September 11, 1990', *Public Papers, 1990*.
123. Bush, 'Address to the 46th Session of the United Nations General Assembly in New York City, September 2, 1991', *Public Papers, 1991*.
124. Michael Duffy and Dan Goodgame, *Marching in Place: The Status Quo Presidency of George Bush* (New York: Simon & Schuster, 1992) 183.
125. Bush, 'Address to the United Nations, September 2, 1991'.
126. Bush, 'Address Before a Joint Session of the Congress on the State of the Union, January 29, 1991', *Public Papers, 1991*.
127. Bush and Scowcroft, *World Transformed*, 491.
128. Ibid., 566.

7 Bill Clinton and the 'Indispensable Nation'

1. Quoted in William G. Hyland, *Clinton's World: Remaking American Foreign Policy* (Westport, CT: Praeger, 1999) 17.
2. See, for example, Larry Berman and Emily O. Goldman, 'Clinton's Foreign Policy at Midterm', in Colin Campbell and Bert A. Rockman, eds, *The Clinton Presidency: First Appraisals* (Chatham, NJ: Chatham House, 1996).
3. Emily O. Goldman and Larry Berman, 'Engaging the World: First Impressions of the Clinton Foreign Policy Legacy', in Colin Campbell and Bert A. Rockman, eds, *The Clinton Legacy* (New York: Chatham House, 2000) 230.
4. Ibid.
5. Quoted ibid., 233.
6. William J. Clinton, 'Address to the UN General Assembly, New York City, September 27, 1993', Press Release, White House Office of the Press Secretary. All of Clinton's speeches and pronouncements cited in this chapter are taken from White House press releases. They can also be found in the multi-volume *Public Papers of the Presidents of the United States: William J. Clinton*.
7. Anthony Lake, 'From Containment to Enlargement: Address at the School for Advanced International Studies, Johns Hopkins University, Washington, DC, September 21, 1993', *US Department of State Dispatch*, vol. 4, no. 39 (September 27, 1993).
8. Dumbrell, *American Foreign Policy*, 189.
9. James M. McCormick, 'Clinton and Foreign Policy: Some Legacies for a New Century', in Steven E. Schier, ed., *The Postmodern Presidency: Bill Clinton's Legacy in US Politics* (Pittsburgh: University of Pittsburgh Press, 2000) 60.
10. Clinton, 'Address to the UN General Assembly, September 27, 1993'.

11. Madeleine K. Albright, 'Use of Force in a Post-Cold War World: Address at the National War College, National Defense University, Fort McNair, Washington, DC, September 23, 1993', *US State Department Dispatch*, vol. 4, no. 39 (September 27, 1993).
12. Hyland, *Clinton's World*, 25.
13. Lake, 'From Containment to Enlargement, September 21, 1993'.
14. Clinton, 'Address to the UN General Assembly, September 27, 1993'.
15. Albright, 'Use of Force in a Post-Cold War World, September 23, 1993'.
16. Lake, 'From Containment to Enlargement, September 21, 1993'.
17. Clinton, 'Address to the UN General Assembly, September 27, 1993'.
18. Clinton, 'Remarks by the President on American Security in a Changing World, George Washington University, Washington, DC, August 5, 1996'.
19. Clinton, 'Second Inaugural Address, January 20, 1997'.
20. McEvoy-Levy, *American Exceptionalism*, 121.
21. Quoted in Dumbrell, *American Foreign Policy*, 181.
22. Ibid., 190.
23. Lake, 'From Containment to Enlargement, September 21, 1993'.
24. Dumbrell, *American Foreign Policy*,183, 189.
25. Martin Walker, *Clinton: The President They Deserve* (London: Fourth Estate, 1996) 259.
26. See Stanley A. Renshon, *High Hopes: The Clinton Presidency and the Politics of Ambition* (New York: Routledge, 1998) ch. 10.
27. Quoted in Dumbrell, *American Foreign Policy*, 180.
28. Walker, *Clinton*, 33.
29. Ibid., 1–6.
30. Quoted in Dumbrell, *American Foreign Policy*, 180.
31. Clinton, 'Announcement of Lifting of Trade Embargo on Vietnam, February 3, 1994'.
32. Clinton, 'Statement on the Normalization of Diplomatic Relations with Vietnam, July 11, 1995'.
33. Clinton, 'Remarks by the President in Toast Remarks at State Dinner, Presidential Palace, Hanoi, Socialist Republic of Vietnam, November 17, 2000'.
34. Clinton, 'Inaugural Address, January 20, 1993'.
35. Michael G. MacKinnon, *The Evolution of US Peacekeeping Policy Under Clinton: A Fairweather Friend* (London: Frank Cass, 2000) ch. 2.
36. Albright, 'Use of Force in a Post-Cold War World, September 23, 1993'.
37. Ibid.
38. US Department of State, *The Clinton Administration's Policy on Reforming Multilateral Peace Operations, May 1994* (Washington, DC: US Department of State, Bureau of Public Affairs, 1994) 4–5.
39. Hyland, *Clinton's World*, 21.
40. Quoted in Karin von Hippel, *Democracy by Force: US Military Intervention in the Post-Cold War World* (Cambridge: Cambridge University Press, 2000) 8.
41. Quoted ibid., 7.
42. John F. Harris, 'A Man of Caution: National Security Adviser Samuel Berger Steers a Tight Course on Kosovo', *Washington Post National Weekly Edition*, May 24, 1999, 7.
43. von Hippel, *Democracy by Force*, 60–1; Hyland, *Clinton's World*, 56–9.
44. Clinton, 'Remarks by the President, The Rotunda, Woolsey Hall, Yale University, New Haven, Conn., October 9, 1993'.

45. von Hippel, 61.
46. Clinton, 'Remarks by the President on *Meet the Press*, November 7, 1993'.
47. von Hippel, 63.
48. Ibid., 78
49. Quoted Ibid.
50. Senator Robert Byrd, a Democrat and Chair of the Senate Appropriations Committee, had been criticizing the administration's Somalia policy since June. See MacKinnon, *US Peacekeeping*, 65–7.
51. 'Situation in Somalia: Let Us Declare Victory and Safely Withdraw' (House of Representatives – October 5, 1993) *Congressional Record*, vol. 139, no. 133, H7382.
52. 'Withdraw United States Troops from Somalia Now', ibid.
53. Linda B. Miller, 'The Clinton Years: Reinventing US Foreign Policy', *International Affairs*, vol. 70, no. 4 (1994) 627; quoted in MacKinnon, *US Peacekeeping*, 78.
54. MacKinnon, *US Peacekeeping*, 78.
55. Ibid., 79–80.
56. Ibid., 108.
57. Quoted in Walker, *Clinton*, 262.
58. Silber and Little, *Death of Yugoslavia*, 287–8.
59. Walker, *Clinton*, 265–6.
60. Hyland, *Clinton's World*, 39.
61. Clinton, 'Statement on the Sarajevo Marketplace Shelling, February 9, 1994'.
62. Walker, *Clinton*, 275.
63. Clinton, 'Radio Address, February 19, 1994'.
64. Richard Sobel, *The Impact of Public Opinion on US Foreign Policy Since Vietnam: Constraining the Colossus* (Oxford: Oxford University Press, 2001), 189.
65. Silber and Little, *Death of Yugoslavia*, ch. 28.
66. Clinton, 'Statement on the Bosnia-Herzegovina Arms Embargo, August 11, 1995'; Clinton, 'The President's News Conference with President Kim Yong-sum of South Korea, July 27, 1995'.
67. Clinton, 'Statement on the Arms Embargo, August 11, 1995'.
68. Clinton, 'The President's News Conference, May 23, 1995'.
69. Clinton, 'The President's News Conference, June 3, 1995'.
70. Clinton, 'Statement on the Bosnia-Herzegovina Arms Embargo, August 11, 1995'.
71. Silber and Little, *Death of Yugoslavia*, ch. 29.
72. Clinton, 'Opening Statement at a News Conference before the Balkan Proximity Peace Talks, October 31, 1995'.
73. Clinton, 'Address to the Nation on the Bosnian Peace Agreement, November 27, 1995'.
74. Clinton, 'Statement on the Bosnian Peace Agreement, November 21, 1995'.
75. Ibid.
76. Clinton, 'Address to the Nation, November 27, 1995'.
77. Clinton, 'Remarks to the Committee for American Leadership in Bosnia, December 6, 1995'.
78. Clinton, 'Address to the Nation, November 27, 1995'.
79. Richard Holbrooke, *To End a War* (New York: Modern Library, 1999) xv, 360.
80. Strobe Talbott, 'Remarks by Deputy Secretary Talbott at a State Department Town Meeting, Washington, DC, November 1, 1995', *US State Department Dispatch Supplement*, vol. 6, no. 5 (December 1995).
81. Clinton, 'Address to the Nation, November 27, 1995'.
82. Holbrooke, *End a War*, 361.

83. Walker, *Clinton*, 282.
84. Clinton, 'Opening Statement, October 31, 1995'.
85. Talbott, 'Remarks at a State Department Town Meeting, November 1, 1995'.
86. Ibid., 47.
87. Clinton, 'Address to the Nation, November 27, 1995'.
88. Goldman and Berman, 'Engaging the World', 227.
89. Michael MccGwire, 'Why Did We Bomb Belgrade?' *International Affairs*, vol. 76, no. 1 (January 2000) 1–23.
90. Clinton, 'Address to the Nation on Airstrikes Against Serbian Targets in the Federal Republic of Yugoslavia (Serbia and Montenegro), March 24, 1999'.
91. Clinton, 'Interview with Dan Rather of CBS News, March 31, 1999'.
92. Quoted in Barton Gellman, 'With No Credible Alternative, the Allies Turned to Bombing', *Washington Post National Weekly Edition*, March 29, 1999, 16.
93. MccGwire, 'Why Did We Bomb Belgrade?' 14.
94. Clinton, 'Remarks on the Situation in Kosovo, March 22, 1999'.
95. Clinton, 'Remarks on the Situation in the Balkans and an Exchange with Reporters, April 5, 1999'.
96. Clinton, 'Address to the Nation, March 24, 1999'.
97. Clinton, 'Interview with Dan Rather, March 31, 1999'.
98. John F. Harris, 'And if Airstrikes Weren't Enough…?' *Washington Post National Weekly Edition*, April 5, 1999, 9.
99. Barton Gellman, 'Is This "Immaculate Coercion"? The Limits of Reliance on Air Power Become Clear in Kosovo', *Washington Post National Weekly Edition*, April 5, 1999, 6.
100. Quoted in ibid.
101. MccGwire, 'Why Did We Bomb Belgrade?' 17.
102. Ibid., 16–18.
103. Clinton, 'Interview with Dan Rather, March 31, 1999'.
104. *Gallup Poll: Public Opinion* 1999 (Wilmington, DE: Scholarly Resources Inc., 2000) 32.
105. Michael Dobbs, 'Post-Mortem on NATO's Bombing Campaign', *Washington Post National Weekly Edition*, July 19–26, 1999, 23.
106. Goldman and Berman, 'Engaging the World'.
107. *Gallup: Public Opinion* 1999, 34–41.
108. *Gallup Poll: Public Opinion* 2000 (Wilmington, DE: Scholarly Resources Inc., 2001) 422.
109. *Gallup: Public Opinion* 2000.
110. McEvoy-Levy, *American Exceptionalism*, 141.
111. McCormick, 'Clinton and Foreign Policy', 61.
112. Ibid., 67.
113. McCormick, 'Clinton and Foreign Policy', 73.
114. Barton Gellman, 'US Strikes at Iraqi Targets,' *Washington Post*, December 17, 1998, A01.
115. Eugene Robinson, 'US Steps Up Attack on Iraq', *Washington Post*, December 18, 1998, A1.
116. Andrew J. Bacevich, 'The Clinton Doctrine: Don't Ask', Washington Post, January 3, 1999, C5; quoted in Goldman and Berman, 234.

8 Conclusions: American Exceptionalism and the Legacy of Vietnam

1. George W. Bush, 'Statement by the President in His Address to the Nation, September 11, 2001', Press Release, The White House Office of the Press Secretary. All speeches and remarks by President Bush cited in this chapter are taken from White House press releases.
2. Quoted in Sharon Krum, 'Bush's Secret Weapon,' *The Guardian*, May 7, 2002, G2 p. 9.
3. *The National Security Strategy of the United States of America*, The White House, September 2002.
4. Bush, 'Remarks by the President in Photo Opportunity with National Security Team, September 12, 2001'.
5. Bush, 'Address to a Joint Session of Congress and the American People, September 20, 2001'.
6. Bush, 'Remarks by President Bush and President Megawati of Indonesia in a Photo Opportunity, September 19, 2001'.
7. R. W. Apple, Jr., 'Afghanistan as Vietnam', *New York Times*, October 31, 2001.
8. Michael R. Gordon with Eric Schmitt, 'US Putting Off Plan to Use G.I.s in Afghan Caves', *New York Times*, December 27, 2001.
9. Michael R. Gordon, 'A Vigorous Debate on US War Tactics', *New York Times*, November 4, 2001; Apple, 'Afghanistan as Vietnam'.
10. Bush, 'Address to a Joint Session of the Congress, September 20, 2001'.
11. Simon Jeffrey, 'Amnesty Demands an Inquiry as Hundreds Die in Fort Siege', *The Guardian*, November 28, 2001.
12. Michael Byers, 'US Doesn't Have the Right to Decide Who Is Or Isn't a POW', *The Guardian*, January 14, 2002, 18.
13. Bush, 'Radio Address to the Nation, September 15, 2001'.
14. Bush, 'The President's State of the Union Address, January 29, 2002'.

Select Bibliography

Baritz, Loren. *Backfire: A History of How American Culture Led Us into Vietnam and Made Us Fight the Way We Did*. New York: Ballantine, 1985.

Bell, Daniel. 'The End of American Exceptionalism'. *The Public Interest* (Fall 1975) reprinted in Bell, Daniel, *The Winding Passage: Essays and Sociological Journeys 1960–1980*, pp. 245–71. New York: Basic Books, 1980.

——. ' "American Exceptionalism" Revisited: The Role of Civil Society'. *The Public Interest*, no. 95 (Spring 1989) pp. 38–56.

Brands, H. W. *What America Owes the World: The Struggle for the Soul of Foreign Policy*. Cambridge: Cambridge University Press, 1998.

Brzezinski, Zbigniew. *Power and Principle: Memoirs of the National Security Adviser, 1977–1981*. London: Weidenfeld & Nicolson, 1983.

Bush, George and Brent Scowcroft. *A World Transformed*. New York: Alfred A. Knopf, 1998.

Campbell, Colin and Bert A. Rockman, eds. *The Clinton Presidency: First Appraisals*. Chatham, NJ: Chatham House, 1996.

——. *The Clinton Legacy*. New York: Chatham House, 2000.

Cannon, Lou. *President Reagan: The Role of a Lifetime*. New York: Touchstone, 1991.

Carter, Jimmy. *Keeping Faith: Memoirs of a President*. New York: Bantam, 1982.

Dumbrell, John. *The Making of US Foreign Policy*. Manchester: Manchester University Press, 1990.

——. *The Carter Presidency: A Re-evaluation*. Manchester: Manchester University Press, 1993.

——. *American Foreign Policy: Carter to Clinton*. Basingstoke: Macmillan – now Palgrave Macmillan, 1997.

Falk, Richard A., ed. *The Vietnam War and International Law*, 4 vols. Princeton, NJ: Princeton University Press, 1968–76.

Fischer, Beth A. *The Reagan Reversal: Foreign Policy and the End of the Cold War*. Columbia, MO: University of Missouri Press, 1997.

Fisher, Louis. *Presidential War Power*. Lawrence, KS: University Press of Kansas, 1995.

FitzGerald, Frances. *Fire in the Lake: The Vietnamese and the Americans in Vietnam*. New York: Atlantic-Little, 1972; Vintage Books, 1989.

——. *Way Out There in the Blue: Reagan, Star Wars and the End of the Cold War*. New York: Simon & Schuster, 2000.

Ford, Gerald R. *A Time to Heal: The Autobiography of Gerald R. Ford*. New York: Harper & Row, 1979.

Fousek, John. *To Lead the Free World: American Nationalism and the Cultural Roots of the Cold War*. Chapel Hill, NC: University of North Carolina Press, 2000.

Freedman, Lawrence and Efraim Karsh. *The Gulf Conflict 1990–1991: Diplomacy and War in the New World Order*. London: Faber & Faber, 1993.

Fulbright, J. William. *The Arrogance of Power*. New York: Vintage, 1966.

Gelb, Leslie H. and Richard K. Betts, *The Irony of Vietnam: The System Worked*. Washington, DC: Brookings Institution, 1979.

Greene, Jack P. *The Intellectual Construction of America: Exceptionalism and Identity from 1492 to 1800*. Chapel Hill, NC: University of North Carolina Press, 1993.

Greene, John Robert. *The Presidency of Gerald R. Ford*. Lawrence, KS: University Press of Kansas, 1995.

——. *The Presidency of George Bush*. Lawrence, KS: University of Kansas Press, 2000.

Gustainis, J. Justin. *American Rhetoric and the Vietnam War*. Westport, CT: Praeger, 1993.

Haig, Alexander M., Jr. *Caveat: Realism, Reagan, and Foreign Policy*. London: Weidenfeld & Nicolson, 1984.

Herring, George C. *America's Longest War: The United States and Vietnam, 1950–1975*. 2nd edn. New York: Alfred A. Knopf, 1986.

Hill, Dilys M. and Phil Williams, eds. *The Bush Presidency: Triumphs and Adversities*. Basingstoke: Macmillan – now Palgrave Macmillan, 1994.

Hippel, Karin von. *Democracy by Force: US Military Intervention in the Post-Cold War World*. Cambridge: Cambridge University Press, 2000.

Hiro, Dilip. *Desert Shield to Desert Storm: The Second Gulf War*. New York: Routledge, 1992.

Holbrooke, Richard. *To End a War*. New York: Modern Library, 1999.

Holsti, Ole R. and James N. Rosenau. *American Leadership in World Affairs: Vietnam and the Breakdown of Consensus*. Boston: G. Allen & Unwin, 1984.

Hunt, Michael H. *Ideology and US Foreign Policy*. New Haven: Yale University Press, 1987.

Huntington, Samuel P. *American Politics: The Promise of Disharmony*. Cambridge, MA: Belknap Press, 1981.

Hyland, William G. *Clinton's World: Remaking American Foreign Policy*. Westport, CT: Praeger, 1999.

Isaacs, Arnold R. *Vietnam Shadows: The War, Its Ghosts, and Its Legacy*. Baltimore, MD: Johns Hopkins University Press, 1997.

Karnow, Stanley. *Vietnam: A History*. New York: Viking Press, 1983.

Kendrick, Alexander. *The Wound Within: America in the Vietnam Years, 1945–1974*. Boston: Little, Brown, 1974.

Kyvig, David E., ed. *Reagan and the World*. Westport, CT: Greenwood Press, 1990.

Lepgold, Joseph and Timothy McKeown. 'Is American Foreign Policy Exceptional? An Empirical Analysis'. *Political Science Quarterly*, vol. 110, no. 3 (Fall 1995) pp. 369–84.

Levy, David W. *The Debate Over Vietnam*, 2nd edn. Baltimore, MD: Johns Hopkins University Press, 1995.

Lipset, Seymour Martin. *American Exceptionalism: A Double-Edged Sword*. New York: W. W. Norton, 1996.

MacKinnon, Michael G. *The Evolution of US Peacekeeping Policy under Clinton: A Fairweather Friend*. London: Frank Cass, 2000.

McCormick, James M. 'Clinton and Foreign Policy: Some Legacies for a New Century', in Steven E. Schier, ed. *The Postmodern Presidency: Bill Clinton's Legacy in US Politics*, pp. 60–83. Pittsburgh: University of Pittsburgh Press, 2000.

McCrisken, Trevor B. 'Exceptionalism', in Alexander DeConde, Richard Dean Burns, and Fredrik Logevall, eds. *Encyclopedia of American Foreign Policy*, 2nd edn, vol. 2, pp. 63–80. New York: Charles Scribner's Sons, 2001.

McEvoy-Levy, Siobhán. *American Exceptionalism and US Foreign Policy: Public Diplomacy at the End of the Cold War*. Basingstoke and New York: Palgrave – now Palgrave Macmillan, 2001.

MccGwire, Michael. 'Why Did We Bomb Belgrade?' *International Affairs*, vol. 76, no. 1 (January 2000) pp. 1–23.

Melanson, Richard A. *American Foreign Policy Since the Vietnam War: The Search for Consensus from Nixon to Clinton*, 2nd edn. Armonk, NY: M. E. Sharpe, 1996.

Mervin, David. *George Bush and the Guardianship Presidency*. Basingstoke: Macmillan – now Palgrave Macmillan, 1996.

Morris, Kenneth E. *Jimmy Carter: American Moralist*. Athens, GA and London: University of Georgia Press, 1996.

Mueller, John E. *War, Presidents, and Public Opinion*. New York: John Wiley, 1973.

Powell, Colin L. with Joseph E. Persico. *My American Journey*. New York: Random House, 1995.

Reagan, Ronald. *An American Life*. London: Hutchinson, 1990.

Ryan, David. *US Foreign Policy in World History*. London: Routledge, 2000.

Schlesinger, Arthur M., Jr. *The Cycles of American History*. Boston: Houghton Mifflin, 1986.

Shafer, Byron E., ed. *Is America Different? A New Look at American Exceptionalism*. Oxford: Clarendon Press, 1991.

Sheehan, Neil. *A Bright Shining Lie: John Paul Vann and America in Vietnam*. New York: Vintage Books, 1988.

Shultz, George P. *Turmoil and Triumph: My Years as Secretary of State*. New York: Charles Scribner's Sons, 1993.

Silber, Laura and Allan Little. *The Death of Yugoslavia*, rev. edn. London: Penguin, 1995; 1996.

Smith, Gaddis. *Morality, Reason, and Power: American Diplomacy in the Carter Years*. New York: Hill & Wang, 1986.

Sobel, Richard. *The Impact of Public Opinion on US Foreign Policy Since Vietnam: Constraining the Colossus*. Oxford: Oxford University Press, 2001.

Stephanson, Anders. *Manifest Destiny: American Expansion and the Empire of Right*. New York: Hill & Wang, 1995.

Tucker, Robert W. and David C. Hendrickson. *The Imperial Temptation: The New World Order and America's Purpose*. New York: Council on Foreign Relations Press, 1992.

Turley, William S. *The Second Indochina War: A Short Political and Military History, 1954–1975*. Boulder, CO: Westview Press, 1986; reprint, New York: Mentor, 1987.

Vance, Cyrus. *Hard Choices: Critical Years In America's Foreign Policy*. New York: Simon & Schuster, 1983.

Walker, Martin. *Clinton: The President They Deserve*. London: Fourth Estate, 1996.

Weinberg, Albert K. *Manifest Destiny: A Study of Nationalist Expansionism in American History*. Baltimore, MD: Johns Hopkins Press, 1935; Chicago: Quadrangle, 1963.

Weinberger, Caspar. *Fighting for Peace: Seven Critical Years in the Pentagon*. London: Michael Joseph, 1990; New York: Warner Books, 1990.

Whitcomb, Roger S. *The American Approach to Foreign Affairs: An Uncertain Tradition*. Westport, CT and London: Praeger, 1998.

Wills, Garry. *Reagan's America*. New York: Penguin, 1988.

Woodward, Bob. *The Commanders*. New York: Simon & Schuster, 1991.

Index

Printed and bound by CPI Group (UK) Ltd, Croydon, CR0 4YY